D0485373

LEONARD
COHEN
HALLELUJAH

A NEW BIOGRAPHY   TIM FOOTMAN

Leonard Cohen - Hallelujah
by Tim Footman

A CHROME DREAMS PUBLICATION
First Edition 2009

Published by Chrome Dreams
PO BOX 230, New Malden, Surrey,
KT3 6YY, UK
books@chromedreams.co.uk
WWW.CHROMEDREAMS.CO.UK

ISBN 978 1 84240 472 0

Copyright © 2009 by Chrome Dreams

Edited by   Cathy Johnstone
Cover Design   Sylwia Grzeszczuk
Layout Design   Marek Niedziewicz

All rights reserved. No part of this book may be reproduced without
the written permission of the publishers.

A catalogue record for this book is available from the British Library.

Printed in the UK by CPI William Clowes Beccles NR34 7TL

LEONARD
COHEN
HALLELUJAH

A NEW BIOGRAPHY   TIM FOOTMAN

ABOUT THE AUTHOR

Tim Footman first encountered the words and music of Leonard Cohen in the early 1980s, through the medium of a budget six-track EP on the Pickwick label; he was particularly taken by the beret the singer was sporting in the cover photo.

He is the author of *Welcome To The Machine: OK Computer and the Death of the Classic Album* (2007) and *The Noughties 2000-2009: A Decade That Changed the World* (2009), and he contributed a chapter to the collection *Radiohead and Philosophy* (2009). He has also written about music, pop culture, philosophy and overpriced restaurants for *The Guardian*, *Mojo*, *Time Out*, *Careless Talk Costs Lives*, *Plan B*, *Zembla*, *Drowned In Sound*, the *Bangkok Post* and the *International Journal of Baudrillard Studies*, among other publications. From 1999 to 2001 he was Editor of the *Guinness Book of Records*.

He has lived on three continents, but always seems to find his way back to London.

CONTENTS

PREFACE
Let us prepare mythologies

Yah, Kone, said Roshi very softly. You should write more sad.
– 'Roshi', from *Death Of A Lady's Man* (1978)

Leonard Cohen was born in 1949.

That's not what the reference books tell us, of course. The official story states that Leonard Norman Cohen came into this world as the Sabbath arrived, on Friday, September 21st, 1934, the second child of Nathan Cohen and Masha, *née* Klinitsky-Klein, respected pillars of Montreal's Jewish middle class. They tell us that young Leonard subsequently attended Westmount High School, that he had an older sister named Esther and a Scottish terrier named Tinkie, not to mention a chemistry set. He played hockey and he played the clarinet, and he wasn't very tall. And all these things are doubtless true.

But Leonard Cohen, the Leonard Cohen we know; the Pope of Mope; the Bedsit Bard; the sometime Buckskin Boy; the composer of music that allegedly makes you want to slash your wrists; the Jewish Buddhist; the philanderer; the drinker; the smoker; the occasional opium fiend; the man who talks to Greek daisies; the poet; the novelist; the raconteur; the unlikely gun fetishist; the bad monk; the worse singer; the potential permanent advisor to the Minister of Tourism of the People's Republic of Trinidad that never happened; the guy who wrote that song in *Shrek*; he only came into existence in 1949, when he a) discovered the life and works of the Spanish poet and playwright Federico García Lorca, b) bought his first guitar, for $12 from a Montreal pawn shop, and c) attended his first concert, by the blues musician Josh White. It was then that the Cohen combination, intellectual and sexual, brooding bohemian and unlikely babe magnet, poet and rock star, began to coalesce.

Or did it? Maybe that spark came five years earlier, on the day of Cohen Senior's funeral; the day on which his nine-year-old son scrawled some commemorative lines, then tucked the paper into the folds of the dead patriarch's bow tie, and buried it in the garden. Or maybe not until 1957 (by which stage he'd already published his first book of poems), when he took the hallucinogen peyote at the top of Mount Royal, the peak that gives Montreal its name, and gazed out onto the city that had spawned him; a conscious, self-conscious nod to every writer before him, from Samuel Taylor Coleridge and Arthur Rimbaud to Aldous Huxley and William S Burroughs, who had sought to open the doors of perception just a little wider than normal hinges permit.

Wherever we allow the story to begin, the fact remains that That Leonard Cohen (see above) is about far more than the sum of his books and poems and songs. He works long and hard at his Art, but has devoted almost as much effort to the pursuit of Being An Artist. Assuming the mantle of the creative bohemian, the right cafe, the right cigarettes, came before any words. His choice of typewriter (an Olivetti) was, one gets the feeling, as significant as a thousand lines that came from it. And any consideration of one of those lines that he typed or a chord that he strummed or a note that he groaned must be set alongside the wine and the women, the island of Hydra and the Chelsea Hotel and Mount Baldy. 'Famous Blue Raincoat' (from his third album, *Songs of Love and Hate*, released in March, 1971) is no less important than the famous blue raincoat (a Burberry, purchased in London) that inspired it. He's a stylish fellow, that Cohen.

There's a difficulty, though. In many ways, Cohen's life is as much a scrupulously crafted artefact as any of his songs, and that's a lot of crafting. We know that a single piece can have an elephantine gestation period: 'Hallelujah', for example, took around 18 months before it reached a condition with which its author was happy, and has subsequently endured further revisions. Others have taken longer, being tried out and rejected for successive albums, until they eventually meet with their creator's approval, a process that's been known to take over a decade. It's a routine that disguises its own art. As the singer Kathryn Williams says of Cohen's songs, "They're massively laboured over to not sound laboured."[1] He's too good a wordsmith to let a mixed metaphor or a cliché get through quality control. Conversely, he's not a supremely gifted musician, so the chords and riffs that would come so easily to a facile genius have to be dragged screaming from his imagination, which accounts for them being a little bruised and bloodied.

So if he works so hard at his art, who is to say that the life that Cohen presents, the drugs and guitars and islands and rainwear and that bloody banana, hasn't undergone a similarly rigorous fine-tuning? As one interviewer declared, in 1975, "When you meet him, whether or not you know his writing, you can't help but recognize immediately that he is his own creation."[2] While he's no media slag, he has given many interviews over the years, often recounting the same anecdotes and the same one-liners but the details and the tales and the telling do tend to shift a little from one version to another. He's never felt the urge to play jazz as such (see Chapter Eighteen), but his interviews are masterly examples of improvisation on a theme – the theme, more often than not, being his own reality.

And when art and life come together, things get really interesting. He offers biographical interpretation of songs such as 'Suzanne' and 'Seems So Long Ago, Nancy', and then casually moves the goalposts; or newly unearthed evidence challenges his account, as with 'Sisters Of Mercy'; or, as in the case of 'Chelsea Hotel # 2', he lets slip a crucial detail then spends the rest of his life apologising for his lapse in gallantry. In recent years, he's claimed that even when a song, such as 'Famous Blue Raincoat', was inspired by real events, he can't remember the details, and isn't sure whether the song was accurate in the first place. His attitude to his own past, his own persona, has clearly changed over the years. As the sonorous narration to an early documentary about him explained, when he was still best known as a poet:

Cohen collects his letters and makes certain that he is heavily photographed. He does this simply because he feels he's becoming an

9

important writer and that such material will someday be of value; and yet he is totally devoid of arrogance.[3]

A decade and a half later, on his 1979 tour, he seems remarkably laid back about the extent to which critics and fans might want to draw conclusions from his own words, as he discusses the story and motivations behind 'Suzanne':

So the next verse moves easily, you know onto the idea that Jesus was a sailor, sank beneath your wisdom like a stone. So you know you could establish a real coherence in the song if that was where you went, you know, if you liked to do those sort of things.[4]

And yet, even if he's happy to have his work picked over, he's careful about how he's perceived as a man. We know he still keeps a meticulous archive of drafts, letters and memoirs, annotating his work and life in minute detail; but much of it is in his own handwriting, literally and metaphorically. Everything we see of him is filtered through that wry, half-smiling persona. As he says, "the archive is the mountain, and the filtered work is the volcano."[5] And ultimately, just as the choice of what comes out of that volcano is Cohen's alone, so is the choice of what goes into the mountain. Everybody knows the dice were loaded, the fight was fixed. What they disagree about is what the result really should have been.

Because, just as Cohen's words are open to interpretation and opinion, so is his life. In his 75 years of wandering and wondering, the tales have been told so often that they acquire their own 'truthiness', to coin a Colbertism. Was he really persuaded to go to Greece solely by the suntan on a London bank clerk? Did he and his Zen master Roshi really bond over cognac? Whose account of the Phil Spector sessions – two self-mythologists, albeit one nicer than the other – should we believe? And what really happened to all that money? Cohen himself admits that his accounts – not to mention his accounting – may be flawed: "I'm blessed with a certain amount of amnesia and I really don't remember what went down," he mused in 2009. "I don't review my life that way."[6] This biography makes no claim to be definitive, because there really is no such thing as definitive. It's more about the telling than the tale.

That said, this book set out to be a biography, and (mostly) keeps to the rules of the form. It's pretty rigorously chronological, tracing Cohen's transition from awkward, middle-class childhood to a youth of bohemian aspirations; initial fame as an exciting poet and novelist who never quite lived up to his original promise, commercially at least; and then his most famous incarnation, as a romantic-cum-existential troubadour whose relative lack of commercial clout was balanced by a small but devoted fan base and an ability to reinvent the mode of his art without sacrificing the essential qualities of its content. Elements that can't be neatly compartmentalised in that structure – his relationship, respect-cum-rivalry, with Bob Dylan, and the belated success of his song 'Hallelujah', are given room to stretch out in the Appendices.

Before we get back to Montreal, some acknowledgements are due. To Rob Johnstone, for initiating the project and overseeing it with his usual cheerful efficiency; to Ron Cornelius, John Lissauer and John Simon for offering up their memories; and to Stephen Scobie for thinking and pointing in the right directions. Many years ago, Ian Rogers suggested tea and oranges in Halifax, Nova Scotia, and Leslie Topp argued for Cohen against Costello in Oakville, Ontario. Thank you both, wherever you are. Thanks to Noel Boivin, Sandra Goroff, Simon Kyte, Valerie Polichar and Les Stanley, for reminding me that Cohen fans come in all shapes, sizes and flavours. Etta James, Camera Obscura, Captain Jack Harkness, Henry Blofeld, Nicholson Baker, Twitter and Yorkshire Tea offered a little respite in the darker moments, especially when it came to the third album. And love and thanks as ever to my parents, to the Powell gang, and to Small Boo, who made meringues and drew pictures on the fridge when I needed them most.

Leonard Cohen: Hallelujah was, for the most part, typed on an iBook G4 that half-way through decided to stop providing full stops;

sadly, it seems to have perished in the attempt. In the words of a better writer than I:

Death to this book or fuck this book...

Tim Footman
London/Bangkok, 2009

CHAPTER ONE
I want to be the kind of hero

I don't have much of a sense of my own work. I don't have much of
a memory, and I'm not at all given to reflection and nostalgia.
– Leonard Cohen, 1988

Very well, let's play this as straight as we can. Leonard Norman Cohen was indeed born on Friday, September 21st, 1934, in Montreal, Quebec, Canada.

His father, Nathan, was an engineer, but spent most of his adult life working for the family clothing business, the Freedman Company, with his brother Horace. He had served in the Canadian Army during World War I, and suffered as a result of his wounds for the rest of his life. Nathan's grandfather Lazarus was originally from Lithuania and arrived in Canada in 1869, following a period spent living in Scotland. Lazarus was a rabbi, but also a successful and respected businessman; his son Lyon co-founded Canada's first Jewish newspaper.

Nathan, Lyon's oldest son, married Masha Klein in 1927. Masha was also from Lithuanian rabbinic stock, being the daughter of Solomon Klinitsky-Klein, who had arrived in Canada as recently as 1923, having escaped the pogroms under which the Jews of Eastern Europe suffered in the early 20th century; the family had spent some time in England, then sailed to Halifax, Nova Scotia. Lyon Cohen had advised the family on their relocation, and soon the Klinitsky-Kleins moved to Montreal. Solomon, a noted scholar, was even more eminent in Jewish circles than Lazarus Cohen, having authored several guides to the language and meaning of the Talmud, the record of rabbinic teaching and discussion that forms a core document in Jewish life.

The combination of religious lineage and business success gave the Cohen family status and respectability within Montreal society, but they were also an isolated minority in several senses. For a start, people who spoke English as a first language, although culturally and economically dominant, were outnumbered two to one by Francophones in the city, and to a much greater degree in Quebec as a whole. Moreover, although the city's anti-Semitism was less overt than the brutal persecution that had driven Lazarus Cohen and Solomon Klinitsky-Klein from Europe, it still existed. Many of the major social and educational institutions made a conscious effort to restrict the numbers of Jews crossing their threshold, or excluded them entirely; Montreal's prestigious McGill University, which Leonard Cohen would enter in 1951, was known to keep discreet tabs on the ethno-religious affiliations of its undergraduates, following the tradition of Harvard and other American Ivy League colleges. It was scant consolation that the main worry was that Jews were considered "too clever" and might outshine the hearty sons of the Anglo-Saxon elite.

Never entirely accepted by the Anglicans, the Cohens also found themselves at a distance from much of Montreal's Jewish community; they spoke English (Masha with a strong Lithuanian accent) in preference to Yiddish; they lived in posh Westmount, some distance from The Main, where the Jewish population was most densely concentrated. Before he was born, Leonard seemed destined for life as a halfway outsider; tolerated, even respected, but rarely fully loved and treasured by wider society. It was a role he would grow to accept, and eventually to relish. It defined him and, in many ways, his art.

Young Leonard's upbringing was physically, if not emotionally comfortable. His father's experiences during the First World War had left physical and mental scars, and his was a distant presence in the lives of his children. However, his ordered, almost Victorian mode of life dominated the household. His children seldom saw him without a suit and tie, even during vacations, and he expected similar standards of formality from his offspring; he was still wearing spats, even occasionally a monocle, into the 1940s. One of Nathan's few interests beyond work and the synagogue was making home movies, and footage of a young, carefree Leonard on his little tricycle seems to crop up in every documentary made about his life.

Even though his son chose the nominally unconstrained life of an artist, he has always expressed his need for discipline and order, in himself and in society as a whole. The closest the family came to disreputability was a friend of Leonard's mother who managed to make a living as a professional gin rummy player. Masha was rather more demonstrative, although she too was prone to depression, and Leonard's relationship with her would have its peaks and troughs until her death in 1978. However, she was always more forgiving than her husband of her son's unconventional tendencies, as he recalled in 2008:

My mother was a Russian Jew, a generous Chekhovian spirit, very accepting in her way... She was alarmed when she saw me running around Montreal with a guitar under my arm, but she was very kind in her observations. She would occasionally roll her eyes, but that was about as far as it went.[7]

The Cohen family was wealthy enough to afford servants, and much of the day-to-day responsibility for looking after the children was handed to an Irish nanny who exposed young Leonard to the rituals of her Catholic faith. It was the beginning of his long ecumenical journey, absorbing elements of various spiritual traditions as he progressed towards his own vision of transcendent truth, or at least an approximation of it.

Nathan Cohen's death in January, 1944, was the first significant trauma of Leonard's life. Aside from the emotional loss, Jewish tradition now bestowed on him a notional role as the head of the household, a heavy burden for a nine-year-old boy, and one that would persist even after his mother's uneasy second marriage, to a man named Harry Ostrow. Leonard would return to the loss of his father in his fiction and poetry, and it is very easy to place a quasi-Freudian, psychological interpretation on some of his later relationships with older men: were the likes of Irving Layton and Joshu Sasaki Roshi simply literary and spiritual mentors, or emotional replacements for the father that Cohen never properly knew?

As Leonard entered his teens, he became more than aware of the burden of responsibility upon him. Not only was his family well respected within Montreal's Jewish community, but he was also heir to long rabbinical traditions on both parents' sides. His bar mitzvah (the ceremony in which a Jewish male symbolically attains manhood, at the age of 13) was laden with even more significance than it would have been for many of his friends, but rendered incomplete by the absence of his father. Leonard was now effectively the man of the house; not just a son, but an ersatz father and husband as well. In adult life, he would bemoan his own perceived inadequacy in both roles.

However, there were growing distractions from the looming burdens of business, community and synagogue. Cohen's adolescence coincided with the post-war years in which young North Americans experienced a growing emancipation from the social norms that had dominated the lives of their parents and grandparents. Although Canada and the United States had both fought in the Second World War, they had for the most part (with the exception of the Japanese attack on Pearl Harbour in 1941) escaped the destruction that befell much of Europe. A new spirit of economic optimism expressed itself as a vibrant strand of consumer capitalism, much of it targeted at a new breed – the teenager. For the first time, music, clothes, soft drinks were marketed directly at the young; and the language the marketers used, however subtly, was based on the universal teenage obsession with sex.

There is no evidence that young Leonard Norman Cohen was any more consumed by lust than his contemporaries. However, his bubbling hormones did express themselves in unusual ways, often with farcical results. He became interested in hypnotism, after reading a 19th century book on the subject, and became quite adept at it; he managed to put one of the household servants into a trance, and proceeded to undress her, although bringing her out of the trance proved to be less straightforward. Feeling that his short stature was hampering his chances with girls (it already prevented him from getting into many of the movies frequented by his taller classmates), he experimented with stuffing Kleenex into his shoes, but came to grief when he attended a dance with the ad hoc lifts in place. Both traumas are recounted for laughs in Cohen's first novel, *The Favourite Game* (1963); the latter prompts the mock-theological speculation that "this must be what Hell is like, an eternal Bunny Hop with sore feet, which you can never drop out of."

For the moment, however, Cohen's rutting urges were sublimated into his growing interest in literature and music. These had their roots well before his near-simultaneous discovery of García Lorca and the guitar. The rituals of the Jewish religion, with their sung recitations, were an early influence, and young Leonard had particularly enjoyed reading the Book of Isaiah at the side of his maternal grandfather, Rabbi Klein. The key attraction for Leonard was not spiritual, however, but simply the chance to spend time with his grandfather; the desire to sit at the feet of a holy man transcended the source and nature of the holiness that motivated him. This was a phenomenon that would be repeated many years later.

Leonard also loved Isaiah for its literary qualities. It includes attacks on the idolatory and injustice that was prevalent among the Jewish people at the time (the 8th century BC) and extensive prophecy that has variously been interpreted as referring to the State of Israel or the coming of Jesus Christ. Themes from the prophetical work would crop up in his writing many times in the coming decades. Although it wasn't a notably bookish household, Nathan Cohen did have bound volumes of Chaucer, Milton and the Romantic poets, as much for show as for his own enlightenment; he had liked the idea of literature, if not the reality. Leonard read them with far more passion than his father ever expressed.

The revelations of 1949, however, forced him to look outside the cultural traditions into which he was born. García Lorca was perhaps an unlikely role model, not least because of his homosexuality. But his sexual otherness, coupled with his status as a political martyr – he was shot by Nationalist forces during the Spanish Civil War – was immediately appealing to a young man beginning to chafe against the clammy expectations of his family and community. Moreover, although García Lorca was not sexually attracted to women, his plays were noted for their strong, passionate, intelligent female characters, the type to

17

whom Cohen found himself increasingly attracted; a modern equivalent would be the feisty, larger-than-life females who inhabit the films of the gay Spanish director Pedro Almodóvar. The doomed poet and playwright became inextricably linked with the young man's interest in music when he took tuition from a Spanish flamenco guitar player who, as if fulfilling all the worst stereotypes applied to Cohen's work, committed suicide after giving just three lessons.

Cohen already had a conventional grounding in music, with childhood tuition in piano and tonette (a plastic wind instrument, similar to a recorder). He subsequently attained a decent level of skill on the clarinet, an instrument inextricably linked with the klezmer music of Eastern European Jewry. But mastering the guitar was not at that time the sort of accomplishment that existed as a rite of passage for the children of the respectable bourgeoisie; learning it was something Cohen chose for himself. A guitar was (except when in the respectable hands of a classically-trained master such as Andrès Segovia) the instrument of gypsies and buskers, a conspicuous, consciously selected badge of outsiderness. Were Cohen the sort of adolescent given to such gestures, it could have been perceived as a sign of defiance.

The themes of rebellion and music reconnected with Cohen's ethnic and religious roots in 1950, when he became a counsellor at a Jewish summer camp. Whereas the tight-knit Jewish middle classes of Montreal were united in social and political conservatism (and were thus passively amenable to the deadening control that the Roman Catholic Church maintained over many of the city's civic institutions), there was another tradition at work at Camp Sunshine, where the fireside singalongs carried a distinctly radical slant. Folk music, as performed by the likes of Woody Guthrie and the Weavers (featuring Pete Seeger) was enjoying a renewed burst of popularity in North America, and many of the lyrics were politically charged. For the first time, Cohen saw a link between his own Jewishness and a more general sense of resistance, whether it was expressed against the historical evils of Hitler and Franco, or the racism and capitalist exploitation of contemporary North America. This was out of step with the mainstream mood, especially next door in the United States, where many folk musicians came under the baleful gaze of anti-Communist watchdogs such as the House Un-American Activities Committee. The 1950s, it must be remembered, was an era of political paranoia and social conformity as well as youthful exuberance.

The songs that Cohen learned around the campfire, combined with the heady blend of Lorca and testosterone, prompted his first serious attempts at poetry. His motives, however, were far removed from the fist-shaking radicalism of Guthrie and Seeger, as he later explained:

I wrote notes to women so as to have them. They began to show them around and soon people started calling it poetry. When it didn't work with women, I appealed to God.[8]

It's a theme that would persist. In the coming years, Cohen's songs and poems would oscillate between paeans of anguished, lustful longing and psalms of rueful, theological contemplation. It was part of his appeal that it was often rather difficult to tell the two apart.

CHAPTER TWO
The Montreal poem factory

"The two qualities most important for a young poet are arrogance and inexperience."
– Irving Layton

Despite his peculiar and, at the time, rather unfashionable interests in gay Spanish poets and socialist folk singers, Cohen was far from being a social outsider while he was a student at Westmount High School. He was president of the Student Council, involved with the yearbook and drama club, and played a number of sports, including ice hockey, and claimed to be "about the ninth best defenceman in the class".[9] He had many friends, although, in keeping with the casual religious apartheid persisting in Montreal society during that period, they were almost exclusively Jewish.

Yet at the same time, he was beginning to concoct an image of aesthetic non-conformism that placed him in implicit opposition to the structures of school and the wider community. In common with his hero Lorca, his was not a violent rebellion, rather a constant reminder that there might be another path which the sheep-like majority would never consider following. His admission to the marginally freer environment of McGill University, where he was a student rather than a pupil, simply allowed him to pursue these bohemian tendencies with more abandon.

In his four years at university, he made token efforts to assume skills befitting the sort of life his family might have wished for him, balancing his fascination for literature (his passion for Lorca now matched by an equivalent love of WB Yeats) with courses in accountancy and commercial law.

However, even his English lessons were neglected; it was beyond the classroom and the library that Cohen was acquiring his real education. One particular interest was in debating and public speaking. In his Westmount yearbook he had declared his ambition to be a "world famous orator", and at McGill he became president of the Debating Union in his final year. Hinting at his future tendency of being dissatisfied with his lot, and also his philosophical love of paradox, he used his new position to attempt to close down the society.

Debating was fun for a while, but Cohen derived greater satisfaction from the informal gatherings of students, teachers and hangers-on who found themselves united by their passion for poetry, their sense that it was something significant, even something powerful:

We really wanted to be good writers, good poets, great poets. We really took seriously Shelley when he said that poets are the unacknowledged legislators of the world. An incredibly naïve description of oneself, but we certainly fell for that. We thought it was terribly important, what we were doing. Maybe it was. Who knows?[10]

This ambition was focused by his involvement with a Montreal-based literary magazine called *CIV/n* (from Ezra Pound's abbreviation for 'civilisation'). This innovative publication specifically sought to find new voices in Canadian poetry, moving on from the slightly sentimental narratives of the past. There was a palpable sense of mission, almost a revolutionary spirit; in the words of AM Klein, from his long work 'Portrait of the Poet as Landscape', the *CIV/n* group sought:

To find a new function for the déclassé craft
archaic like the fletcher's; to make a new thing;
to say the word that will become sixth sense;
perhaps by necessity and indirection bring
new forms to life, anonymously, new creeds[11]

Many of the figures associated with the magazine were older and more established than Cohen, including two who became significant mentors to the young writer: his teacher Louis Dudek and the poet Irving Layton. It was Dudek who had symbolically 'knighted' the 20-year-old Cohen with his own manuscript of a poem called 'The Sparrows', signifying that he was no longer just a dabbler in poetry; and he would be instrumental in publishing Cohen's first book, although their tastes in and views on poetry would become very different. But it was Layton who would remain one of the staunchest champions of Cohen's literary credentials in the coming decades. Already a recognisable face and voice in Canadian media, he shared Cohen's budding fascination with women (he would marry five times before his death in 2006) and also offered a blueprint for the creation of a public image, although Layton's pugnacious mouthiness (similar in some ways to the American author Norman Mailer) was rather different from Cohen's eventual persona as a wry, enigmatic sage. In his poem 'For My Old Layton', from the 1964 collection *Flowers For Hitler*, Cohen would pay tribute to the older man's

paragraphs of love, hidden,
like a cat leaves shit
under stones

Many another poet would have been offended, but this neatly encapsulates Layton's subversive, bad-boy image, entranced by his own poetic gifts, yet mistrustful of the cultural baggage that surrounds it. He had a particularly hearty contempt for critics.

One element of Cohen's writing that Layton encouraged from the beginning was the need to focus on his Jewish heritage. This was not from any particular theological perspective (Layton's interest in religion as such was never as profound as Cohen's, and he classified himself as a free-thinker from an early age) but more from the passion that could be found in the rhythms of the Jewish scriptures, most specifically the prophetical writings. It was something that would carry over in the transition from Cohen As Poet to Cohen As Songwriter. Songs such as 'Story Of Isaac' (1968), 'Who By Fire' (1974), 'The Window' (1979), 'Hallelujah' and 'If It Be Your Will' (both 1984), and 'I Can't Forget' (1988) all have a basis in the stories or rituals of his faith; the form of the poems in *Book Of Mercy* (1984) is derived from the Book of Psalms.

The McGill poetry scene was select, not just from a sense of elitism or self-importance, but because there were very few people who were particularly interested. Over 30 years later, Cohen recalled:

You've got to understand that the English writing scene in Montreal is tiny. It's a French city and the actual number of people writing in English is very small. It didn't have any prestige or prizes at the time. Not even any girls. But a few of us were on fire and we'd write for each other and any girl that would listen.[12]

In addition to that self-imposed isolation from the mainstream, many in the group were Jewish, or from a recent immigrant background, or both. As well as Cohen, Dudek and Layton, these included the writers Eli Mandel and Cid Corman and the sculptor Stanley 'Buddy' Rozynski. It seemed as if to be a poet, one's outsider status had to be declared in advance.

Although Cohen's main creative focus during his McGill years was as a poet, he hadn't forgotten those few lessons from an unhappy Spaniard, nor the songs learned at Camp Sunshine. He formed a band within Hillel, the Jewish students' group; and with his school friend Mike Doddmann, and a mysterious bass player known only as Terry, he made up a country and western trio, the Buckskin Boys, playing cover versions at school and community dances and making occasional opportunistic forays into calypso music. As his notoriety as a poet developed, he would also begin to perform his verses with musical accompaniment, a pianist or guitarist at first, eventually appearing on occasion with a band of up to a dozen jazz musicians. But these were still strictly recitations of previously composed verses, and the seemingly natural progression to writing words with a specific view to having them sung to music would not come for several years.

For the time being, though, Cohen's musical endeavours were carried out purely for fun and spare cash, with no sense that in 50 years' time he might possibly be doing the same sort of thing before audiences of 100,000 people. As he later said:

There was never any sense that this would have any future, that there was anything but the moment. No sense of a career involved at all. The word 'career' always had a very unattractive and burdensome resonance in my heart. My idea was mostly to avoid participating in that activity called 'career' – and I've been pretty much able to avoid it.[13]

If music did have any major benefits at this stage, it was as an aid to Cohen's pursuit of women. Having overcome his early hang-ups about his height, he was developing into something of a ladies' man, insofar as the still conservative social structures of 1950s Canada would allow him, and the combination of sex and art made him a campus celebrity. As one of his contemporaries at McGill put it:

Already in college he bore the trace of a wound, the aura of a lover, the mantle of the artist. His father had died when he was nine years old. His poems about the body of "Freia" a mere consonant away from the girl we recognized as Freda, won for him the erotic distinction of a Shelley, a DH Lawrence. So bold a lover was bound to be as sure a poet.[14]

Freia was indeed Freda, an art student named Freda Guttman, and this relationship would persist even when she went to college in Rhode Island. As an artist, she was a willing co-conspirator in his creative escapades, while the fact that she was from a respectable Jewish family made her acceptable to the protective Masha Cohen, who never really got over Leonard's decision in 1953 to move out of the family home and share rooms with his friend Mort Rosengarten.

Even after Cohen and Guttman's romantic attachment ended, they would remain friends (a pattern that has persisted, give or take a few exceptions, in his subsequent dalliances). Guttman would also have a role in his first post-university work, the project that would, in a modest way, introduce him to a wider public. Impassioned readings and flamenco riffs were no longer enough. Leonard Cohen was going to write a book.

Although he had bowed to family pressures and entered law school upon graduating from McGill, he was fooling nobody, least of all himself. The poet Louis Dudek, one of his early mentors, was in the process of organising a series of volumes to give a wider audience to young Montreal poets, and asked Cohen to submit a selection. Freda Guttman provided illustrations for the book, which had an initial print run of just 500 copies.

Let Us Compare Mythologies is the work of a young writer, a novice feeling his way, although the overall quality is remarkably good, considering the fact that many of the poems were written by a teenager. Plenty of the themes that Cohen would revisit are already evident, alternating between religion and sex, or combing the two, as in 'Lovers', where an affair takes place against the background of an anti-Jewish pogrom. 'Elegy', meanwhile, suggests that he had still not come to terms with the death of his father, although some of the imagery ("his fluttering winding-sheet") has distinctly Christian undertones. 'The Song of the Hellenist', among other titles, points towards later Greek adventures. At his cleverest, Cohen echoes the witty metaphysical poets of the 17th century. 'The Fly', about an insect that disturbed his contemplation of the sleeping Freda, nods and winks towards John Donne's 'The Flea', both writers using a bug to communicate frustrated male lust. He's at his least convincing, strangely, when he lurches towards song. 'Prayer For Messiah' reads almost like a parody of the sort of radically tinged folk music he would have sung by the fireside at Camp Sunshine ("O sing from your chains", indeed.)

Critical response at the time of publication was generally positive, although there was some unease from older, more conservative reviewers over Cohen's fascination with the (to them) more disturbing aspects of life. Northrop Frye, already one of the most respected names in Canadian criticism, said that he looked forward to reading more from Cohen, and was especially taken by his treatment of Jewish themes, although "the erotic poems follow the usual convention of stacking up thighs like a Rockette chorus line".[15] On similar lines was this, from the literary magazine *The Fiddlehead*:

Mr. Cohen's greatest weakness is an overuse of images of sex and violence, so that at its worst his work becomes a sort of poetic reductio ad absurdam of the Folies Bergeres and of Madame Tussaud's Chamber of Horrors.[16]

The notion that a New York dance troupe, an elderly French nightclub and a cheesy London tourist attraction might be reliable yardsticks for unspeakable depravity demonstrates the aesthetic gap that had opened up between Cohen's generation and its predecessors. *Let Us Compare Mythologies* was a modest but representative example of a cultural shift that was suffusing all media at the time: the beats, the absurdists and the angry young men in literature and theatre; the French New Wave and kitchen sink realism in film; rock 'n' roll, political folk, bebop and free jazz in music. It was not just a transition from the precedent set by an earlier generation, it was a fundamental rejection of much of what they stood for.

Unfortunately for the fragile sensibilities of Frye, Donaldson and their like – the sort of critics who aroused the wrath of Irving Layton – things were going to get rather sexier and considerably more violent.

CHAPTER THREE
How many people in this city

"I remember sitting in a coffee shop in the Village, and I'd heard about a new spirit, a sweet spirit and I remember sitting there taking my paper placemat and writing in big letters 'KILL COOL!'"
– Leonard Cohen, 1992

The first edition of *Let Us Compare Mythologies* sold out quickly, further cementing Cohen's reputation as an exciting prospect on the Canadian literary scene. But the key word is 'Canadian'. Cohen himself later recalled the self-delusion and self-indulgence of his little writerly clique: "If we sold 400 books of poetry in Canada we considered ourselves to be well on the way to immortality."[17] As his biographer Ira Nadel later remarked, the English-speaking world as a whole was in thrall to the US Beat generation of Jack Kerouac and William Burroughs, and epochal works such as Allen Gingsberg's 'Howl' (1956). In the same period, the archetypical Canadian poem was EJ Pratt's 'Towards The Last Spike' (1952), an epic about the completion of the national railroad. So in a national context, Cohen's early verses were:

...pretty tame stuff, but for Canada, woah, great! Here is a young writer, found his voice, wasn't embarrassed to write nakedly about subjects that other poets had been much more discreet about.[18]

And while a few hundred Montreal intellectuals, a great many of whom were probably his friends, were sufficiently impressed to buy his first volume, this scorn for conventional discretion wasn't going to make his fortune, or even permit him to make a decent living from his writing.

His next move fulfilled both his practical and his bohemian aspirations. Postgraduate study at Columbia University, one of the fabled Ivy League of East Coast colleges, would add a patina of respectability to his frankly mediocre degree from McGill, and might actually help him get a proper job. His half-hearted attempts to engage with legal study had, as might have been expected, come to nothing, and stints working in his family's various factories were unsatisfactory for all concerned. Moreover, García Lorca, the hero of his adolescence, had studied at Columbia in the 1920s, and his mentor Louis Dudek had acquired his doctorate there in 1951 – it seemed a perfect fit.

The university, fabled alumni notwithstanding, was a disappointment; the Romantics and contemporary American literature were as unfulfilling as the law when they were confined to the classroom. Even the chance to write a term paper about his own poems didn't excite his critical faculties. But Columbia did have the distinct advantage that it was situated in New York City, whose jazz clubs and coffee shops made Montreal seem distinctly parochial. While he was studying, Cohen had a short-lived relationship with a fellow student named Anne Sherman, significant because it was his first serious entanglement with a woman who was not Jewish. He also briefly made the acquaintance of Jack Kerouac, just as the Beat movement that he exemplified penetrated the mainstream consciousness. "Yeah, I met Kerouac one evening," he recalled nearly 40 years later. "He was lying under a dining room table, pretending to listen to some jazz record while the party swirled on round him." But one drunken encounter didn't open that many doors. "I wasn't really invited to join the Beats as they went in their jalopies across the States. I did feel a certain kinship; but I don't think they considered my poetry was good enough to be included in their anthologies. They never invited me to submit my poems to their magazines." He failed to penetrate the self-consciously cool inner sanctums of Manhattan's counter culture, with its beards and bongos; the beret he sported was as much a nod to the francophone culture of his home town as it was a signifier of hip. He slunk back to Montreal, where he found the situation was much the same:

I was always only on the fringe. I liked the places they gathered,
but I was never accepted by the bohemians because it was felt that
I came from the wrong side of the tracks. I was too middle-class,

I was Jewish among the French Catholics. I didn't have the right credentials to be at the centre tables in those bohemian cafes.[19]

He was included on the album *Six Montreal Poets* as the voice of youth alongside the likes of Dudek and Layton, but it had long been obvious that those who were determined to be full-time poets usually don't get to eat. From the stifling sanctuary of his mother's house, Cohen made (relatively) serious efforts to find a career. While working for various family concerns in the city, with interludes yet again as a summer camp counsellor, he sought an opportunity that might combine excitement and stability, especially if it got him out of Montreal. His efforts to join the Pinkerton Detective Agency and the Hong Kong Police came to nothing when it turned out that he'd received a suspended sentence for resisting arrest and other public order offences in 1954. (Cohen had maintained, to no avail, that he'd simply been watching a group of over-exuberant McGill students celebrating a football victory, and was in the wrong place when the police arrived.) He also applied for a number of teaching jobs, although his modest academic credentials were of little help here.

In retrospect, there's an air of half-heartedness in Cohen's attempts to find a place in the real world, a place that might have made his father proud. He still saw his role as being a poet, and poets had a responsibility to look the part, to play their assigned role. In this, they were abetted by the panoply of critics and media commentators, happy to reinforce their aura of moody otherness. In the introduction to a televised discussion of his second novel, a few years later, the presenter Paul Soles set the stage for the writer thus:

Poets in this racing, challenging, highly paced day and age are not easily absorbed into the community, perhaps never were. We're inclined to feel separated from them because they respond to the world in a very sensitive way.[20]

One wonders how well such sensitivity might have gone down in the Hong Kong Police.

Despite the setbacks and frustrations, Cohen was still writing poetry, as well as performing it in the Montreal clubs that now seemed like a pale imitation of the Greenwich Village dives that he'd frequented in 1956-1957. He also made some tentative attempts to write drama (in collaboration with Irving Layton) and fiction, although none of these experiments would be made available for public consumption. He even started a literary magazine, called *The Phoenix*, which turned out to be rather less successful than *CIV/n*, and went on to help run an art gallery, which was driven out of business by a fire.

Cohen might have remained a small footnote in the annals of Canadian literary could-have-been-contenders had he not enjoyed two lucky breaks in 1959. The first was the acceptance of his second volume of verse by the prestigious Toronto publishing firm of McClelland & Stewart. Although this arrangement was hardly going to make his fortune (and in the end the book wouldn't be published until 1961), it was a sign that his work might have some kind of appeal beyond the incestuous camaraderie of the Montreal literary scene. Jack McClelland had offered him a contract not because he was a drinking partner, or past student, or the physical manifestation of some vague notion of literary promise, but because his poems were good enough to offer the possibility of critical and commercial success. In the neurotic hierarchy of writers, this could be seen as his first *proper* book.

The second stroke of fortune came when the Canada Council awarded him a scholarship worth $3,000. It was a pleasant surprise, but it forced him to a decision; he had to respond to the conflicting pressures from his family and community, who saw him as something of an aimless aesthete who really ought to knuckle down and get a proper job; and the beautiful people of New York and Montreal to whom he was just another bourgeois who tried that little too hard to be hip, and whose beret was worn at slightly the wrong angle.

In the end, he determined to turn his back on the lot of them.

CHAPTER FOUR
European monasteries

The intellect of man is forced to choose
Perfection of the life or of the work
– WB Yeats, 'The Choice'

Cohen's decision to use the Canada Council money to fly to London was based on impeccably artistic reasoning: he wanted to be in the heartland of English literature, to be able to summon up the ghosts of Shakespeare and Milton to act as muses to his creative vision. The reality was rather less romantic, as he touched down in December, 1959, during a particularly wet and gloomy British winter. Almost his first purchase was a blue Burberry raincoat, which would later achieve a modicum of fame on its own account. Many years later, he would still complain that "living in England is like living in a cabbage."[21]

He lodged in Hampstead, an area of north London then and now dominated by the wealthy, liberal-leaning intelligentsia, with friends of Mort Rosengarten's parents. His hostess Stella Pullman offered the right balance of discipline and encouragement, insisting that he produce at least three pages of work each day, on the Olivetti typewriter he bought for £40; the novel he was working on would eventually be published as *The Favourite Game*, although it had started life as *Stars For Neatness*.

Despite Cohen's desire to pay homage to the pillars of the literary canon, most of his activities were distinctly low-brow, albeit enjoyable. In the company of Nancy Bacal, a friend since the days of Westmount High School, he particularly enjoyed the semi-legal clubs and parties frequented by the growing population of Caribbean immigrants; this was the subculture then being depicted by Colin MacInnes in novels such as *City of Spades* and *Absolute Beginners*. It was an atmosphere where art, politics and crime danced together in sweaty basements, fuelled by exotic music – the mento and R&B that served as precursors to ska and reggae – and the best marijuana in London. One of his acquaintances was a hustler and pimp called Michael de Freitas, who restyled himself Michael X (and subsequently Abdul Malik) upon joining the Nation of Islam. Michael X had grand schemes to foment a revolution in his native Trinidad, and even offered a government role to Cohen.[22]

It must have given him quiet satisfaction to have been mixing in circles far more dangerous and exotic than those frequented by the New York beatniks who had spurned him a few years before; although it may only be coincidence that of the two pubs on his street in Hampstead, the William IV and the King of Bohemia, he preferred to frequent the former. Cultural self-improvement blurred with debauchery again when he visited Dublin, nominally to pay tribute to one of his poetic heroes, WB Yeats. He did manage to attend the Abbey Theatre, which had been a creative hub for Yeats, Sean O'Casey, JM Synge and other figures of the Celtic Revival, although the original building had burned down in 1951; in any case, the Irish trip metamorphosed into something of a pub crawl.

By the spring of 1960, Cohen had completed the first draft of his novel (then known as *Beauty at Close Quarters*), as well as revisions to his new poetry collection. The weather in London had barely improved. According to legend, after a visit to the dentists, he stepped out of an Underground station in the financial district, and through the rain spotted a branch of the Bank of Greece. A teller let him know that the weather was rather more agreeable in his homeland, and the deal was pretty much done. As Cohen told the tale a few years later, the teller was defying the vile weather by wearing sunglasses: and "that was the most eloquent protest against the landscape that I had seen."[23]

In fact, he had long been attracted to Greek culture, and a number of poems in *Let Us Compare Mythologies* include Hellenic references. In London, he had already made the acquaintance of Jacob Rothschild, scion of the legendary banking dynasty, who told him of the island of

Hydra, where his mother owned a large house. It was home to a thriving colony of artists, most of whom were considerate enough to speak English. By mid-April Cohen was out there and instantly felt at home, as he recalled more than 40 years later:

I felt no culture shock, on the contrary, I felt that everywhere else I'd been was culture shock, and this was home. I felt very much at ease in Hydra... every corner, every vision – just looking out the corner of your eye – whatever you saw, whatever you felt, whatever you held was beautiful, and you didn't have to say those words to yourself, it was just... When you picked up a cup you knew by the way that it fitted into your hand that it was the cup that you always had been looking for. And the table that you sat at, that was the table that you wanted to lean on, and the wine, that was ten cents a gallon, was the wine that you wanted to drink, the price you wanted to pay.[24]

It was an underdeveloped place, with intermittent supplies of electricity, and water drawn from wells; the only mode of transport, aside from walking, was by donkey. Nonetheless (or more likely because of this primitive rigour), it attracted a diverse community of writers, artists and musicians, and its popularity as a movie location was also growing. Cohen had found a community of cool that welcomed him, although he was still slightly wary of the dangerous-looking young men who hovered as the boats came in, doubtless up to no good. "They were the hipsters of Piraeus," he later recalled, "the guys who developed modern bouzouki music. They made our hipsters look like kindergarten kids."[25] Cohen had finally discovered someone cooler than Jack Kerouac.

As is often the case in artistic communities, very little art actually got done. Creative energies were chiefly expended on drinking and fucking, the latter more often than not in the company of someone you weren't really supposed to fuck. Romantically unattached when he arrived on Hydra, Cohen was at first an amused observer of the coital merry-go-round on the island, until he met a Norwegian named Marianne Ihlen.

She was nominally in a relationship with her novelist compatriot Axel Jensen, and had a son by him. However, their association was as fraught and complex as any other on Hydra, and when Axel transferred his affections to an American painter, Cohen and Marianne became lovers. It was Cohen's most significant relationship up to that point.

Cohen's domestic stability was further assured in September, when he used a bequest to buy a three-storey house on the island. It gave him a secure base in which to work, as well as a home for Marianne and Axel Junior; the three of them were, to all practical purposes, a family. It was, on the face of it, an idyllic environment. He wrote more poetry, fine-tuned his novel, and listened to music: country and western from US Armed Forces radio; Greek songs from the local stations; and the few LPs he'd brought from Canada, Ray Charles being a particular favourite at the time. He also consumed industrial quantities of hashish, amphetamines and LSD, which occasionally distracted him from his work:

I have a lot of acid stories, as everyone does. At the side of my house there was a kind of garbage heap that during the spring would sprout thousands of daisies, and I was convinced I had a special communion with the daisies. It seems they would turn their little yellow faces to me and smile whenever I started singing or addressing them in a tender way.[26]

Things weren't quite perfect, however. Although his monetary outgoings on Hydra were minimal (his house had cost $1,500, which he had inherited after the death of his grandmother), so was his income. His second poetry collection was not scheduled for publication until the following year, and McClelland & Stewart were still undecided about the fate of his novel. He realised that the only way to maintain an ideal lifestyle was to criss-cross the Atlantic, earning money in Canada, and then spending as little as possible of it in Greece. In an odd way, he was living the life of an immigrant labourer, scrabbling for cash to feed his family back home; the odd twist was that 'home' was abroad. But it could have been worse. "I was living on $1,100 a year," he later said:

> It was a very good, very peaceful time, except for these convulsions of anxiety, when I'd go back to Canada to make some money. Yeah, I worked in an office. I ran an elevator, I did a great deal of journalism, I sold some short stories.[27]

Cohen's never-ceasing conflict between bourgeoisie and Bohemia had, it would appear, once more resolved itself as stalemate. It wasn't to last.

CHAPTER FIVE
The Spanish voices laugh

"The fact that the lines I write don't come to the end of the page doesn't qualify me as a poet."
– Leonard Cohen, 1961

Cohen had attended Columbia University partly in emulation of Federico García Lorca, and had been rather disappointed with the experience. But at least he hadn't been in risk of his life, which is what happened the next time he followed in the footsteps of his idol.

Lorca had followed his New York interlude with a three-month sojourn in Cuba; but that wasn't the only connection that Cohen made between the poet and the island. In 1959, Fidel Castro had toppled the corrupt, plutocratic, Mafia-backed regime of Fulgencio Batista, and was creating what he saw as a socialist Eden in the back yard of the United States. The thematic, romantic link with the Spanish Civil War – the conflict that had claimed Lorca's life – was obvious. Castro and Lorca were clearly political and cultural soulmates, although Fidel's views on homosexuality might have provoked a little frostiness between the two men. Cohen, who had no problems with being something of a cultural tourist, went to see what was going on.

Apart from his romantic/political instincts, he was also deeply attracted to the notion of placing himself in danger, of stepping outside his comfort zone, even further than Hydra (although of course geographically closer to his homeland). His father's experiences in the First World War, and his knowledge of the way his people had suffered under Russian and German oppression, made him aware of what a safe, privileged life he had led up to this point. He explained the motivation for his trip to Cuba in the 1965 documentary:

The real reason was a deep interest in violence. I was very interested in what it really meant for men to carry arms and to kill oth-

er men and how attracted I was exactly to that process... That's getting closer to the truth; the real truth is that I wanted to kill or be killed.[28]

Unfortunately, his romantic preconceptions of Cuba turned out to be somewhat misplaced. The popular upheaval that had swept aside Batista's dictatorship had also closed down many of the casinos and brothels, and tainted the louche, easygoing sleaze of Havana's bars and restaurants with an aura of collective earnestness. García Lorca would not have found much to enjoy. That said, Cohen found enough night-life, music and company to amuse himself.

His yearning to see death and violence seemed more likely to be fulfilled. The political situation was growing more serious, especially after the United States deployed a force of anti-Castro Cubans in the debacle that would become known as la Batalla de Girón, or the Bay of Pigs invasion. Cohen's Canadian passport gave him some degree of protection – woe betide any red-blooded *Yanquis* in Havana that summer – although there was an air of paranoia that tended to place any foreigner under suspicion. His mother sent a worried message to the Canadian embassy asking him to return, as did Irving Layton. Cohen's publisher Jack McClelland also expressed disquiet, although that was partly because Cohen had gone to Cuba without checking the page proofs of the new book, *The Spice-Box Of Earth*, potentially holding up publication.

In the end, Cohen's luck ran out, and he was arrested on suspicion of being an American spy. He was, however, eventually able to convince the soldiers that he was a supporter of the revolution, and even had his photograph taken with them. In fact, so convincing was his display of camaraderie that it rebounded on him when, towards the end of April as he was trying to leave the country, officials saw the picture and made the deduction that he was a Cuban *militano* trying to defect with a forged passport. Only by taking advantage of a distraction on the tarmac did he manage to give his teenaged guard the slip and make it onto the plane back to Miami.

Cohen's experiences in Cuba inspired a few poems, although their content was mainly directed away from the island: notably 'The only tourist in Havana turns his thoughts homeward', which imagined what Canada would be like if it aped Castro's oppositional anti-Americanism, in increasingly absurd terms ("let us dump asbestos on the White House... let us terrorize Alaska... let us threaten to join the U.S.A. and threaten to pull out at the last moment") and would be published in Cohen's third collection, *Flowers For Hitler*. But the most lasting effect of his visit was to sweep away much of his political idealism; Castro was just another dictator, not the liberator of the oppressed masses he claimed to be. This political agnosticism, verging on cynicism, was a trait that would set Cohen apart from his contemporaries in the 1960s. While his fellow artists became involved in the great social issues of the decade (such as Vietnam, race relations, gay and women's rights) Cohen was rarely drawn to explicit comment. Only in 1992, when he was nearly 60, would his recorded output veer anywhere near a statement of political belief; and when it did, he revealed himself to be something of a contrarian, well out of step with the liberal attitudes espoused by his fellow artists.

To the relief of his friends and family, Cohen made it back to Montreal by early May, in time for the publication of *The Spice-Box Of Earth*. It was, inevitably, a more mature collection than its predecessors, and also demonstrated a wider range of interests. The title is a reference to the Havdalah, the ceremony that marks the end of the Sabbath, at nightfall on Saturday, during which participants traditionally inhale the scent from a box of spices, to remember the sweetness of the day of rest. The fact that Cohen's spice box is stuffed with earth might suggest a glum dullness to contrast with the transcendence of the religious ceremony. In fact, he wanted it to represent the excitement of reality, as opposed to the symbolism of ritual, as he explained in a radio interview in 1961:

> *I wanted to designate a kind of variety of experience. I wanted this book to be the kind of book that you could dig into and find many kinds of emotions and many kinds of encounters.*[29]

His fascination with the paradoxes of Judaism extended to the poems themselves, particularly 'The Genius', which investigated the historical reinventions of Jewish identity, from "the ghetto Jew" to Dachau, via the Inquisition, Broadway and (fleetingly) economic success. He also paid tribute to his virtual mentor, AM Klein, depicting him as "the weary psalmist", an allusion to the Biblical story of David to which he would return in the 1980s; further Old Testament allusions, to the Song of Solomon, came in 'Beneath My Hands':

> *your small breasts*
> *are the upturned bellies*
> *of breathing fallen sparrows.*

But there was more to the collection than Judaism: the ache of absence ('I Long To Hold Some Lady', 'For Anne'); the essential otherness of the writer ('I Wonder How Many People In This City'); the self-delusion of freedom that besets humanity ('A Kite Is A Victim'). 'You Have The Lovers' depicts an enclosed, possibly half-imagined amatory nexus that reads like a blueprint for Cohen's controversial second novel, *Beautiful Losers*.

The Spice-Box Of Earth was not simply a niche product for the self-appointed literary elite; its commercial success (the first print run sold out in weeks) demonstrated its broad appeal, by the standards of modern poetry. When, in 2006, it was identified as one of Canada's 100 most important books, its champion JS Porter explained its charm: "Nothing human is alien to Cohen's wide-embracing heart."[30]

Of course, populist appeal can have its pitfalls. In a generally positive review in *Canadian Literature*, David Bromige cautioned – with a degree of foresight – about Cohen's occasional tendency to adopt the clichéd language of popular music:

> *A poet, if he wishes to keep his poems alive, must watch closely for those words whose meanings have decayed, and drive them away from his work. These are words like "heart," ruined by bad poets and successful song-writers; like "lovely" and "splendid," destroyed by advertising media. Leonard Cohen is obviously aware of the obsolescence of "heart," for it can be no accident that it does not appear once. But other ruined words – "beauty," "gold-*

en," and "glory," for example – frequently recur. And when a poet as perceptive as Leonard Cohen uses these words and others of like ambiguity, there are grounds for belief in his partial lack of creating consciousness. But only partial.[31]

It was an appeal, a supplication to the bohemian aspect of Cohen's psyche, to reject the financial lures of bourgeois success; and for the next few years at least, Cohen would allow the beatnik in him to predominate. In July, he set sail again for his Greek island.

CHAPTER SIX
On the very threshold of greatness

"I think that's a good thing for anyone to be, a brilliant failure. I can't stand success. It's obscene."
– Leonard Cohen, 1963

Back on Hydra, Cohen resumed his relationship with Marianne and continued to work on his novel. He was disappointed by the fact that Jack McClelland had passed on the chance to publish it; in fact, Mc-Clelland didn't really think his prized young poet should be dabbling with prose fiction at all. But the relationship between the two men remained cordial. Cohen's indulgences on the island, as he reported in a letter to the publisher, were "hashish, cognac and neurotic women",[32] although this turned out to be a watered-down list of his preferred substances. An encounter in Montreal with the Scottish junkie writer Alexander Trocchi had introduced him to the joys of opium, although his first experience with the drug had rendered him temporarily blind. He got used to its effects, and found a local pharmacist who could supply the drug discreetly.

He would not have defined himself as an addict to any of these substances (except possibly the women, neurotic or otherwise); he saw alcohol and drugs as sacraments, and as aids to the process of physical and creative self-mastery. As he explained in a television interview in 1966:

You can co-operate with the vision that alcohol gives you; you can co-operate with the vision that LSD gives you; I mean, all those things are just made out of plants and they're there for us and I think we ought to use them; but there's another kind of high to get

from refusing to use them. You know, there's all kinds of possibili-
ties. Asceticism is a high too. Voluptuousness is a high.[33]

It was on Hydra that Cohen had begun his serious investigation of
religious and spiritual pursuits beyond the teachings of Judaism. Axel
Jensen was an early influence in these studies, which focused on Asian
philosophies, with particular reference to *The Tibetan Book Of The
Dead* and the *I Ching*. The latter was of particular interest to Cohen,
and he can be seen using it with some Montreal friends in the documentary *Ladies And Gentlemen... Mr Leonard Cohen*. Also known as
The Book Of Changes, it is a book of Chinese hexagrams intended to
help the reader divine the future, and it became hugely popular among
the hippies and flower children of the late 1960s and early 1970s. It
was also around this time that Cohen became a vegetarian, a lifestyle
he would maintain until about 1968. Perversely, the return to meat coincided with the point at which he became seriously interested in Buddhist meditation.

Meanwhile, the London-based publisher Secker & Warburg had
agreed to publish his novel, provided there were substantial revisions;
Cohen also acquired an agent, Sheila Watson at David Higham Associates. She objected to his proposed title, *Beauty At Close Quarters: An
Anthology*, calling it "terrible, vulgar and out of keeping with the style
of the novel"; alternatives they discussed included *Buried Snows, Wandering Fires* and *Winged With Vain Desires*.[34]

Possibly wary of the peripatetic lifestyle of their new author (were
they aware of his cavalier response to the proofs of *The Spice-Box Of
Earth*?), Secker insisted that he needed to come to London to work on
revisions for the new novel. He moved back in with the Pullmans in
Hampstead. He was still depressed by London's damp and cold – especially because he now had the delights of Hydra with which to compare it – but he also returned to the West Indian clubs he'd enjoyed
so much on his first visit. There he discovered a new pastime, new to
him at least – the Twist. By 1962, this global dance craze (spawned by
Chubby Checker's hit single of two years before) was on the wane, but

to Cohen, who had been in voluntary exile from most manifestations of popular culture, it was something fresh and fascinating. It also rescued him from the meticulous tedium of the editorial process.

His obligations to Secker discharged, and having finally decided on a title – *The Favourite Game* having edged out promising late contenders including *Fields Of Hair* and *The Moving Toyshop* – he returned to Hydra. There he was visited by his mother, who remained blissfully unaware of Marianne's existence for the duration of her stay; not only was she a gentile, but she was also divorced, and her association with Leonard, the scion of a rabbinical caste, would have been considered shameful if the more orthodox members of Montreal Jewry had been made aware of the situation. Having survived this interlude, Cohen went to New York to meet his publishers at Viking, who would be bringing out the US edition of the novel. It finally saw the light of day in the autumn of 1963.

In an interview he gave on Canadian TV in 1963, Cohen dismissed the notion that *The Favourite Game* was a fictionalised self-portrait:

> *The emotion is autobiographical because the only person's emotions I know about are my own. The incidents are not autobiographical. I apologise. I'm terribly sorry. I cringe before the tyranny of fact but it is not autobiographical. I made it up out of my little head.*[35]

In fact, anyone who had known Cohen even slightly during his teens and twenties would have known this to be nonsense. *The Favourite Game* hardly bothers to hide its autobiographical roots. It's the story of Lawrence Breavman, born into a well-off Jewish family in Montreal; his father dies young, and he has a difficult relationship with his neurotic mother. In a more private context, in a letter to Jack McClelland, Cohen did qualify his denial that the novel might owe more than a little to the author's own life: "Lawrence Breavman isn't me but we did a lot of the same things," he wrote. "But we reacted differently to them and so we became different men."[36] Breavman adores and pursues women, finds employment in a factory and a summer camp, and somehow manages to become a literary celebrity. The author's experiments with hypnotism, and his tragic-comic attempt to make himself taller with wads of Kleenex also come into play. Apart from Cohen and his family members, his friend Mort Rosengarten appears in the form of Krantz; his New York lover Anne Sherman is Shell; the "divine idiot" Martin Stark is based on Robert Elkin, one of the children under Cohen's supervision at summer camp (although Elkin was spared Martin's grisly fate).

In literary terms, it's a *Künstlerroman*, a novel that traces the emotional and intellectual development of a character into adulthood as an artist. But *The Favourite Game* is rather more than a thinly-disguised account of the writer's own life. It is peppered with literary and other cultural references, as if Cohen is desperate to impose some aesthetic resonance on the misadventures of a bright, horny teenager. Dylan Thomas, Robert Frost, Gerard Manley Hopkins and WH Auden all receive name checks; "Canadians are desperate for a Keats" he wails at one point, although he's never arrogant enough to suggest that he might adopt the mantle. The fragments of Breavman's poetry are Cohen's own, from *The Spice Box of Earth*, making the biographical connections irresistible.

And it's not only poets that hover; Breavman tells Krantz that "we're walking into a European movie", and there seems to be a conscious effort to replicate the nonchalant cool of French *nouvelle vague* filmmakers. Aside from the stylised existentialism of the genre, François Truffaut's *Jules et Jim* (1962), with its dangerous emotional tensions between two men and a woman, is echoed as Breavman and Krantz follow the stranger towards Sherbrooke, and a similar dynamic arises later within the relationship between Shell, Gordon and the mutely adoring Roger.

And yet *The Favourite Game* is a novel. Henry James and Joseph Conrad also enjoy passing references, and both were identified by the literary critic FR Leavis in his 1948 book *The Great Tradition* as the pinnacle of English novel writing. Leavis's theories would have been earnestly debated in the classrooms of McGill in the 1950s, and the coffee shops nearby.

However, this is far from an ego trip. Breavman/Cohen is a gauche, self-obsessed young man who leaves a trail of emotional destruction wherever he goes, disappointing family, friends and lovers alike. "The dialogue" with which he and Krantz bond is wittily absurd, but is ultimately a substitute for the emotional maturity that neither of them can yet attain, and just as much an escape from reality as the obsessive routines of the autistic Martin Stark. Although Breavman achieves a degree of success by the end of the narrative, it's not at all clear whether he's actually grown up at all.

The nearest literary models are not James or Conrad, however, but two more modern authors. JD Salinger's *The Catcher In The Rye* (1951) was a key text in the post-war development of youth culture, and there are clear similarities between the anti-heroes of the two books; although Breavman is calmer and possessed of a more calculating self-awareness than Salinger's Holden Caulfield. The most obvious model, though, is James Joyce's *A Portrait Of The Artist As A Young Man* (1916), which depicts a similarly priapic, slightly obnoxious youth in late-19th century Dublin; Cohen had studied the book at McGill, as part of a course run by the Canadian novelist Hugh MacLennan. What *The Favourite Game* lacks by comparison is the massive spiritual crisis equivalent to that undergone by Joyce's Stephen Dedalus; a sermon on the torments of hell transforms him temporarily into a priggish, self-denying state of Catholic fundamentalism. Only when he has his emotional epiphany, seeing a beautiful young woman paddling in the sea does he come to the belated realisation that transcendent joy is also possible in the real world, without necessarily running the risk of eternal damnation.

Breavman's chafing against the norms of society, especially religion is a key component of the book: witness his discomfort at his father's funeral, and the childish bellowing of "FUCK GOD!", which would have been distinctly shocking in 1963, with authors such as DH Lawrence (another candidate for Leavis's 'Great Tradition'), Henry Miller and John Cleland having been banned in the United States until 1959. But the closest he comes to articulating a spiritual position is his throwaway line to Wanda: "We all want to be Chinese mystics living in thatched huts, but getting laid frequently." Probably unwittingly, Cohen is expressing what would eventually become a summary both of his life and of his art, the uneasy balance of the spiritual and physical. But Wanda doesn't see it that way, and she just runs off.

The Favourite Game is an enjoyable novel, but hardly a great one. Cohen himself was not particularly proud of it even as it was being published, although the subsequent award of the Prix litteraire du Québec, worth $4,000, may have reconciled him to its charms. His second novel, the controversial *Beautiful Losers*, is probably more highly regarded by critics today; but Cohen's debut still has its supporters, such as the critic and academic TF Rigelhof, who has identified it as being among the 10 greatest Canadian novels ever. [37]

However, its real value is as a marker towards Cohen's later literary development. It's as if the author is obsessed with testing boundaries, but more those of society than of his own talents as a writer. Aside from the childish blasphemy and expletives, it deals with a number of subjects that were rare in fiction in the early 1960s, such as masturbation and menstruation; this risqué element may have helped persuade *Cavalier* magazine, a sub-*Playboy* men's periodical, to publish an extract. In addition to the sex, there's a troubling strain of violence that resurfaces throughout the narrative. At first it is restricted to animals: pet rats are variously disembowelled, drowned and starved; a live bullfrog is dissected; a cat has its brains dashed out on a sidewalk. These weird episodes prefigure the climactic discovery of Martin's crushed body, which persuades Breavman to return to Montreal. Whereas Joyce's Dedalus is propelled into manhood by a glimpse of petticoats, Cohen's alter ego is awoken by a violent death.

While Joyce's *Portrait* is still read and enjoyed today, its true significance is in its status as a sort of dry run for *Ulysses*, widely lauded as one of the most significant, influential novels of the 20th century.

The inevitable question was whether *The Favourite Game* might be a first step to something bigger, a Great Canadian Novel, or at the very least a novel that communicated the essence of Montreal in the same way that Joyce depicted Dublin in *Ulysses*. There are a few nods towards Joyce's later masterpiece; for example, Mrs Breavman's single-sentence rant at the end of Book II, echoing Molly Bloom's inner monologue at the conclusion of Joyce's epic.

But the closing pages of *The Favourite Game* hint instead at other creative directions, as Breavman sits in a restaurant in Montreal:

> *The juke-box wailed. He believed he understood the longing of the cheap tunes better than anyone there. The Wurlitzer was a great beast, blinking in pain. It was everybody's neon wound. A suffering ventriloquist. It was the kind of pet people wanted. An eternal bear for baiting, with electric blood.*

Cohen was indeed a sort of literary pet but, as yet, not enough people seemed to want to allow him on the furniture.

CHAPTER SEVEN
The gargoyles of guilt

"I don't know, everybody has become kind of loony"
– Leonard Cohen, 1966

The Favourite Game earned some positive reviews, but sales were paltry, not helped by the fact that the novel remained unpublished in the author's native land until 1970; before that point, the only version available to Canadian readers was the expensive import of the British Secker edition.

Despite this, Cohen was by now a celebrity, amongst the Canadian literati at least. His relative youth, and his tendency to deal with often difficult subject matter, gave him an unsought reputation as the cultural voice of the young. When a crew from the National Film Board of Canada filmed Cohen and three other poets (including Irving Layton) on a reading tour in 1964, the footage was re-edited to make it a documentary about Cohen alone.

Ladies And Gentlemen... Mr Leonard Cohen is interesting not so much for what it tells us about Cohen at the time, but because of what it tells us about the way he was perceived by the cultural establishment. The sequences of Cohen sleeping, waking, bathing, drinking in Montreal bars, strolling soulfully in the parks of his childhood are all staged or, as Cohen remarks later in the film as he watches the footage, "not entirely devoid of the con". But the tone in which he is presented suggests bohemian danger; even his professional life is conceived in terms of sex and drugs: "He picks up a prize or pushes a book." He stands in front of a young audience, saturnine in a leather jacket, like the academic he never became.

The film also speaks of a time when it was considered quite normal to make a film about a poet who wasn't dead or the winner of a Nobel Prize (yet).[38] Although Cohen had the ear of the young, he was still depicted as coming from the world of art. Footage of him jamming on guitars and harmonicas with his long-time friends Robert Hershorn and Mort Rosengarten is depicted simply as goofing around; the narrator's remark that "He listens largely to pop music" is uttered with barely concealed condescension. Back then, real poets didn't go in for that sort of thing.[39]

The recital footage included in the film demonstrates the extent to which Cohen's writing style had changed; his new pieces tended to be shorter, less lyrical, not afraid to shock, and the proposed title for his next collection, *Opium For Hitler*, was par for the course. Jack McClelland was uneasy about the change in direction, and said so. However, possibly aware of the hurt he'd caused by rejecting the writer's first novel, and appreciating the value of the Cohen brand (although he would never have thought about it such a crass manner), he agreed to publish the book.

Like *The Favourite Game*, *Flowers For Hitler* (the title under which the new book was finally published) pushes against the standards of taste that were prevalent in North America in the early-to-mid-1960s. In particular, as the title suggests, the poems frequently refer to the events of World War II, still fresh in the memories of many. Any Jew whose forebears had left continental Europe before the Final Solution had ground into action must have felt conflicting pangs of relief and guilt, and a nagging sensation of "what if?"

Stylistically, the poems display the influence of the Beat movement; not so much the laconic existentialism of Jack Kerouac, but the swirling rage of Allen Ginsberg's 'Howl' (1955). Unlike Kerouac, Ginsberg had become a friend of sorts, visiting Cohen at his Hydra hideaway; in 1977, he would provide backing vocals, alongside Bob Dylan, on the *Death Of A Ladies' Man* album. It's interesting to compare the *Hitler* poems with those of the so-called Liverpool poets (Adrian Henri, Roger McGough and Brian Patten) who were also Beat aficionados, and were fascinated with the weird detritus of pop culture; in Cohen's case, this surfaces in the form of Miss Canada ('Business As Usual'), Abbot and Costello ('Disguises') and Jack Benny's violin ('Congratulations'). But it's his invocations of the Nazis: Hitler the aspiring architect; Goebbels the failed novelist; the banal vital statistics of Adolf Eichmann that really provoked sharp intakes of breath upon publication. Today, although these names are still bywords for evil, they don't necessarily provoke the same degree of visceral loathing; imagine, for a modern-day comparison, sardonic squibs about the frustrated teen-age dreams of the 9/11 attackers.

Although many of the poems in *Flowers For Hitler* are formally imaginative, and some of Cohen's droll couplets raise a smile, it does have the feel of a writer getting things out of his system. As one contemporary critic put it:

> *It's useful to think of* Flowers for Hitler *as the author auditioning himself for all the parts in an unwritten play. Useful because it underlines the process of self-recovery and self-discovery that is at the center of these poems.*[40]

Retrospectively, the performance for which *Flowers For Hitler* was a preparation can be identified as being Cohen's next book, his second published novel. In contrast with *The Favourite Game*, which had been composed across a meandering, four-year span of revisions, deletions and interminable title changes, *Beautiful Losers* was produced in two concentrated bursts of activity in 1964 and 1965. The author went for days at a time without eating, fuelling his 12-hour typing sessions with amphetamines and Ray Charles records. Soon after he sent the finished manuscript to McClelland & Stewart, he collapsed from a combination of exhaustion and sunstroke, although he seems almost to have enjoyed the situation, as he described in an interview the following year:

> *I think there are certain times in your life when, if you don't stop, things just stop for you. You get a fantastic singlemindedness when you are lying in one place hallucinating. For me, it ended a lot of things. I would like to say that it made me saintly.*[41]

The publishers were somewhat perplexed by what he sent; the text seemed to have made the same sort of stylistic leap that Joyce had managed between *Portrait* and *Ulysses*. While Cohen's fiction debut had been a challenging text, it did pretty much keep to a conventional narrative form, with a beginning and an end. By comparison, the new work was difficult, abstract, allusive, dotted with interior monologues, historical diversions, radio broadcasts, soul music, passages in French and Greek, sound effects, even magazine advertisements; in an explicit nod to Joyce, the dialogue had no quotation marks, instead being prefaced with long dashes. It was self-involved, self-referential, maybe a little self-indulgent, definitely, defiantly post-modern; as one critic later put it, "fiction that is also about fiction".[42] The language was often coarse, obscene even; the characters were mostly unlikeable; there was sex and violence aplenty.

Beautiful Losers also picks up from *The Favourite Game* in its meme of a *ménage a trois* (a conceit that also ties it to the Leopold-Molly-Boylan triangle in *Ulysses*). The protagonists are the unnamed narrator, obsessed with the historical figure of Catherine Tekakwitha, a 17th century Iroquois and Canada's first saint; his wife Edith, who has committed suicide by squatting at the bottom of an elevator shaft and waiting for the car to crush her; and his deranged friend F., who claims supernatural abilities and has also been sexually involved with Edith. There is little action as such; instead, the reader is confronted with pages of reminiscence and monologue, to the extent that one wonders whether the whole thing is intended to be the deluded imaginings of the narrator. There are weird historical interludes about cannibalism ("Strawberries taste like pork, too.") and the torture of missionaries, juxtaposed with contemporary pornography. ("Actual Photos of Male and Female Sex Organs and Excrement.")

Apart from the challenging structure and the off-putting language, there was another problem. Although *The Favourite Game* was clearly and recognisably set in Montreal, it was to a great extent an Everyman narrative, with which many a clever, unfocused young reader could identify. The content and context of *Beautiful Losers*, by contrast, are specifically Canadian, in fact specifically Québecois. Two decades ago, in his novel *Two Solitudes*, the writer Hugh MacLennan (also a professor at McGill during Cohen's time at the university) had addressed the apparent incompatibility and lack of understanding between Canada's two main cultures. In the early 1960s, French-speaking Quebec separatists had begun a bombing campaign in Montreal, and Cohen depicted F. as one of their number. Although Cohen's first language was English, his Jewish identity meant that he didn't identify particularly with the English-speaking, Anglican establishment in his home city; his instinctive loyalty was to Quebec he believed, whether or not it was part of a wider, Anglophone-majority Canada. *Beautiful Losers* offered a political and cultural challenge, as well as formal difficulties.

Jack McClelland's unease was born out. Many big book-stores were wary of devoting too much space to such a problematic volume. The critics did not help, balancing praise for Cohen's audacity with acknowledgement that this was a difficult, often dispiriting book, which many readers simply would not get. The review in the *Toronto Star* was typical, saying that it was both "the most interesting Canadian book of the year" and also "the most revolting book ever written in Canada".[43] The English writer John Wain (once a member of the so-called 'Angry Young Men' wave of British novelists and playwrights, roughly the transatlantic equivalent of the Beats) warned Canadian readers that the book ought to provoke a period of self-examination:

> ...*fragments of contemporary politics are flung at the reader in a thick, pelting shower, and from it emerges both a personal tragedy and a judgment on Canadian life... Mr. Cohen has a real theme, the frightening vacuum of modern Canada and the Canadian's uncertainty as to who he is and where his allegiances lie, both historically and in the present. I hope it will be widely read in spite of all.* [44]

Although *Beautiful Losers* was in some ways ahead of its time (a few years later, after Cohen had become a household name, it would sell far more than it had on its initial release), it could also be argued that it had slightly missed the boat. Obscenity actions in the United States and the United Kingdom a few years before had raised public awareness and interest in "challenging" volumes such as *Lady Chatterley's Lover*. While there were clearly plenty of readers attracted by the possibility of titillation in a respectable wrapper, there was no doubt that authors such as Lawrence had become totems in the battle for freedom of expression. It was not a battle of his making, but it was one he was prepared to join, as he explained on a Canadian TV show that dealt with the critical reaction to the novel:

I don't think that anybody really considers the censor's opinion of your work definitive. The censor is in disrepute. The censor's having a hard time... People are really having more fun in an obvious kind of way. People are professing their appetites in a franker kind of way although they're probably not getting turned on very much. Society seems to be making a lot about orgasms and appetites and freedom; so that by writing a pornographic novel you're forced into the role of a very minor hero.[45]

Unfortunately for Cohen there were any number of books being challenged on the grounds of taste and decency, and his got a little lost in the deluge. The publication of *Beautiful Losers* coincided with the successful (albeit short-lived) banning in the UK of *Last Exit To Brooklyn* by the American Hubert Selby, Jr. In some ways, *Beautiful Losers* was too difficult to be a bestseller, and yet not difficult enough to be a fully fledged *cause célèbre*. As with all his previous books, the author's public persona received a boost (lots of appearances on Canadian TV shows flirting raffishly with interviewers asking why he wrote such a dirty book) while actual sales figures remained depressingly low.

Decades later, Cohen was asked to provide a preface for the first Chinese translation of the book; he seemed, if not embarrassed by the book itself, slightly bemused by the passions it provoked:

This is a difficult book, even in English, if it is taken too seriously. May I suggest that you skip over the parts you don't like? Dip into it here and there. Perhaps there will be a passage, or even a page, that resonates with your curiosity. After a while, if you are sufficiently bored or unemployed, you may want to read it from cover to cover. In any case, I thank you for your interest in this odd collection of jazz riffs, pop-art jokes, religious kitsch and muffled prayer - an interest which indicates, to my thinking, a rather reckless, though very touching, generosity on your part.

Beautiful Losers *was written outside, on a table set among the rocks, weeds and daisies, behind my house on Hydra, an island in the Aegean Sea. I lived there many years ago. It was a blazing hot summer. I never covered my head. What you have in your hands is more of a sunstroke than a book.*
Dear Reader, please forgive me if I have wasted your time. [46]

At the time of writing, Leonard Cohen has not published another novel.

CHAPTER EIGHT

He wants to trade the game he knows for shelter

"I cleared my famous throat."
– *Beautiful Losers* (1966)

The disparity between the critical reputation of *The Beautiful Game* and its commercial performance forced Cohen to confront a few harsh realities, as he would recall in a 1993 interview:

> *It became quite clear to me that I couldn't make a living as a writer without going to the university or something like that, and that was a kind of revelation, because I had thought, 'How wonderful, I'm getting published, and as the night follows the day, everything's going to work out.' I've never had a clear sense of career. I just felt that the work was going to establish me in some kind of economic reality that would allow me to pay my bills. But it didn't happen that way. In hindsight, it sounds absurd.*[47]

His disillusionment with the literary life was reinforced by the sales figures for his next volume of poetry, *Parasites Of Heaven*. To be fair, it's a half-hearted addition to the Cohen canon, lacking even the shocking-for-its-own sake vigour of *Flowers For Hitler*; its only real interest for anyone but the Cohen completist lies in the fact that several of the poems would be resuscitated in the next stage of his career.

Cohen's decision to enter the music business was sudden, and at the same time long delayed. He was by no means a novice or inexpert musician, having played guitar at summer camps and with his Jewish and country bands as far back as the early 1950s. Later, he had performed his poems to a musical accompaniment in Montreal clubs.

His next musical phase began in February, 1966 at, of all places, the 92nd Street YMCA in New York, when he concluded a poetry recital with a composition called 'Traveller'; he would later record it as 'The Stranger Song'. He reprised the song three months later, along with early versions of 'Suzanne' and 'So Long, Marianne' on an edition of the Canadian TV show *Take 30*, which was otherwise devoted to discussion of the furore provoked by *Beautiful Strangers*. Host Adrienne Clarkson gave an introduction that seemed, in its *de haut en bas* way, to be redolent of the references to "pop music" in the commentary to the NFB documentary broadcast the previous year:

Leonard, in fact, wishes not to be a poet, but a kind of modern minstrel. He's become very excited by the music of the mid-60s and the kind of music that comes pouring out of the transistor radios into the ears of young people.[48]

Unfortunately, the minstrel himself was almost as distanced from the beating heart and transistorised ears of youth culture as Clarkson. His long spells in the isolated paradise of Hydra had cut him off from many of the contemporary developments in popular music. The closest he'd come to 'pop' in the conventional sense was his passing fascination for the Twist, a dance craze that had already become the preserve of drunken aunties at weddings rather than hip young trendsetters. To attempt a reinvention as a pop star at the age of 31 did seem to be a radical step, as absurd in its own way as his notion that poetry might pay its way. The 1960s was a decade that put a premium on youth, and Cohen was, in the weird chronology of popular music, a middle-aged man.

What little recent music he did know came in the form of the country hits played on US forces radio, when he'd been able to pick it up from his battery-operated transistor on the island. Cohen had long been an admirer of the doomed country pioneer Hank Williams, although by the middle of the 1960s, Williams's raw, white howl had been supplanted by the lush, over-orchestrated 'countrypolitan' sound, which had increased the popularity of the music far beyond its Southern heartland.

Nonetheless, Cohen set out for Nashville, home of the Grand Ole Opry and headquarters of the country music industry. But he didn't make it; for reasons that remain unclear, he stopped off in New York City, which would become his base for the next couple of years.

His feelings about New York were mixed. He was excited by its aura of danger and decadence, and its ethnic complexities that made Montreal's linguistic duality seem straightforward. But at the same time, this was the city that had rejected him a decade before, deeming him insufficiently bohemian. Maybe now, with a few well-received books on his resumé, the welcome would be warmer.

He soon made the acquaintance of a group of writers and performers who had taken the sounds of British and American folk music – the sounds that formed the roots of Cohen's beloved country songs – and invested them with contemporary political resonance. Bob Dylan, Joan Baez, Judy Collins and others like them were among the first musicians to achieve commercial success with what could loosely be labelled 'protest music'; unsurprisingly, the programmers for the army stations to which Cohen listened on Hydra had tended to avoid their songs about the evils of war and racial intolerance. He had become intrigued by some of Dylan's songs, much to the bemusement of his fellow Montreal poets, who failed to appreciate the wordplay between the consumptive harmonica solos.

The sounds were new to Cohen, and yet, at the same time, he instinctively understood them. Dylan and Baez were following a tradition that led from The People's Songbook, the source of many of the radical anthems he'd sung at summer camp in the 1950s, and old leftists such as Pete Seeger, who had played in Montreal at the invitation of Sam Gesser, the man behind Cohen's first ever recording, *Six Montreal Poets*. This new generation of folk singers (others included Dave Van Ronk, Phil Ochs, Tom Paxton, Tim Hardin, David Blue and Canada's own Buffy Sainte-Marie) maintained the political integrity of Seeger and his ilk, but in many cases had managed to convert it into success on the pop charts. This was a model to which Cohen could aspire, shifting units without sacrificing his art, with acclaim from literary critics and *Billboard* magazine alike.

Unfortunately, by 1966, the pure folk sound (essentially just voice and acoustic guitar, with optional harmonica breaks) seemed almost as tired as the Twist. Dylan himself, the unchallenged leader of the pack, outraged folk purists by 'going electric' at the Newport Festival the previous year; already he had moved on from explicitly political songs (such as the anti-war 'With God On Our Side') to more oblique, surreal expressions of personal discontentment. He had performed with the majority-Canadian rock outfit that would eventually become known as The Band; Cohen's arrival in New York coincided with Dylan releasing his double album, the organ-heavy *Blonde On Blonde*, most of which had been recorded in Nashville.

In fact, 1966 has a fair claim to being the absolute qualitative peak of popular music, as the commingling influences of the British invasion, black soul from Detroit and Memphis, innovative production techniques on the West Coast (exemplified by the work of Brian Wilson and Phil Spector), a new spirit of political and social activism and increased use of drugs among the young, spawned a dizzying array of music.[49] Apart from Dylan's masterpiece, this was the year of the Beatles' *Revolver*, the Beach Boys' *Pet Sounds*, the Rolling Stones' *Aftermath*, The Who's *A Quick One* and the Byrds' *5th Dimension*; of 'Reach Out I'll Be There' and 'Sunny Afternoon' and 'Good Vibrations' and 'Land Of 1000 Dances' and 'It's A Man's Man's Man's World' and 'Summer In The City' and 'River Deep Mountain High'. Cohen's poetry and fiction had failed to reach a wide audience partly because his stylistic complexity was too advanced for many potential readers. Now he found his musical education to be behind, rather than ahead of the curve.

Fortunately, Cohen's New York contacts were not restricted to peaceable folkies. He was living in the Chelsea Hotel, the nexus of the city's bohemian scene for many decades; previous occupants had included Dylan Thomas, Édith Piaf, Brendan Behan, Jean-Paul Sartre and William Burroughs. Although they wouldn't actually meet for a few years, Bob Dylan's residency crossed over with Cohen's, as did that of a promising young guitar slinger named Jimi Hendrix. His location gave also gave him access to a bevy of attractive young women, despite the fact that he was nominally still in a relationship with Marianne Ihlen, who was by then living with her son in a loft on the Lower East Side.

One who particularly attracted him was the actress, model and aspiring singer Christa Päffgen, better known as Nico. She was an associate of the artist Andy Warhol and performed with his protégés the Velvet Underground (whose front man Lou Reed was in turn an admirer of Cohen's writing, and got him to sign his copy of *Flowers For Hitler*). Nico, who claimed to prefer younger, prettier men, failed to succumb to Cohen's advances, which only added to the long-running fascination he felt for her: his songs 'Joan of Arc' (1971), 'Take This Longing' (1974) and 'Memories' (1977) would all to a greater or lesser extent be inspired by her. The fact that Nico, who had been born in Germany shortly before the outbreak of the Second World War, was a junkie and quite possibly a neo-Nazi can only have bestowed on her a strange sort of transgressive allure to the descendant of rabbis.[50] Rather less fraught was his fling with the Texan blues-rock singer Janis Joplin, then fronting the band Big Brother and the Holding Company; Cohen remembered the encounter in lubricious detail in 'Chelsea Hotel #2', from the album *New Skin For The Old Ceremony* (1974).

But the most important encounters with women that Cohen enjoyed in New York were strictly platonic. The first was with Mary Martin, a Canadian music executive and friend of Robert Hershorn, who had played banjo in Cohen's Hillel band. Martin was now working for Albert Grossman, manager to Bob Dylan; it was she who had pushed for Dylan to take on the Hawks (later to become The Band) as his backing group in 1965.

Martin was none too impressed with Cohen's singing voice, but she did like his songs, and suggested that he should get in touch with the singer Judy Collins, whose successful recording career dated back to 1961. Unlike many members of the folkie set, Collins was strictly an interpreter of other people's material, and was always on the look-out for new songs. Her reluctance to write her own songs was allegedly a reaction to a false accusation of plagiarism over a high school essay about TS Eliot's play *The Cocktail Party*.

It's unclear how immediately Collins became convinced of Cohen's prowess. Collins later recalled:

Leonard wasn't sure whether his songs were legitimate enough. He was a published poet and he used to go to these little poetry meetings at quaint scholarly places in Canada, but he certainly hadn't sung in public before, although he had sung the songs to a couple of very patient friends.[51]

Collins and Cohen got to know each other over an Italian meal, following which she asked him to return the next day and let her hear what he was about musically. Collins wasn't immediately won over, but she heard potential, and advised Cohen to go back to Montreal and work on the two songs he'd played for her. While he was back in his hometown, another opportunity presented itself, when CBC offered him the chance to present his own TV show. Had the possibility arisen 18 months before, he might have taken it; but now he was sure he wanted to be making art, not just talking about it, as he explained, in slightly hyperbolic terms, to a Canadian journalist:

The cosmic rules changed from whatever they were before... A major change occurred last year, something comparable to the beginning of the Renaissance. A lot of people now sense the change and are baffled. They feel the world has gone crazy, and they can't get their hands on what is happening. To get along, you have to become part of the chaos.[52]

He duly called Judy Collins from his tiny rented apartment on Aylmer Street and played 'Suzanne', based on his poem 'Suzanne Takes You Down', about a female friend, the wife of a Montreal sculptor. Collins was convinced, and included 'Suzanne' and 'Dress Rehearsal Rag' on her next album, *In My Life*. The other songwriters represented on her record provide a neat summation of the contrasting influences on Cohen's style: the folk stylings of Dylan ('Just Like Tom Thumb's Blues', from *Highway 61 Revisited*) and his Scottish doppelganger Donovan ('Sunny Goodge Street'); versus the melancholy European cabaret of Bertolt Brecht and Kurt Weill ('Pirate Jenny', from *The Threepenny Opera*) and Jacques Brel ('La Colombe'). The presence of Lennon and

McCartney (the title track) is a reminder of how big, how all-pervading, how *compulsory* the Beatles were in the mid-1960s; Cohen is one of the few major performers of the era whose recorded work betrays little or no evidence of ever having heard them.

Apart from her admiration for the quality of his songwriting, Collins saw something that Mary Martin had missed in Cohen's grave, gravelly baritone, and cajoled him to perform in public. On April 30, 1967, he appeared as her guest at an anti-nuclear benefit show. He began to play 'Suzanne', then walked off the stage, the reason, according to which source you choose to believe, being a broken string, tuning problems, or stage fright. Collins later said that the crowd had loved the gesture, presuming it was something deliberately avant-garde; nevertheless, she persuaded him to try again, and his brief spot was a storming success.[53]

Collins continued to support the nascent tunesmith, recording three more songs ('Bird On The Wire', 'Hey, That's No Way To Say Goodbye' and 'Priests') on her 1967 album *Wildflowers* and campaigning to get him added to the bill of the 1968 Newport Folk Festival, as part of a songwriting workshop alongside Joni Mitchell (with whom Cohen was then having a fling), Janis Ian and Tom Paxton. Meanwhile, Cohen was chivvying Collins to pick up a pen; her first composition, 'Since You Asked', was included on *Wildflowers*. In 2008, Cohen recorded a spoken-word version of the song on the Collins tribute album, *Born To The Breed*.

Although Cohen socialised easily with many in New York's folkie set, in some quarters there was a sense that he had not really paid his dues as a musician; and yet his lack of experience also seemed to give his work an air of freshness. The Canadian singer-songwriter Buffy Sainte-Marie summarised both these responses in an article she wrote for the long-running folk magazine *Sing Out!*:

He lacks musical training and whether or not the original quality of his melodies comes from simply not knowing what he is doing is not the point... He has the delicious gall to ask us, who do not even know him, to follow him into a completely original and sometimes scary mind of words without the aid of any of the old folksy musi-

cal clichés we are used to holding on to as a guide-rail... It's like
losing track of time; or realizing you've outgrown your name; or
getting off at Times Square and walking into the Bronx Zoo; you
don't know how it happened or who is wrong, but there you are.[54]

Cohen's performance at the New York benefit had won over a sceptical Mary Martin, who arranged another meeting, this time with
John Hammond, a senior artists and repertoire executive at Columbia Records. Hammond followed the same relaxed audition process as
Collins had done; a meal, then a one-to-one performance. After hearing Cohen play half a dozen of his compositions, he told the nervous
artist: "You got it, Leonard."

CHAPTER NINE
She gets you on her wavelength

"And then sweeping up the jokers that he left behind,
You find he did not leave you very much, not even laughter."
– 'The Stranger Song'

"I don't remember any early influences. I think I stole from every-
body I ever heard."
– Leonard Cohen, 1971

Executives at Columbia were wary about John Hammond's new pro-
tégé, although the A&R man could boast an unrivalled history of star-
making going back to the 1930s. He had had a major role in the discovery of Benny Goodman, Count Basie, Big Joe Turner, Billie Holiday,
Pete Seeger, Josh White (who Cohen had seen playing live at the age of
14), George Benson, Aretha Franklin and Bob Dylan. Before his death
in 1987 he would help Bruce Springsteen and Stevie Ray Vaughan on
the way to glory. He had proved the doubters wrong before: Bob Dylan's damp squib of a first album had led to the weird-voiced Minnesotan being dubbed 'Hammond's folly'.

Dylan's success had set a useful precedent for Cohen in that his lack
of a conventionally lovely singing voice was no longer a particular issue (although, to be fair, it was one of Hammond's earlier discoveries,
the jazz singer Billie Holiday, who had kicked that door wide open as
long before as 1933). Cohen remained insecure about his vocal abilities, although as Marty Machat, who would later become his manager,
said: "None of you guys know how to sing. When I want to hear singers, I go to the Metropolitan Opera." Cohen was heartened by this, as
he explained in 1988:

*I certainly never had any musical standard to tyrannise me.
I thought that it was something to do with the truth, that if you
told your story, that's what the song was about.*[55]

It was a feeling prevalent among many of his musical contemporaries. While the folk boom was host to a number of technically excellent singers (Judy Collins being a prime example), feeling and attitude and authenticity also counted for something. What was more significant, from a marketing point of view, was Cohen's age: he was nearly 33 when he signed with Columbia, and looked older. Moreover, with a publishing history going back more than a decade, there was no way the label's PR people could get away with shaving a few years off his biography. This was, after all, an era when youth was at an absolute premium. Pete Townshend of The Who had declared (through his mouthpiece, Roger Daltrey) that he hoped he'd die before he got old; the Berkeley Free Speech activist Jack Weinberg implored his friends never to trust anyone over 30. But Hammond's instincts trumped any fashionable outbursts of gerontophobia.

Hammond initially took charge of the sessions, bringing in the classically trained double-bass player Willie Ruff and, at Cohen's request, a full-length mirror; he had become so used to practising in front of his own reflection, he wanted to carry the habit on in the studio.

However, the bulk of the work (and the producer credit) went to John Simon, who would later achieve acclaim for his collaborations with The Band, Blood, Sweat & Tears and Janis Joplin's group Big Brother and the Holding Company, but was at that time best known for overseeing The Cyrkle's insubstantial folk-pop hit 'Red Rubber Ball' (1966). Many of Cohen's biographers have asserted that the job went to Simon because Hammond was unwell, and that Cohen and the producer had "a torrid relationship".[56] Simon himself remembers things a little differently. "I took over the gig from John Hammond, who wasn't moving quickly enough for Leonard as far as scheduling sessions while LC was waiting in the Chelsea hotel," he says.[57] Moreover, although there were heated differences over Simon's arrangements of the songs, the two men actually got on relatively well. "He was my genial host during the Montreal Expo back then," recalls Simon, referring to Cohen's

64

concerts during the World's Fair held in the summer of 1967. "Before the New York sessions, we worked together at my parents' empty house and he stayed up all night reading in my dad's library." What may have provoked creative tension was that, despite Cohen's relative inexperience in a recording environment, he had very strong opinions on how he wanted his music to sound. Simon, meanwhile, was aware of some of the disquiet being expressed by Columbia executives about John Hammond's latest discovery, and felt that sanding down a few of the rough edges would make commercial sense; after all, wasn't Cohen's main reason for becoming a singer to achieve the financial security that poetry could not offer?

In the end, Simon's additions were discreet and sensitive: for examples of what could have gone wrong, one could refer to the pizzicato strings that defaced Buddy Holly's last recordings, as if to turn him into a bespectacled Bobby Vinton; or the simpering choirs that Phil Spector smeared over the Beatles' *Let It Be* album. One of his signature features was to use a female voice as a backing sound, in the space where a horn or string section might otherwise appear. (The vocals on Cohen's album were provided by Simon's girlfriend at the time, Nancy Priddy, later the mother of TV and movie star Christina Applegate.) Priddy's wordless syllables cushion Cohen's voice without smothering it; it was a technique to which Cohen would return time and again in his later recordings, sometimes prioritising the female vocals to the extent that he effectively becomes a backing singer on his own recordings.

This was his first album, however, and he didn't want to be usurped before he'd even begun. After getting everything in the can, Simon left the final mixes to the featured performer. "I know he was unhappy with some of the charts and subsequently pulled in some street musicians to play," recalls the producer. "I wasn't around for those changes." In fact, because of the recording technology available at the time, four-track tape, it was impossible to remove many of Simon's additions from the recordings without starting all over again. The "street musicians" Cohen used included members of the psychedelic group Kaleidoscope, featuring future session legend David Lindley; they can be heard on the finished versions of 'So Long Marianne' and 'Teachers'.

65

Cohen's own view of the final result is best expressed by his note on the lyric sheet of the album, entitled *Songs Of Leonard Cohen*:

> *The songs and the arrangements were introduced. They felt*
> *some affection for one another but because of a blood feud,*
> *they were forbidden to marry. Nevertheless, the arrangements*
> *wished to throw a party. The songs preferred to retreat behind*
> *a veil of satire.*

Nearly a decade later, he was more charitable about his producer, acknowledging that "John Simon was great, and much greater than I understood at the time."[58]

The accusation most frequently levelled at Cohen by his detractors over the years is that his music is depressing, dirge-like, the stuff of suicides in dank attics; his supporters point instead to his wry sense of humour. The above suggests that, at the beginning of his recording career, he was still taking himself and his work a little seriously – unless, of course, he was joking.

The suits at Columbia were, it seems, underwhelmed by the finished product, sending it to shops on December 26, 1967 – reckoning, perhaps rightly, that few children would have been eager to find Cohen's musings in their stockings on Christmas morning. The cover design appears to have received little thought: a sepia head shot of the performer, taken in a photo booth in Montreal, with the album's title in lettering that may have appeared cutting-edge at the time, but now looks dated to the point of self-parody. The picture on the back is a kitschy painting of the Anima Sola, a traditional Catholic image representing a soul in purgatory (and not, despite some retrospective join-the-dots detective work by Cohen fans obsessed with later references to female saints, Joan of Arc or Bernadette of Lourdes). Half-assed as it was, this would by no means turn out to be the worst packaging to adorn Cohen's recorded work.

The music stands up rather better. Several of the songs have stayed in Cohen's live set four decades later, and have been recorded by artists as diverse as Roberta Flack, Harry Belafonte, Nina Simone, Nana Mouskouri and the Lemonheads. Side one opens with 'Suzanne', already a minor classic thanks to Judy Collins's rendition. It was inspired by Suzanne Verdal, a Montreal acquaintance who was particularly fond of a tea blend called Constant Comment, which was flavoured with dried orange rind (the "tea and oranges" in the first verse). That said, Cohen has recently indulged in a little historical revisionism with regard to a specific meaning or inspiration:

It was never about any particular woman. For me it was more about the beginning of a different life for me. My life in Montreal and my life wandering alone in those parts of Montreal that are now very beautifully done up and in those days, it was the waterfront. I used to wander around down there and I used to go to that church a lot.[59]

"That church" is the chapel of Nôtre Dame de Bon Secours, which houses "our lady of the harbour", the statue of the Virgin Mary that faces the water, blessing ships as they leave the city. This isn't the Montreal of Victorian Jews, or even the Montreal of bohemian poets; it's the home of the Francophone, Catholic majority (notwithstanding Suzanne's patronage of the Salvation Army); the Montreal that little Leonard encountered when his Irish nanny took him to church. The angelic softness of Nancy Priddy's voice adds to the sacred flavour.

'Suzanne' has become a definitive Cohen song; perhaps *the* definitive Cohen song, the one that even Cohen-haters don't mind (and of which the true Cohen devotees might admit to becoming a little sick). That it appears as the first track on Cohen's first album – as if the Rolling Stones had opened their account with 'Satisfaction', or Dylan with 'Like A Rolling Stone' – suggests a supreme confidence and a fully developed musical personality; or perhaps just an urgent desire to get his best work to the attention of the listening public. The British comedian Arthur Smith, in his 2000 stage show *Arthur Smith Sings Leonard Cohen* (later recorded for BBC radio), describes seeing Cohen playing live in Paris in 1976: "When we left, he was on his twelfth encore. Six of them were 'Suzanne'."[60] It's almost certainly an exaggeration, but it does communicate the extent to which the song has become identified with its creator.

Cohen has always insisted that he never had a sexual relationship with Mme Verdal; he claims that he would not have wanted to betray his friendship with her husband, and in his words, "the purity of the event was not compromised by any carnality and the song is almost reportage."[61] Similarly pure was his encounter with the teenagers (Barbara and Lorraine) who crashed in his hotel room in Edmonton, Alberta, a scenario depicted in 'Sisters of Mercy', which he also peppers with religious references. He wrote the song as he watched them sleep, a transaction he describes as "my confession"; he is a worshipper, a supplicant before women, even the ones who don't succumb to his eloquent wooing. 'Sisters' is one of the few songs that Cohen had completed at one sitting, without submitting to a protracted process of letter-by-letter revision. What was revised (once again) was the back story to the song. Cohen originally claimed, with an apparent desire to configure himself in the role of a romantic knight errant, that he had met the two girls in a snowstorm, and offered them refuge in his room; this was the version he gave in the notes on his first *Greatest Hits* album. It later transpired that the truth was a little more mundane, and that he had met them at a party thrown by a philosophy professor at the University of Alberta. He hadn't enjoyed the party, and in some ways they had rescued him – a story that does fit the meaning of the lyrics rather better.[62]

By contrast with the chaste (or choosy) Suzanne and Barbara and Lorraine, many women did succumb, of course, a situation that provoked several other songs on the album. 'So Long, Marianne' concerns the decay of his relationship with Marianne Ihlen, whose loyalty had been stretched to breaking point. The arrangement (with hoedown fiddles and a rat-a-tat snare drum) gives an uneasy, brittle edge to what might otherwise be a self-pitying wallow. 'Hey, That's No Way To Say Goodbye' is another break-up ballad, although just to confuse the issue, it's about the end of a tryst that took place while Cohen was still supposedly attached to Marianne; in his own words, "I was with the wrong woman, as usual."

Both songs are sad, that quality that quickly came to characterise Cohen's work, to the point it became a stereotype, a cliché. And yet at the same time, they are also ruefully positive, in a 'that-which-doesn't-kill-me-makes-me-a-better-chronicler-of-life's-agonies' kind of way. This can't be said for the album's closer, 'One Of Us Cannot Be Wrong'. The ode to jealousy and self-laceration is punctuated with whistling and yodelling that degenerates into atonal yelps; a hint of the more ascetic, stripped-down sound Cohen would use on his next two albums. It offers a lyrical template, in its cocktail of obsession, violence and guilt, with the sort of material Cohen's devotees such as Nick Cave would start to produce in the 1980s.

Elsewhere, Cohen offered a number of lyrical bon-bons to readers of his fiction and poetry: like 'Suzanne', 'Teachers' is based on a poem in *Parasites Of Heaven* ('I Met A Woman Long Ago'), and deals with the various spiritual mentors, the "teachers of the heart" that Cohen had been investigating, and with whom he was growing progressively disillusioned. Also from *Parasites* is 'Master Song', which deals with the potentially damaging effect of false gurus, as Cohen later explained:

I think in those days there was much concern with the idea of masters and disciples, with the idea that some people knew a lot more than you did; and the world was one vast monastery, in which we were all laboring to acquire enlightenment. I think the song treats that vision sardonically.[63]

'Master Song' also alludes to the sort of *ménage à trois* depicted in *Beautiful Losers* (and also to an extent *The Favourite Game*). The latter would remain a recurring theme of Cohen's writings well into the 1970s, although any attempt to infer specific biographical inspiration from the author would be deflected with a plea of faulty memory. 'The Stranger Song', meanwhile, was a revised version of 'Traveller', the piece he had performed in his very first singing engagements in the first half of 1966.

Reviews were polite but not ecstatic; *Rolling Stone* broke it down as "three brilliant songs, one good one, three qualified bummers, and three are the flaming shits." The reviewer also felt that Cohen (or maybe Simon) was trying and failing to emulate the innovative production techniques being pioneered by the Beatles and others: on 'One Of Us Cannot Be Wrong', he suggested, "the arrangement fades into a hilarious cacophony – but the Beach Boys did this kind of thing better in *Smiley Smile* (and they aren't even poets)."[64] In the *New York Times*, Donal Henahan compared Cohen unfavourably with Dylan (a pairing that would become more, not less common in the coming years), but suggested that the market was ripe for "a spell of neo-Keatsy world-weariness" and that Cohen might be the best candidate to supply this.[65]

Sales figures reflected the critical response: Cohen was not another 'Hammond's Folly', but neither was he the 'New Dylan' that many at Columbia were seeking. The old Dylan had returned from the recording hiatus that had followed his 1966 motorcycle crash; his comeback album, *John Wesley Harding*, was released almost simultaneously with *Songs Of Leonard Cohen*, which may have accounted for the modest sales of the latter. Interestingly, in view of Henahan's comments, the critic Christopher Ricks later declared that Dylan was not just "neo-Keatsy" but the equal, perhaps even the superior of the 19th-century romantic poet; an argument that some interpreted as a microcosm of the clash between high and low culture.[66]

The comparisons between Cohen and Dylan as songwriters were inevitable, if a little simplistic. However, the effect of Simon's production, especially with regard to the female harmonies, was to provoke comparisons with more commercially-oriented folk acts such as Peter, Paul and Mary or the Mamas and the Papas, and late-60s harmony pop groups such as the Left Banke and the Association. Parallels were even drawn with some of the poppier tracks (such as 'Sunday Morning'; 'Femme Fatale') on the Velvet Underground's first album, featuring Cohen's crush Nico.[67] Dylan's eponymous debut album, released in 1962, had featured nothing but voice, acoustic guitar and harmonica; the overall sound of Cohen's next two suggests that this was the sort of approach the artist might have preferred.

Today, the consensus among music reviewers is that *Songs Of Leonard Cohen* has its merits, but isn't in the very top rank of Cohen's recordings. Again, the production is held partly to blame for this, although there are some vociferous fans of Simon's efforts, including the critic Robert Christgau:

Cohen's actually far more vulgar than people think he is, and that's good, I like that about him. I'm glad he's not Joni Mitchell, whose first album is very spare and to me completely unlistenable.[68]

That, however, was the retrospective view. In 1968, Cohen's debut only tangentially troubled the *Billboard* charts, but did better in Europe; especially in Britain, where it reached the Top 20. This prompted a couple of further visits to London, to appear on a TV show hosted by the ex-pat American singer Julie Felix, and then to record a TV concert of his own, as well as taping a session for the DJ John Peel on the BBC's relatively new pop station, Radio One. He was no longer the impoverished novelist cowering from the rain in his still-not-famous blue raincoat. He was, if the word didn't seem too inappropriate, a star; far more so than he was in New York.

Maybe the collective desire for neo-Keatsiness was on the other side of the Atlantic. In any case, it was a pattern that would repeat itself more much in Cohen's career, giving him an absurdly low profile in the country that would eventually become his adopted home. For a 20-year-old starting out as a singer, such results in the single most important market for recorded popular music would have constituted an acceptable calling card; for a 33-year-old making one final attempt to earn a decent living from his creativity, it was more than a little disappointing.

CHAPTER TEN

The beauty of the word

"And I'll leave you with one broken man
Whom I will teach you to repair."
– 'You Know Who I Am'

In an interview published shortly after the release of his second album, Cohen seemed eager to become part of the mushrooming youth counterculture from which he'd previously felt excluded, both on account of his age, and also by his physical isolation on Hydra. "I've been on the outlaw scene since I was 15," he told the *New York Times*. "I had some things in common with the beatniks, and even more things with the hippies. The next thing may be even closer to where I am."[69]

There's a distinct air here of a man keen to prove his counter-cultural credentials. The reference to his 15th year is not accidental; that was the point at which he discovered the writings of García Lorca, and when he had his first guitar lessons. It's quite feasible to date his rejection of Westmount normality from that period. What's odder is his self-proclaimed allegiance to the beatniks (who spurned him in New York and Montreal) and the hippies (with whom he had little in common beyond his prodigious drug consumption). While Cohen's skills as a performer and writer were attracting plaudits, he was hardly in the vanguard of youth culture. The last sentence is prescient, however, as from the end of the decade his work would often be lumped together with the genre that went under the ludicrously vague label of "singer-songwriter", a progression from the 60s folk boom; others on the list would include Jackson Browne, Tim Buckley, Nick Drake, Richie Havens, Carole King, Gordon Lightfoot, Don McLean, Joni Mitchell, Randy Newman, Carly Simon and James Taylor.

Hovering over them all, however, was the spirit of Bob Dylan. At this point, Cohen and Dylan had never been in the same room together, although they had many mutual acquaintances, both from the folkie set and within Warhol's Factory clique, as well as being signed to the same record company by the same talent scout. But by the time Cohen had established himself in New York, Dylan had embarked on his 18-month hiatus, traumatised by the pressure of touring, adulation and drugs. (The extent to which his motorcycle crash in July, 1966 was a catalyst or a convenient excuse for his withdrawal is a point of debate among Dylan obsessives and may never really be properly resolved.) The fact that Dylan's comeback was recorded in Nashville – Cohen's intended destination when he'd set out on his unlikely musical odyssey – must have seemed like the height of bad manners. Moreover, the sparse instrumentation of *John Wesley Harding* (no strings or female syllables there) was presumably the sort of sound that Cohen had envisaged for his own debut, which John Simon had resisted.

So if Cohen was attempting to get ahead of the curve and pre-empt the "next big thing", his subsequent move seemed rather perverse. He followed his original itinerary and went down to Nashville, Tennessee, two years later than planned, where he used the same producer (Bob Johnston) and studio as Dylan had used for his comeback. It was almost as if he wanted to make a tribute album.

He also emulated Dylan's acquisition of a rural base, by moving into a small house about half an hour's drive from Nashville. This he rented from Boudleaux Bryant, co-writer, with his wife Felice, of numerous hits for the Everly Brothers, as well as Buddy Holly's 'Raining In My Heart'. Jettisoning the meat-free diet he'd enjoyed for three years or so, he acquired a gun, and made efforts to shoot small game. His move was partly practical, so as to be close to the capital of country music, but there was almost an element of image manipulation at work; he was preparing mythologies one again. As Ira Nadel puts it:

He was striving to move the music out of the self. He was living on this remarkable little farm in Franklin, Tennessee... He was influenced by the isolation of that, and that fit his romantic notion of the artist, out of Byron, out of Shelley, even out of Blake; he is a bard.[70]

But these weren't the only lifestyle changes for someone who'd once been a committed urbanite. Having finally said so long to Marianne, and ended his entanglement with Joni Mitchell, Cohen now took up with a 19-year-old Floridian named Suzanne Elrod. They had met in New York during Cohen's brief, strange flirtation with Scientology,[71] and they began a tempestuous relationship that would last for the best part of a decade. It may or may not have been an attraction that Suzanne, unlike Marianne, was Jewish; although it's unlikely that this made the relationship ideal in the eyes of Cohen's mother and other relatives, it probably didn't hurt. Suzanne moved in with Cohen at the Chelsea Hotel, and also followed him to Hydra and Montreal. Then, despite his initial resistance to cohabitation in Franklin, perhaps wanting to keep his professional and domestic lives separate, she joined him in the farm cabin in Tennessee.

Country music itself was changing, taking Nashville with it to an extent. Artists such as Johnny Cash (with whom Bob Johnston had also worked), Willie Nelson and Buck Owens were creating a grittier sound, closer to the Hank Williams records that Cohen had loved as a teenager, when he was playing with the Buckskin Boys. Dylan and The Byrds – especially in the period when Gram Parsons was a member – had identified common ground between country music and the counterculture. It was unusual to have a Jewish Canadian poet pitching his tent in the capital of American country music, but it didn't seem as downright bizarre as it might have done five years previously.

Johnston had assembled a trio of seasoned session musicians: Charlie Daniels, later to branch out on his own account with hits such as 'The Devil Went Down To Georgia'; Ron Cornelius; and Elkin 'Bubba' Fowler. Between them, the five men would provide the vast majority of the instrumentation, although there were occasional self-indulgences, such as a spree to France to record voices for the Resistance anthem 'The Partisan'. The song, by Anna Marly and Hy Zaret, was the first cover version Cohen had recorded, having picked it up from *The People's Songbook* when he was working as a camp counsellor in 1950.

Otherwise, all the tracks were Cohen's own compositions, many of them having been written during his first visit to Los Angeles, in early

1968. 'The Story Of Isaac' is particularly interesting from a biographical perspective, fusing the narrative in chapter 22 of the Book of Genesis (concerning the patriarch Abraham's willingness to sacrifice his son Isaac, a tale to which Bob Dylan had referred in his song 'Highway 61 Revisited') with the writer's own frustrated relationship with his father; "I was nine years old" refers, of course, to Leonard's age when Nathan Cohen died.

But other songs are less straightforward. 'Seems So Long Ago, Nancy' has a particularly complex back story, which seems to change according to who you ask, and when you ask them. Originally, Cohen claimed that it was the story of a friend from Montreal who committed suicide after giving birth to an illegitimate child that was taken away from her;[72] by the late 1970s, he was suggesting to the film-maker Harry Rasky that it was an invented tale, inspired by a woman he met beside the jukebox in an all-night diner in Nashville;[73] David Sheppard suggests that it's a "homage to his Montreal friend Nancy Becal [sic]."[74]

It could of course be argued that imposing empirical, historical meaning upon a song or poem or other work of art is just asking for trouble. Many contemporary listeners were content to have Cohen's records as little more than high-concept mood music for the end of a party; John Walsh identifies 'Nancy' as "the *chanson du choix* of the wretchedly drunk student clutching the lavatory bowl."[75] It was only the hardcore fans that sat alone in their bedsits and college rooms, poring over the lyric sheets as if they were the *I Ching*.

Certainly some of the tracks on *Songs From A Room* seem to be designed so as not to give up an explicit meaning too easily. 'The Old Revolution' would appear to be political, and 'The Butcher' is probably about drugs. 'A Bunch Of Lonesome Heroes', in common with 'The Partisan', suggests some sort of guerrilla warfare, which would have had resonance at the time of the Vietnam War.

But beyond that, the lyrics are gnomic and impenetrable, again, in the best tradition of Bob Dylan. That said, Cohen's fondness for opacity went back many years: long before he was writing songs, the poet and academic ML Rosenthal had suggested that "Leonard Cohen's diminutive poems were lyrics that had little or no meaning." One of his students at New York University countered that, on the contrary:

> *It wasn't the sense of these thin lyrics that mattered; rather, it was the aura that they created, the sense of the mysterious, the unknown that every human being experiences simply by being alive.*[76]

The strongest and most resilient track on *Songs From A Room* is the first, a Cohen classic to rank alongside 'Suzanne' from his previous album – and it's also the most penetrable. 'Bird On The Wire' had already been recorded by Judy Collins and David Crosby, but Cohen's performance would be the definitive one. The sparse arrangement – guitar, bass and Jew's harp, the latter provided by a friend of Cohen's from New York – sums up the stripped-down sound that Cohen had sought in vain for his debut, and the lyrics are something approaching a personal manifesto for the writer. Maurice Ratcliff rather neatly identifies its place in the Cohen canon as being analogous to Frank Sinatra's 'My Way',[77] although its place as a karaoke standard is less assured. Subsequently Cohen himself expressed misgivings about the recording, although in doing so he encapsulated in some ways the aesthetic of his performing style, in which honesty trumps technical ability at all times:

> *I don't like my recording of it, particularly... I wasn't in charge of my voice. But that also produces a kind of authenticity that some people find worthwhile or amusing or entertaining or even instructive. Just singing it the best you can.*[78]

In the song, Cohen – or, if you want to be really picky, the inhabitor of his narrative voice – yearns above all for freedom; freedom as an artist, a writer and a musician, but also, and less attractively, for the have-your-sexual-cake-and-eat-it aspect of the writer's personality. This latter paradox is neatly summed up in the album's packaging; although Cohen was now living with Suzanne Elrod, on the back cover there's a sweet picture of Marianne Ihlen in the house on Hydra. The front image is an improvement on its predecessor, but still no classic:

a monochrome shot of the artist looking decidedly stern, on a white background.

Despite the quintessentially American circumstances of its making, *Songs From A Room* performed just as feebly as its predecessor had done in the United States, while again more than justifying its existence in Europe. It reached number two in the British charts, and also made a real impact in France, not only because of the patriotic, bilingual fervour of 'The Partisan'. Perhaps the overwhelming sense of doomed romanticism appealed to an intelligentsia that had had its hopes raised by the near-revolution of May, 1968, only to see the country declare its confidence in the post-war conservative consensus. *Le Nouvel Observateur* dubbed Cohen "le folksinger de l'année", and the story went around that if a Frenchwoman owned a single record, it would be by Leonard Cohen.[79]

It's a frivolous statistic, of course, but it does sum up Cohen's growing fame, and the persona that he presented; the moody, smouldering existentialist, a pin-up boy for the thinking woman. His stern demeanour was not just a pose, however; he had long suffered bouts of depression, which couldn't help but have an impact on his writing and performances. Twenty years on, he recalled the making of *Songs From A Room*, and offered a justification for the gloomy aesthetic of which he was often accused:

> *I did start to break down around that time. There is a certain bleak quality to that record but it has other redeeming features. I don't think those are bad qualities for a singer necessarily. Everybody lives a life of the heart; everybody knows what it's like to crack up, and I think we cherish that in our singers when they manifest that in song.*[80]

Despite the poor sales of Cohen's records in the United States, Canada remained loyal to its latest favourite son, and his new European audiences found him fascinating. Moreover, his success in a different medium had had a knock-on effect on his book sales. He was still writing poetry in parallel to his songs, and his new volume *Selected Poems 1956-68* contained several new pieces alongside selections from his four previous books. The collection sold 200,000 copies in the United States alone – and he was finally achieving a reasonable level of financial security. *Selected Poems* earned him the Governor General's Award for Poetry, but he politely declined the prize, and the $2,500 that came with it, although he could never come up with a cogent explanation for his refusal. Earlier in the decade, when *The Spice-Box of Earth* had failed to win the same award, he had been crestfallen; now, it seemed somehow less important.

On a material level, Cohen's life seemed to be coming together, but he was still fascinated by many and various manifestations of the spiritual. Having disentangled himself with alacrity from the clutches of Scientology, he was open to new offers, new ideas.

CHAPTER ELEVEN
A saint does not dissolve the chaos

"The world is vast and wide. Why do you put on your robes at the sound of a bell?"
– Zen koan

Judaism is far more than a religion. It's a culture, a tradition, a heritage, a set of rituals, a way of life, a community, an ethnicity. While it is possible to be converted to Judaism, it's a fairly uncommon practice; the easiest way to become a Jew is to have the right parents. And once you're there, it's pretty much impossible to get out. Even if you renounce God and reject all aspects of Jewish life, you're still Jewish; many non-believers were sent to the death camps.

In many ways, Cohen was a poor Jew, especially by the austere standards of his rabbinical grandfathers. Drugs and fornication and foul language aren't usually part of the deal, although drinkers are welcome, even encouraged. But he still considered himself Jewish, keeping the Sabbath on Hydra, attending synagogue when in New York and Montreal. Deep down, he believed.

And yet the religious mosaic of Montreal maintained its spell; Cohen still remained curious about other routes to God, striving not for an alternative to the faith of his ancestors, but for an adjunct to it. He found it, strangely enough, in a wedding invitation.

The link was an American called Steve Sanfield, who had met Cohen on Hydra; the fact that Sanfield sold drugs at the time made the connection almost inevitable. He had later moved on to Los Angeles, where he became involved in a Rinzai Zen Buddhist group under the tutelage of a Japanese monk called Joshu Sasaki, known by the title Roshi, literally 'elder teacher'. Sanfield crossed paths with Cohen again in 1967, when the latter was recording his debut album in New

York, and Cohen expressed an interest in his friend's new lifestyle and beliefs.

This was a time when Eastern religions and philosophies – specifically Hinduism, Buddhism and traditions that merged elements of the two – were becoming highly fashionable among Western youth. The Beatles, inevitably, were at the forefront, attending retreats with the Maharishi Mahesh Yogi, and even travelling to his ashram in India. Over the next few years, every self-respecting esoteric philosophy would attract a rock star or two, with lead guitarists particularly welcome: Pete Townshend of The Who became a follower of Meher Baba; Sri Chinmoy attracted Carlos Santana and John McLaughlin; head Byrd Roger McGuinn joined the Subud sect; and George Harrison remained a devotee of Hare Krishna for the rest of his life. Jimmy Page's later fascination with the Satanist mystic Aleister Crowley was a rather more sinister manifestation of the same phenomenon.

Cohen knew about the principles of Zen, of course, and was fascinated by the apparently self-contradictory questions – *koan* – it involved (for example: "What is the sound of one hand clapping?") He was also interested in the rigorous self-discipline that was core to its practice. The fasts that he had endured while writing *Beautiful Losers* had been informed by Jewish traditions of asceticism, of achieving spiritual and personal growth by reining in the physical appetites of the human body.

However, he was also aware of his own human frailties, his desires for the fleshly pleasures of life; for sex and drugs and, in his own quirky way, rock and roll. His speed-fuelled self-denial on Hydra had already resulted in a physical and emotional breakdown. So it was in a spirit of intellectual curiosity rather than committed yearning that he travelled to Los Angeles for Steve Sanfield's wedding at the Cimarron Zen Center. The sight of Roshi preaching abstinence while knocking back cups of sake (Japanese rice wine) appealed to Cohen's love of contradiction and complexity. He realised that becoming involved in Zen practice was compatible with his Jewish identity and beliefs, and even with his enjoyment of the bacchanalia that constituted life as a rock musician. Like his friend Allen Ginsberg, who had become involved with the Hare Krishna movement, he understood that practising meditation was not a severing of his links to Jewish culture and belief. As he explained in 2008, when he had been following Roshi for nearly four decades:

The school of Buddhism that Roshi comes out of and his particular take on it, which is very unusual, there's no deity that is affirmed or rejected, so it doesn't really come in conflict with one's family religion.[81]

Although his commitment to Zen would ebb and flow over the years, Cohen's devotion to meditation certainly helped him retain an amused detachment about the more egregious activities that characterised the business in which he found himself. Before he'd even recorded his first album, he had mistakenly signed over the rights to three songs – 'Master Song', 'Dress Rehearsal Rag' and, most importantly, 'Suzanne' – to a publisher called Jeff Chase, who would not relinquish them until 1987. Cohen also discovered that his own publishing company, Stranger Music, was part owned by Mary Martin, who had introduced him to John Hammond and was acting as his de facto manager. His producer Bob Johnston introduced him to lawyer Marty Machat, who handled his affairs for the next two decades; it was only after Machat's death in 1988 that things began to unravel again.

Despite his discovery of the benefits of meditation, Cohen was still prone to bouts of depression and self-doubt. In 1973, after the poor critical reception of his first live album, he expressed his disillusionment with many aspects of the music business in no uncertain terms, provoking a spate of "Cohen Quits!" headlines. Inevitably, his words had been twisted: "I said, 'But I don't want to see a headline: Leonard Cohen quits music business and goes into monastery',"[82] he explained. "I mean, how can I quit? I've never been in it." His ability to be in the game and apart from it, at one and the same time, was quintessentially Zen – a Cohen *koan*.

CHAPTER TWELVE
When I am on a pedestal

"The shadows I live with are numberless."
– 'Gloomy Sunday'

In 1970 Cohen embarked on his first tour, starting in Germany. The 1960s were over, culturally as well as literally; the previous December, the murder of an 18-year-old youth by Hell's Angels 'security' during the Rolling Stones' set at the Altamont Free Festival had wiped the last vestiges of innocence, love and peace from the scene.[83]

Nobody was murdered at Cohen's gigs, but there were a few close-run things, some of them possibly explained by Cohen's heavy drug use at the time. He offered Nazi salutes to the punters in Hamburg, and took the entire audience back to his hotel in Copenhagen; at a festival in Provence, the whole band mounted the rickety wooden stage on horseback.

In August he played at the Isle of Wight Festival, in front of a crowd estimated at anywhere between 300,000 and 800,000. Others on the bill over five nights included Miles Davis, The Who, Chicago, The Doors, Jethro Tull, Free and Sly and the Family Stone; Cohen had the disadvantage of following Jimi Hendrix, playing what would be one of his last concerts. Worse, he went on near the very end of the festival (only Richie Havens would follow him), in front of an audience that was exhausted, strung out and restive; several food stalls had been set alight shortly beforehand. The reaction of the audience and media was mixed, with the British music press being particularly unkind, although by that point there can have been very few people on the island who were fully in command of their critical faculties. Footage of the performance suggests that Cohen and his band were on good form, although the tempos were exceptionally slow; drugs and tiredness almost certainly played their part. Cohen himself appreciated the exposure, but didn't enjoy the experience:

The band and myself were sleeping in this sort of trailer, we were supposed to go on at midnight and the whole thing was delayed so we all flaked out in this trailer. They woke us up and we got up there in this kind of daze and everyone was asleep in the audience, well a lot were sleeping. I think our music fitted in well with the general mood of the wipeout that everybody felt. I feel that the conditions of that festival were very unpleasant.[84]

Back in Nashville with the same band (now christened 'the Army' following the rigours of their European campaign), he began work on his third album, to be known as *Songs Of Love And Hate*. Regular gigs had boosted his confidence as a performer and his voice, if never a thing of beauty, is stronger and less wayward than on the previous albums. The starkness to which he aspired on *Songs From A Room* is leavened by strings, horns and choir, and occasionally perked up with drums. However his songwriting mojo would seem to have retreated a little. Some of the compositions here were several years old, and while there is nothing wrong with returning to old material, and remaking it, there is a feeling that some of the songs were simply rejects from earlier sessions, resuscitated to fill a gap where inspiration should be.

Songs Of Love And Hate does contain at least one copper-bottomed classic, in 'Famous Blue Raincoat', inspired by the garment Cohen had purchased to protect himself from the ravages of the London winter in 1959. The subject matter is yet another eternal triangle, the three points being the narrator, his lover – the recipient of his letter – and Jane, the woman who replaced her. However, Cohen claimed some time later that although the scenario was somehow based in fact, he'd forgotten the full details, and the true identities of the other people involved:

I always felt that there was an invisible male seducing the woman I was with; now, whether this one was incarnate or merely imaginary I don't remember. I've always had the sense that either I've been that figure in relation to another couple or there'd been a figure like that in relation to my marriage. I don't quite remember, but I did have this feeling that there was always a third par-

ty, sometimes me, sometimes another man, sometimes another woman.[85]

Cohen's weirdly formal sign-off ("Sincerely, L Cohen") is at once funny and moving; in common with so many men, his downfall is his inability to express his deepest emotions. The sepulchral verse is balanced by a sweetly keening chorus, that this author can't help comparing to Leo Sayer's 'When I Need You', but please don't let that affect your enjoyment.

The other keeper on the album is 'Joan Of Arc', another song reflecting Cohen's fascination with the iconography of Catholicism, refashioned as a gentle, faintly Gallic waltz, made eerie by being simultaneously sung and recited; this technique would resurface in Cohen's recordings in the 2000's, when his croaky *sprechgesang* was set alongside the voices of singers such as Sharon Robinson and Anjani Thomas. Despite the religious symbolism, it's very likely that it was written about Nico, the Teutonic maiden who had never succumbed to his charms; the pointed use of the word "heroine" may be a reference to her narcotic of choice.

Droll wordplay aside, much of the album is pretty bleak, comprising the sort of songs that Cohen-haters and Cohen-mockers point to when they suggest that he just makes music to accompany whimpering and wrist-slashing. The Biblically portentous 'Last Year's Man' is marred by a children's chorus (recorded at a London stage school, so Cohen and Bob Johnston were simply asking for trouble). 'Dress Rehearsal Rag', meanwhile seems too indebted to Bob Dylan in 'Positively 4th Street' mode. When Cohen first performed it in 1968, he introduced it by referring to a "Czechoslovakian" (actually Hungarian) song called 'Gloomy Sunday' that became associated with suicide and despair, although the notion that it was actually banned to discourage self-harm is an urban myth.[86] Maybe to protect the mental equilibrium of his more sensitive listeners, Cohen has avoided the song in recent years.

'Avalanche' exchanges downbeat self-loathing for an air of non-specific loathing, exacerbated by Paul Buckmaster's menacing string section. In fact, it has some of the brooding, coiled aggression that would come to characterise the post-punk genre of Gothic rock in the early

1980s; it's little surprise that Nick Cave wanted to get his jaws round couplets such as "Your laws do not compel me / to kneel grotesque and bare" on the first Bad Seeds album, released in 1984.

A couple of songs attempt to lift the gloom. 'Diamonds In The Mine' is a strange collision of reggae and up-tempo country, once again with a Dylan-esque sneer; 'Sing Another Song, Boys' is also energetic, despite being taken from the Mandrax-drenched Isle of Wight set. However, both seem artificially imposed on the overall mood, which is glum to the point of self-parody. The cover isn't so great, either: white lettering on black, with an inexpertly cut head shot of an unshaven Cohen, grinning like a beatific hobo.

Songs Of Love And Hate isn't exactly a bad album, but it's somewhat inconsistent, uncomfortably sequenced and Cohen's redeeming wit is in perilously short supply. Instead we get a sort of all-pervading bitterness that in small quantities is invigorating and honest, but across a whole album feels like the complaint of a man who's woken up with a hangover but can't remember the joy of his own drunkenness. In his review for *Rolling Stone*, Arthur Schmidt referred to "the essential stylelessness of the production, or perhaps the lack of stylistic integrity,"[87] which is about right. At first, Cohen was defensive, rebutting the kneejerk accusations that he wallowed in misery, as he expressed to the *NME*:

The songs are empty, and you can put into them what you want to put into them. My voice just happens to be monotonous, I'm somewhat whiney, so they are called sad songs. But you could sing them joyfully too. It's a completely biological accident that my songs sound melancholy when I sing them.[88]

With the perspective of a few years, however, he was more open to acknowledging the problematic nature of his own public persona, and the oppressive nature of the album:

There is a perception, too, of my songs as depressing, but I think that's not the case. One side of the third album I find a little burdened and melodramatic. I think that's the fault of the songs and

85

of the singer. It's a failure of that particular album, but it's not a characteristic of the work as a whole.[89]

Songs Of Love And Hate sold pretty poorly, even in Cohen's core markets of Canada and Europe, although Columbia showed no evidence at this stage that they might want to end their association. All the same, it was clearly time for a change of style and scenery – time to get the hell out of Nashville.

CHAPTER THIRTEEN
I am only whispering

"All you've cost me so far is money and pain."
– *McCabe and Mrs Miller* (1971)

"The mental hospitals are full of people who are artists."
– Leonard Cohen, 1972

Cohen may not have been developing into the neo-Dylanesque gold-mine that the bean-counters at Columbia might have hoped for, but he was carving out a respectable niche as a sage of the counterculture. Indeed, because of the reverse snobbery that inevitably afflicts alternative societies, relative lack of success gave him a sort of existential cool. Bob Dylan had hits; he even had (if you credited him for the success of The Byrds) chart-topping singles. Cohen's vision was just too left-field for that sort of commercial frippery.

Indeed, his absence from the charts, from the transistor radios that Adrienne Clarkson had described with such condescending bemusement, meant that his work was acceptable material for more refined creative media, which might have shied away from anything too explicitly 'pop'. As early as 1969, his music had been adapted by the Royal Winnipeg Ballet in a piece called *The Shining People Of Leonard Cohen*; in 1973, it inspired a revue under the title *Sisters Of Mercy*, which enjoyed a brief, largely panned run at the off-Broadway Theatre de Lys.

Potentially more lucrative was his tentative introduction to Hollywood. A film to be directed by John Boorman (*Point Blank, Deliverance*), to which Cohen was to have contributed songs, was aborted in the early stages; he was also involved in discussions with Franco Zeffirelli about a planned biopic of St Francis of Assisi. The latter film did actually see the light of day, as *Brother Sun, Sister Moon* (1972), but in the event the music would be provided by a different neo-Dylan, in the form of Donovan.

Cohen's Hollywood career finally got underway thanks to the director Robert Altman, who had been very impressed by his debut album when it was released, and now asked to use some of the songs on his "anti-western" *McCabe and Mrs Miller*, starring Warren Beatty and Julie Christie. When the film was released in 1971, Altman used three tracks from the album ('Sisters of Mercy', 'The Stranger Song' and 'Winter Lady') and a brief guitar instrumental that Cohen composed especially for him. Altman would later return to Cohen's music, putting 'Bird On The Wire' on the soundtrack of his 1978 ensemble drama *A Wedding*. Another film-making fan was the German *enfant terrible* Rainer Werner Fassbinder, who incorporated Cohen's music into his movies *Beware Of A Holy Whore* (1971) and *Fox And His Friends* (1975), as well as his TV productions *Like A Bird On The Wire* and the epic *Berlin Alexanderplatz*.

Aside from these contributions, Cohen also appeared in a film on his own account, when Tony Palmer, who had worked with the Beatles, Cream and Frank Zappa, directed him in the semi-documentary *Bird On The Wire* (1972). Cohen loathed it, an emotion not assuaged by the fact that he'd given several hundred thousand dollars to ensure it actually saw the light of day.

Also in 1972, Cohen brought out his first entirely new volume of poetry in six years, not counting the new pieces in *Selected Poems*. *The Energy Of Slaves* is a bitter, introverted collection, reflecting his souring relationship with Suzanne Elrod, a situation that had not been greatly improved by the birth of their first child, Adam. Cohen rarely allowed his relationships to interfere with his pursuit of other women, neither was he averse to commemorating those encounters in his verse: "I could grow to love / the fucking in New York" he crows in 'Far From The Soil'. At the same time, he is glumly aware of his failings and the hurt they might inflict, as demonstrated in 'I Left A Woman': "O go to sleep my faithful wife / I told her rather cruelly".

The title of another piece in the collection is 'The Poems Don't Love Us Any More' and the reader does get the impression that (beyond some kind of primal-scream-ish therapeutic value), Cohen at this point in his career was deriving little pleasure from the craft with which he had first made his name. As a writer, he felt out of place; out of time; unacceptable to the establishment and wary of the charlatans who dominated the counterculture; one untitled poem rails at "all the flabby liars / of the Aquarian Age".

To be fair to poetry, not much else was bringing a smile to his face either. Another European tour seemed to bring out his troublemaking tendencies. In Germany, a country where he was particularly popular, he wound up the Berlin audience with an impersonation of Goebbels; in Jerusalem he would only perform if the whole band was on acid. Even the practice of Zen had become less consoling to him; a snowbound retreat at Roshi's new base on Mount Baldy was such a cold, dispiriting experience that he decamped for an impromptu vacation in Mexico. As he later remarked laconically during a concert, "I've also indulged myself in the various religions and philosophies. But cheerfulness kept breaking through."[90]

A photograph taken by Suzanne of Cohen, with his hair shorn for the retreat, adorned the inside cover of *The Energy Of Slaves* and the front of his next album. With his brutal skinhead crop, fuck-you stare and the title in typewriter font it was by far the best sleeve yet to have wrapped a Cohen record (not a tough call, to be honest), pre-empting the design tropes of punk rock by several years. Sleeve notes by the eccentric artist Daphne Richardson, who had committed suicide in London before the record was released, add to the disconcerting effect of the overall package.

Live Songs, as the title suggests, is a collection of recordings from Cohen's tours of 1970 and 1972. Again produced by Bob Johnston, its main interest lies in the way it demonstrates Cohen's continuing tendency to rewrite his own work, as well as the presence of four songs that don't appear on any studio album, although whether any of them justify their inclusion on musical grounds is another question. 'Minute Prologue' is a self-referential improvisation recorded at the Albert Hall in London; 'Passin' Thru' is a likeable country standard, the sort of thing that would have been second nature to the musicians of The Army; 'Please Don't Pass Me By (A Disgrace)' is a bizarre half-spoken epic recounting Cohen's encounter with a blind beggar in New York;

and 'Queen Victoria', described by David Sheppard as "a dour ordeal of a song"[91] is a musical performance of the poem 'Queen Victoria And Me', originally published in *Flowers For Hitler*. In fact, it's questionable whether this last track qualifies either as "live" or as a "song"; it was taped in Cohen's cabin in Tennessee, with no audience present. In it, Cohen identifies with Victoria's feelings of loss and abandonment following the death of her beloved consort Prince Albert in 1861; although his over-enunciation of the monarch's name suggests a certain level of mockery. Because there's more going on here; in *Beautiful Losers*, the character F refers to the 1963 bomb attack that decapitated the statue of Victoria on Montreal's Sherbrooke Street. By the early 70s, Quebec separatists had moved on from such neo-Dadaist escapades, kidnapping and strangling the provincial government minister Pierre Laporte. Just as the wider global counterculture of the 60s had gone horribly wrong at Altamont, the parallel social changes in Quebec – to which Cohen had offered his support – had turned into something far bleaker, which rather matched the grim mood of the album, subsequently described by Sylvie Simmons as "a miserablist's dream" and "a contender for Most Sombre Live Album Ever".[92] Not only did *Live Songs* sell poorly (hell, Cohen was by now used to such snubs) but the critics didn't much like it either.

The blurry status of 'Queen Victoria' – poem or song, both or neither – mirrored a general feeling about its creator in the early 70s. What exactly was Leonard Cohen, this lugubrious Canuck whose work now adorned the ballet stage and cinema screen as well as concert hall and bookshop? A singer-songwriter? A poet? A novelist? Or just some kind of all-purpose curmudgeonly philosopher, offering ready-made epithets with which his devotees could pepper their chat-up lines?

All were agreed that at the heart of his craft was his ability to manipulate the English language. "Leonard Cohen's fans are word people," as one journalist put it. "For most of them, words have become the first aid station in the preventive detention camp of the feelings."[93] Emotionally and intellectually, he knew what made his audiences tick. And yet there was still a feeling that the grubby recording business was not an appropriate environment for such an artist, that he had in some strange way prostituted his art. The critic and anarchist George Woodcock complained:

If Cohen were not the kind of poet he is, he would never have started on the path of becoming a pop singer, and becoming a pop singer has deleteriously affected his recent development as a poet.[94]

Woodcock's own terminology shows how laughably outmoded his attitude was – "pop singer" puts Cohen on a par with Donny Osmond or David Cassidy – but it probably expresses the feelings of many who were excited by his early writings, seeing in him the potential to become the Canadian Yeats or Joyce (or at least Ginsberg or Kerouac). And now he was just going around taking drugs and screwing women and playing his guitar to hippies who didn't really appreciate his art. Cohen would publish just one more collection of poetry in the decade (the bitter *Death Of A Lady's Man*), and after that the gap between books would grow incrementally longer. And he would never write another novel. It seemed that he, at least, had an idea of what he was, or at the very least, what was expected of him; and critics such as Woodcock would just have to deal with it.

And yet he suffered from the common paradox of those who have experienced sudden success; when he got it, he didn't like it. As he explained in an interview in 1972:

I lived a lot better when I had less money. A lot more luxuriously, and so it's very confusing, as you might imagine. My standard of living went down as my income increased... Believe me, it's just the nature of money. Money in the hands of some people can only decrease their standard of living. I mean I lived a lot better when I had no money. I was living in a beautiful big house on a Greek island. I was swimming every day; writing, working, meeting people from over the whole world and moving around with tremendous mobility. You know, I can't imagine anyone living any better and I was living on about $1,000 a year. Now that I spend many times that I find myself living in hotel rooms, breathing bad air, and very constrained as to movement.[95]

This was a particular problem for artists who had achieved their fame and success in the late 60s, when the whole ethos of popular culture was directed towards an anti-materialist lifestyle, something far closer to the Greek island than to the hotel room. This discomfort, tinged with guilt, about the various roles into which he was forced – roles, remember, that he had fought long and hard to inhabit – persisted for Cohen throughout the decade. Asked why he had begun to reject the label of poet, he replied:

> *It's due to the process of cultural advertising which has the same effects as commercial advertising. Certain words become devalued and not only that but many people rush to embrace the description and I just don't like the company.*[96]

CHAPTER FOURTEEN
Let's all get even

"I'm not really a Jew; just Jew-ish."
– Jonathan Miller

"I don't have to have a song called 'Give Peace A Chance'. I could write a song about conflict and, if I sang it in a peaceful way, then it would have the same message. I don't like these slogan writers."
– Leonard Cohen, 1973

The Yom Kippur War of October, 1973 presented another dilemma to Cohen. Instinctively, atavistically, his sympathies as a Jew were with the State of Israel; moreover, the Egyptian and Syrian forces were in this instance the aggressors, having cynically chosen the Day of Atonement, the holiest point of the Jewish calendar, to launch their attack. However, he also had sympathy with the ordinary Arabs, especially those who had had their land seized by Israel in the aftermath of the Six Day War in 1967. Not, of course, that his political views were held with any great conviction, nor did they provoke in him any particular desire to follow up with actions; he had happily kept his house on Hydra when his more politically sensitive friends were encouraging him to move away in protest against the Greek military junta taking power in 1967.

So it came as something of a surprise when, as the very existence of the Jewish State appeared to be imperilled, Cohen openly backed the Israeli side. Moreover, his support wasn't limited to public statements – he got on plane to Tel Aviv. Of course, it wasn't the first time he'd been attracted to a dangerous political situation; on the other hand, it was a full 11 years since he'd gone to Cuba to see what a revolution might really look like. He was no longer a young, naïve idealist (indeed, Cuba had knocked much of that idealism from him), and no longer even an anonymous, private individual. He was Leonard Cohen, the famous Leonard Cohen, the guy who sings those sad songs.

Cohen's ultimate motivations, and his state of mind over this period, are a matter of some conjecture. The birth of his son Adam had done little to repair his festering relationship with Suzanne, although they had been living together in the house on Hydra for some months. His enthusiasm for Zen had waned after his chilly experiences on Mount Baldy, and his drug use was unabated. Moreover, his last two albums (*Songs Of Love And Hate* and *Live Songs*) and most recent book (*The Energy Of Slaves*) had hardly set the tills alight. The only area of his life that was an uncompromised success was as a live performer, especially when playing to his devoted fans across Europe. But in his current fragile state, incessant touring was inadvisable.

Ira Nadel describes the early part of Cohen's time in Israel as being devoted to the lusty pursuit of women, much of it successful; the Gad Hotel in Tel Aviv was his favoured pick-up joint.[97] But in the midst of this period of priapic adventures, he remembered why he'd come in the first place, and volunteered to join the Israeli armed forces. He'd never been on the peace-and-love wing of the singer-songwriter community, the tradition personified by pacifists such as Joan Baez, and he'd long had a morbid fascination for guns and militarism. He later claimed that, had his father lived, he would probably have entered Kingston Military Academy before joining the Canadian Army,[98] and his father's service revolver remained one of his most treasured possessions. However, the closest he'd come to armed combat was a little hunting when he was living in Tennessee, shortly after he'd renounced vegetarianism. In Tel Aviv, it was decided that the best way he could assist the war effort would be by wielding a guitar rather than an Uzi, and singing to the troops. He played a number of ramshackle concerts alongside Israeli entertainers, and met General Ariel Sharon, later to become the Prime Minister of his country. He also saw action of sorts when his party was fired upon at a captured Egyptian airfield near the Suez Canal. The whole experience reinforced his admiration for the discipline of military life, as he described the following year:

...you get caught up in the thing. And the desert is beautiful and you think your life is meaningful for a moment or two. And war is wonderful. They'll never stamp it out. It's one of the few times people can act their best. It's so economical in terms of gesture and motion, every single gesture is precise, every effort is at its maximum. Nobody goofs off. Everybody is responsible for his brother. The sense of community and kinship and brotherhood, devotion. There are opportunities to feel things that you simply cannot feel in modern city life. Very impressive.[99]

It clearly had a positive effect on Cohen. On the other hand, how his music, then at its bleakest and most morbid, might conceivably aid the morale of the embattled soldiers has never really been explained.

The war came to an end, with Israel bloodied but victorious, at the end of October. Cohen paid a visit to Jerusalem, then travelled alone to Ethiopia, where he wrote songs in the Imperial Hotel in Asmara. Only a few months later, that country too would be thrown into turmoil, when a military coup led to the ousting, and eventually the murder, of Emperor Haile Selassie. He returned to Hydra, and then moved on to New York, to begin work on his next album. Relations with Suzanne were still tense, although the birth in September, 1974, of a daughter – named Lorca, for the hero of her father's adolescence – suggests some degree of reconciliation.

The New York sessions saw Cohen break away from the Army, the Nashville-based performers with whom he had worked since 1968. His new producer was John Lissauer, to whom he had been introduced by Lewis Furey, a musician friend from Montreal. Lissauer created an instrumental palette that was more varied than the stark twang of the Nashville recordings, but without the commercial sweetness that had provoked friction between Cohen and John Simon. Furey's viola, as well as other new components, such as the mandolin and trumpet of Jeff Layton, filled out the sound, making it the most musically interesting of Cohen's recordings up to this point. According to John Lissauer, much of their working pattern was down to instinct:

Leonard played me the songs, and I tried to find a 'frame' or 'setting' for each. I hoped, I guess, to help make the songs seem 'visual'. If he liked the idea and it sounded inspiring to him, we went with it. We never sat around and discussed a philosophy, or had a specific plan to make the album seem a certain way. We just recorded things that seemed right.[100]

Another feature of the sessions was the unlikely presence of Roshi. Following his strange interlude in Israel, and still feeling the effects of his strained relationship with Suzanne, Cohen was making renewed attempts to incorporate Rinzai practice into his life, and he found it comforting to have his master along. The old man didn't interfere; his sole contribution to musical activities was a droll exhortation to his disciple that "you should sing sadder".[101]

The amiable atmosphere within the studio, and the attractiveness of the instrumental settings contrasted with the content and mood of the songs, which are more explicitly autobiographical than anything Cohen had recorded up to this point. Many of them concern the parlous state of his relationship with Suzanne Elrod. 'Is This What You Wanted', based on a poem from *The Energy Of Slaves*, contains a couplet ("You got old and wrinkled / I stayed seventeen") that is so phenomenally impolite that one presumes it must be ironic; although Cohen's selfish philandering throughout his time with Suzanne suggests he might be playing the lack of gallantry straight. The lines about Jesus, Freud and "the Whore and the Beast of Babylon" add a certain intellectual gloss to what is essentially a brutal slanging match; references to manual orgasm and KY jelly sum up the overall tone rather better. In passing, it's interesting to note the essential structure of the song, with the verses following a repetitive motif (the alternating "You" and "I") before a degree of release in the chorus. It's a lyrical format to which Cohen would return many times in his career; consider 'Hallelujah' and 'Everybody Knows'.

'Why Don't You Try' and 'I Tried To Leave You' also hint at passive-aggressive games, nudging a lover to depart because the narrator doesn't have the moral courage to make the move himself. Again, the scenario echoes the state of Cohen's own relationship.

This motif of ambivalence filters through ("I need you, I don't need you") into 'Chelsea Hotel #2', which concerns Cohen's remembrance of his sexual encounter with Janis Joplin in 1967, although he later regretted making the connection public. His claim to have lured Joplin to bed by pretending to be Kris Kristofferson cannot be verified, but if it's true, it's a classic example of his seductive *chutzpah*.[102] In many ways this is the song on the album that most retains the "old Cohen" sound of picked guitar and dark, deep vocals. The best-remembered line, "We are ugly but we have the music", had resonance for both the protagonists: Cohen, who had stuffed his shoes with Kleenex to make himself taller and thus more attractive to the haughty Montreal girls; Joplin, who had been the subject of a vicious fraternity campaign to have her declared "ugliest man on campus" while she was attending the University of Texas.

'Take This Longing' is more ambiguous, and opinion is divided over whether it's about a relationship that Cohen was unable to end (with Suzanne) or one that he was never able to get out of the starting gate (with the unattainable Nico). Or maybe it's just about Cohen's compulsive fascination for womanhood in all its forms. As David Sheppard says:

An intense devotee of womankind since adolescence, Cohen's proclivities for the opposite sex are part and parcel of his personal mythology. If he is disconsolate in song then his misery is about a woman; if he is priapic and voyeuristic then it is a woman's intimacy he craves, and if he is an evocative weaver of images, then it is a woman he is attempting to seduce with alluring language.[103]

Beyond his sexual relationships, Cohen is obsessed with self-examination. 'Who By Fire', effectively a duet with the Jewish singer Janis Ian, is based on a prayer recited during Yom Kippur. It alludes to his renewed identification with Judaism, and the arrangement hints at Hasidic melancholy. Despite his reconciliation with Roshi, he still saw himself as a Jew.[104]

'A Singer Must Die' offers a Kafkaesque scenario in which a performer (either Cohen or an archetype for all artists like him) is condemned "for the lie in his voice". It's a political song, but not the politics of ideologies: the personal politics of honesty and truth. As Cohen later said of it:

> *I guess that's some kind of basic view I hold about the thing, that it doesn't really matter what the singer is speaking of, it doesn't really matter what the song is. There's something I listen for in a singer's voice and that's some kind of truth. It may even be truth of deception, it may even be the truth of the scam, the truth of the hustle in the singer's own presentation, but something is coming across that is true, and if that isn't there the song dies. And the singer deserves to die too, and will, in time, die. So the thing that I listen for is that note of something big manifested that is beyond the singer's control.*[105]

This also ties in neatly with the constant refrain of those who admire Cohen as a singer, in the face of disdain from those who admire technical facility above all things. A flawless soprano might have a lie in her voice; Cohen, for all his faults, is redeemed because his voice sings the truth.

But the highlight of the album, at least from the perspective of biographical criticism is the musically incoherent but lyrically fascinating 'Field Commander Cohen', in which he contemplates the identity crisis of the poet/novelist/songwriter and further muddies the stream by reinventing himself as a sort of countercultural 007, "parachuting acid into diplomatic cocktail parties". In contrast with the sour tone that pervades so much of the album, here Cohen's tongue is rammed so firmly into his cheek it almost pokes through the skin, a facet of his life and personality that's often obscured by the stereotype of the bedsit gloom merchant. As John Lissauer says: "He has a wry and dry sense of humour that surfaces when least expected and most appropriate."

Cohen had originally intended to call the album *Return Of The Broken Down Nightingale* but in the end even he backed off from that level of self-deprecation. It was released as *New Skin For The Old Ceremony*, the first Cohen album not to have the word 'Songs' in its title; the clear intent was that although the words and music were from 1974, the themes that Cohen was discussing were timeless. This was also the first album not to have his picture on the cover, except in the United States; there, the sixteenth-century image representing the spiritual union of the male and female principles was deemed to be too exciting for American consumers.

Even with its newly emasculated cover, the album failed to chart at all in the United States. In Britain, where a bit of censorious airbrushing preserved the figures' modesty, it scraped into the Top 30. But it sold best of all in continental Europe, where the Renaissance angels appeared in all their Jungian glory. There may be a message in there, somewhere. Cohen himself was quietly happy with the results of his labours. "I must say I'm pleased with the album," he said. "I'm not ashamed of it and am ready to stand by it. Rather than think of it as a masterpiece, I prefer to think of it as a little gem."[106] Lissauer concurs: "I don't know how to recognise a masterpiece."

New Skin is a strange album, in which the often beautiful music sometimes seems to operate in a different dimension from the visceral (self?) loathing that seeps through the lyrics. This isn't a bad thing by any means, but it can be a somewhat disconcerting listen. Weirdest of all might be the final track, 'Leaving Green Sleeves', which improvises over the chords and lyrics of the 16th century English air before ending in a bout of cathartic screaming. It may not be such a conceptual leap to compare Cohen's work at this time with the later songs of Abba, where sweetly sumptuous harmonies and inventive melodies provide the vehicle for tales of divorce, despair and betrayal.

Critical response was rather more positive than it had been for the previous two albums. Paul Nelson in *Rolling Stone* disliked the complexity of Lissauer's arrangements, but admired the integrity and honesty of Cohen's songs, comparing him variously to Scott Fitzgerald, Graham Greene, Ingmar Bergman and Ernest Hemingway (and thus adding another few layers of confusion to those who might want to pigeonhole him simply as a songwriter). The reviewer spotted that the personal and particular aspects of the writer's life that informed his songs also resonated with his listeners:

...in the rooms of today, Cohen's predicaments seem both real and reasonable, albeit frightening. All victories, all relationships, may be transitory, but there are many beginnings and many endings to almost everything of importance in a life, and Cohen's art is more cognisant of this than most.[107]

Across the Atlantic, the *NME* also name-checked Bergman, but kept Cohen in his singer-songwriter box, alongside Joni Mitchell and Carole King. However, the reviewer appreciated that Cohen had shed the utter grimness of his recent work, although such things are, of course, entirely relative: "I take these signs to be ones of optimism," he wrote, "and hence can report that Armageddon has been postponed, if only temporarily."[108]

CHAPTER FIFTEEN
Because it is so horrible between us

This isn't punk rock! This is ROCK PUNK!
– Phil Spector, 1977

In fact, despite his intact sense of humour, all was really not well with Cohen. *New Skin* was released shortly before his 40th birthday, a landmark that would entitle him to indulge in a mid-life crisis – if he hadn't been going through one of those for the past 30 or so years. In London to promote (albeit through gritted teeth) Tony Palmer's *Bird On The Wire* film, he gave a number of long interviews to the music weeklies. Anxious to avoid a repeat of the 'monastery' comments that had caused so much confusion (see Chapter Eleven), he rejected the pervasive notion that he might be a depressive. To a journalist from *Melody Maker* he asserted:

> *The image I've been able to gather of myself from the press is of a victim of the music industry, a poor sensitive chap who has been destroyed by the very forces he started out to utilise. But that is not so, never was. I don't know how that ever got around. I would also contest the notion that I am, or was, a depressed and extremely frail individual, also that I am sad all the time.*[109]

However, in conversation with Steve Turner of the *NME* he let his guard down a little, suggesting that the question was not whether he was depressed, but how he dealt with the fact. He acknowledged that he had performed his songs and poems in psychiatric hospitals, explaining that

> *...it was the feeling that the experience of a lot of people in mental hospitals would especially qualify them to be a receptive audience for my work... In a sense when someone consents to go into*

101

a mental hospital or is committed he has already acknowledged a tremendous defeat. To put it another way, he has already made a choice. And it was my feeling that the elements to this choice, and the elements of this choice, and the elements of this defeat, corresponded with certain elements that produced my songs, and that there would be an empathy between the people who had this experience and the experience as documented in my songs.[110]

Whether or not Cohen was medically depressed, his personal life was a mess. He could apparently neither live with Suzanne, nor live without her. He thought of marrying her, but still insisted on maintaining his liaisons with other women; some of them short-term flings, others rather more serious. And work also got in the way. Almost as soon as his new daughter Lorca was born, he threw himself into a 50-date European tour to promote *New Skin For The Old Ceremony*, following this with his first real North American tour, beginning in New York City in November. He toured again in 1976, to support his first greatest hits package. In between, he spent a great deal of time with Roshi, including a trip to Japan, while at the same time deepening his study of his Jewish roots. It certainly appeared that, if Cohen did have some form of underlying mental dysfunction, he was at least trying to address it. On the other hand, his next project suggested that, in the greater scheme of things, Cohen was utterly sane.

Although *New Skin* had sold weakly, Cohen had enjoyed working with John Lissauer, and was planning to do so again. They had even begun writing together – a novel experience for Cohen – with a view to making a new album, provisionally called *Songs For Rebecca*. But then Cohen was diverted by one of the more unlikely projects of his career, when his lawyer Marty Machat suggested that he should spend some time with Phil Spector.

Spector, with George Martin, Brian Wilson and Joe Meek, was one of the men who redefined the role of the record producer in the 1960s; his 'Wall of Sound', employing dozens of instruments playing together in a confined studio space, had distinguished dozens of hit singles in the 1960s. He would subsequently work on the Beatles' *Let It Be* album, as well as solo albums by John Lennon and George Harrison, and projects of varying success with Harry Nilsson, Dion DiMucci and Cher.

At first, the working relationship went smoothly; Cohen stayed at Spector's house in Los Angeles and on the first night they wrote two songs together. Part of Spector's attraction for Cohen was the elemental simplicity of his craft, so much more accessible than his own work, more immediate than the constant revisions that could stretch out for months, even years:

> *Phil is not a great songwriter, but he's a bold one. He's bold enough to employ the most pedestrian melodies, and yet somehow make them absolutely successful. That is why his compositions are brilliant.*[111]

Spector and Cohen had much in common, both being Jewish, both having lost their fathers at a young age. (Spector's by suicide: the title of his first big success, 'To Know Him Is To Love Him', comes from the text on his father's gravestone.) But whereas Cohen was prone to fits of melancholy and discontent, exacerbated at this point by the terminal illness of his mother, Spector was well on the journey from cantankerous eccentricity to full-blown insanity. In 1985, in an interview for German radio, Cohen would attempt to place Spector's behaviour in some kind of context:

> *He's a lot crazier than people say he is. But he's also a very sweet man, and when you meet him one-to-one, he's incredibly hospitable, incredibly generous. But when he has an audience, he becomes a performer of a kind of Medici magnitude; he becomes a medieval tyrant. Then it gets a little tricky.*[112]

"Tricky" was Cohen's laconic, Canadian understatement at its most pointed. When it actually came to recording the album, the tyrant was in charge. Cohen was very interested in guns; Spector was dangerously obsessed with them, regularly wielding a loaded .45 during sessions, at which point he would also be drunk on Manischewitz kosher wine. The story goes that he pointed a gun at Cohen's throat and said "I love you, Leonard," to which the only sensible reply was "I *hope* you love me, Phil."[113] A few years later, the New York punk band the Ramones would tell similar tales of militaristic excesses when Spector produced their *End Of The Century* album; eventually, his megalomania tipped over into tragedy, and in 2009, he would be jailed for the murder of the actress Lana Clarkson. Cohen himself was no stranger to substance-fuelled debauchery, but the sessions coincided with an uncharacteristic phase of chemical abstinence on his part, which was probably a bad move in the circumstances. "I didn't even have the imagination at the time to medicate myself and escape from the situation," he later mused. "I was horrifically sober for most of it and that made it far worse."[114]

Spector used several of the associates with whom he'd crafted the Wall of Sound for acts such as the Ronettes, Crystals and Righteous Brothers, including saxophonist Steve Douglas, drummer Hal Blaine, arranger Nino Tempo and engineer Larry Levine. There was also an unscripted appearance by Bob Dylan and Allen Ginsberg, who happened to be in town, and provided backing vocals on the track 'Don't Go Home With Your Hard-On'. The one person who didn't seem to be involved was Cohen, whose contribution appeared limited to lyrics, which he'd sing once, only to have his contribution used as little more than a guide vocal; he had become a bridesmaid at his own wedding. It must have come as something of a relief when Spector confiscated the tapes, supposedly at gunpoint, and announced that he was going to concoct the final mixes alone.

Death Of A Ladies' Man, as the resulting album was called, is certainly an interesting piece, although the question remains as to whether it is truly a Leonard Cohen work – Cohen himself took to referring to it as "Phil's album" for some time. Not only was the lyricist and nominal singer excluded from the decision-making process, but he also had to compete with the strong vocals of Ronee Blakley, who effectively sings co-lead on three tracks.[115] This sidelining of Cohen as singer would become a noticeable feature of his albums after the 1980s, when the quality of his own voice began to deteriorate to an alarming degree; here, it was not so much an artistic decision – although Blakley's contributions are sumptuous – but a demonstration of Spector's control freakery, his desire to make Cohen as much a tool of his ego as the singers on his 1963 Christmas album had been.

The quality of the songs varies wildly. 'True Love Leaves No Traces', the opener, sets the tone. It's definitively a Cohen song, having been based in part on his own poem 'As The Mist Leaves No Scar', from *The Spice-Box Of Earth*. But Spector smothers him, with Blakley (which is pleasant) and an annoying, tootling flute (which really isn't). Cohen is reduced to the status of a wordsmith for hire, permitted to join in the music making thanks to the indulgence of the big-shot producer. He may as well be mute, shaking a solitary maraca.

On 'Paper-Thin Hotel', Cohen is given more of chance to show his stuff. This is probably the best, most affecting of Cohen's many analyses of the decay of his relationship with Suzanne, although the fact it's she who is depicted having illicit sex, rather than Cohen himself, might be regarded as an act of historical airbrushing worthy of Stalin.

'Memories' is a neat dollop of nostalgia, described by Maurice Ratcliff as what would happen "if Cohen had written the songs for *Grease*",[116] which is cute, although what goes through my head is more akin to a Cohen-helmed production of *The Rocky Horror Show*.[117] With its references to Frankie Laine singing 'Jezebel', it's a reminder that Cohen had been a teenager, and was once as much a devoted pop fiend as the young Spector.

'Don't Go Home With Your Hard-On' is self-indulgent and self-consciously smutty, but cheerfully harmless enough. Less forgiveable is 'Fingerprints', possibly one of the most horrid and pointless things Cohen has ever recorded, as if he'd resurrected the Buckskin Boys to sing about divorce at a square dance.

The title track comes at the end, and offers a tired, resigned coda both to the album and to Cohen's relationship. (Suzanne, who appears on the sleeve with an expression that could curdle powdered milk, would finally leave with the children a few months after the record was released.) "So the great affair is over," he croons, with a sardonic *Weltschmerz* worthy of Dorothy Parker,

But whoever would have guessed
It would leave us all so vacant

And so deeply unimpressed?

Although most critics at the time boggled at the idea of Cohen and Spector working together, contemporary reviews were often very positive. Paul Nelson in *Rolling Stone* gave a thumbs-down to a couple of tracks, but dubbed the title track "one of Cohen's finest songs" and said of the album overall:

> *It's either greatly flawed or great and flawed – and I'm betting on the latter. Though too much of the record sounds like the world's most flamboyant extrovert producing and arranging the world's most fatalistic introvert, such assumptions can be deceiving... Spector displays a good deal of sensitivity toward a type of material (chansons, for want of a better word) with which he's never worked.[118]*

In *Sounds*, self-confessed Cohen sceptic Sandy Robertson was also charmed by the sheer, barmy incongruousness of the project:

> *'Leonard Cohen meets Phil Spector' sounds more like a line from a Lester Bangs article than something you would ever expect to actually become manifest on vinyl, yes? Cohen's dirge-like pessimism would hardly appear to be the perfect fodder for Spector's wall-of-sound cum Richard Wagner ecstatic streetnoise, but amazingly enough it works.[119]*

A few years later, once he'd got over the angst of the sessions, Cohen contemplated the results objectively and not without a little fondness. He referred to the album in ambivalent, contradictory terms as "a grotesque masterpiece"[120] and by 1980 he had written off to experience the fraught experiences of its creation:

> *I think the songs on the record are good. If the treatment was different I think it could have been a very acceptable thing. Even now I see certain aspects of its excellence. Not that I really care, as I should care. But I do think there's something gay and manic about*

the album. The mix is very eccentric, but if you don't happen to be looking for me in it, which unfortunately I was, if you just look at it as a piece of music, it's very interesting. And it gets better. I couldn't stand it at the beginning.[121]

The fact that Cohen could only appreciate the record from an objective distance perhaps says most about it. It has its devotees, many of them outside the normal demographic for Cohen fans. As he recalled with a certain bemused pride: "A lot of the punksters celebrated the album, and wrote me about it and praised me for it."[122] Considered apart from the fraught circumstances of its creation, it's actually a pretty good album – just maybe not a particularly good Leonard Cohen album.

In the autumn of 1978, Cohen brought out a new collection of poetry, his first in six years. It was called *Death Of A Lady's Man*, a variation on the album title to please grammar Nazis and irony connoisseurs alike. The book title referred to a single woman, that of the album to a multitude. Yet, when the album was released, he was still nominally in a relationship; when the book appeared, he was an available bachelor again. The cover bore the 16th century woodcut of the *coniuncto spirituum* that had adorned *New Skin For The Old Ceremony*, and was dedicated to his mother, who had died in February.

Its history was complicated. Cohen had originally submitted the manuscript to McClelland & Stewart over two years previously, well before the horrors of the Spector sessions. It was then called *My Life In Art*, and many of the poems reeked of intense self-examination, both of Cohen as an artist and Cohen as a man. With a certain gruesome inevitability, the tone of the collection provoked the writer to be even more self-critical, and he became neurotic about revisions and layout, even about the quality of the paper. More than once the book was scheduled for publication, and then withdrawn, much to the bemusement of critics and the media. When it did finally make it to the shelves, quite a few wondered why Cohen had bothered.

What's immediately noticeable about *Death Of A Lady's Man* is that many of the poems are accompanied by prose commentaries. In itself, this was not unprecedented. In 1922, TS Eliot's *The Waste Land* had come with pages of notes, explaining many of the philosophical and linguistic references, while adding several more layers of complexity for the critics to chew over; critical editions of the poem include detailed notes on the notes. Vladimir Nabokov's novel *Pale Fire* (1962) was almost entirely composed of commentary on a 999-line poem by the fictitious genius John Shade. Again, the notes simply added to the ambiguity, but to fans of Nabokov, that's the whole point.

Cohen's comments, on the other hand, didn't aim to explicate or decode the poems so much as to reinforce their bitter tone, as if they represent the voice of an onlooker applauding from the sidelines of a street fight. The combination is best summed up by reference to 'Death To This Book', which begins "Death to this book or fuck this book and fuck this marriage." The 'marriage' had been fucked for a long time, of course, and by the time the book appeared, Suzanne had fucked off. And, just as with his relationships, Cohen's inconsistency and indecision had come perilously close to fucking the book to death as well.

The commentary, meanwhile, reads:

> *There hasn't been a book like this in a long time. The modern reader will be provided a framework of defeat through which he may view without intimidation a triumph of blazing genius.*

At which the critics and, for the most part, the reading public, simply shrugged. Many had probably forgotten that Leonard Cohen had ever been a poet in the first place.

CHAPTER SIXTEEN
My masterpiece unsigned

"I've heard all the wild reports;
they can't be right."
– 'The Gypsy Wife'

The frosty reception that *Death Of A Lady's Man* received meant that, once again, Cohen had to examine and consider the question of who he was and what he did, professionally and culturally. Typical of his attempts to place himself in some kind of literary continuum is this, from an interview to promote his *Greatest Hits* package in 1976:

That's the nature of the thing. It's somehow built into the design of a song, the fact that it moves around. And if it doesn't, then it isn't really that thing that we call a song. It could be something else pretty excellent, it could be a poem designed to stand on a page or an esoteric document or a kind of a paradox that could exist on parchment, but you know, a song, its nature is that it moves. You, know I think I have an idea of where I am. There are major writers and there are minor writers. I consider myself a minor writer. That's not just an exercise in modesty, because I love the minor writers, like Robert Herrick. I'm not that kind of writer like Solzhenitsyn, a writer who has a great, great vision. I have a small corner. And I feel more like an inhabitant of that corner than any other kind of description, poet or writer or lyricist.[123]

In practical terms, the fact that Cohen the Poet had been eclipsed by Cohen the Rock Star was not such a big deal. A songwriter whose albums sell modestly is almost certain to make a more secure living than all but the most successful poets. But what must have rankled with

Cohen is that he reached the peak of his poetic craft just as, thanks to Dylan and the Beatles, popular musicians were suddenly attracting the sort of adulation and intense critical scrutiny that had once accrued to poets. When Christopher Ricks first compared Dylan favourably with Keats, it provoked fury in academic circles; but such observations would fairly soon become commonplace. Cohen mischievously said that Dylan was more like Picasso.[124]

But it's one thing to have one's work read and heard and discussed in the context of poetry; quite another to claim to be a poet per se. The academic Stephen Scobie sees Cohen's dilemma as being a matter of fashion and credibility as much as quality:

The curious switch has been that, the more he is taken seriously as a 'rock star', the less seriously he is taken as a 'poet/novelist'. My guess is that nowadays he is seen as a musician who once upon a time, unfortunately, had to establish his credentials as a writer. The Klein poem ['Portrait of the Poet as Landscape'; see Chapter Two] *is again key – the disappearance of the 'poet' from the reputation of modern society. How do you get taken seriously? The conventional way was as a 'poet', and he loved that. The new way (pioneered by Bob Dylan) was as a 'singer/songwriter'; he was good at that too. Somewhere in between, he was a stand-up comedian. In my view, of course, he was (and is) indissolubly all of these things. The songs cannot stand apart from the poems.*[125]

So, in Scobie's view, Cohen as Rock Star exists only thanks to the inspiration of Cohen the Poet, although the former is the one who puts food on the table. For the rest of Cohen's career, we can expect occasional appearances of poetry books, which relatively few people buy, and even fewer read; it's an old saw of the publishing industry that there will always be more producers of poetry than consumers.

And now it was time to be Rock Star again. Or maybe a Jazz Star, of sorts. Cohen had performed with jazz musicians before, of course, reciting poetry to musical accompaniment in the clubs of Montreal in the late 1950s. While he never boasted the technical proficiency to be a proper jazz musician, he had an affinity for the nocturnal bonhomie of the lifestyle, and the existential cool of its practitioners.

His next album was not strictly a jazz record, but it had some of the ambience that had attracted Cohen two decades before, thanks not least to the presence of the Texas fusion band Passenger. Producer Henry Lewy also brought in a mariachi ensemble, a Russian violinist and John Bilezikjian, virtuoso of a Middle Eastern stringed instrument known as the oud. This was world music before the phrase was in common currency, and Cohen enjoyed both the conceptual oddness of these collisions, and the sound they made:

I thought that had some interesting resonances... a Jewish-English-Canadian singing of French independence with a mariachi band from a restaurant in Los Angeles. I thought that had certain interesting harmonics.[126]

The eclectic instrumentation was also reminiscent of *New Skin For The Old Ceremony*, and John Lissauer, the producer of the earlier album, showed up to play piano on 'Came So Far For Beauty', a song he had originally written with Cohen for the abandoned *Songs For Rebecca* project. Garth Hudson of The Band played a little keyboard as well.

This delicacy and musicianship was clearly a reaction against the Wagnerian density that Phil Spector had imposed upon Cohen's songs. This was partly down to the relaxed efficiency that Henry Lewy (who had been introduced to Cohen by Joni Mitchell) brought to the proceedings, as Cohen later recalled:

He had that great quality that Bob Johnston had. He had a lot of faith in the singer, as he did with Joni. And he created an extremely hospitable atmosphere in the studio where things could happen. And things had changed somewhat by then; these were my own songs and the musical ideas were specifically mine.[127]

Cohen's biographer Jim Devlin sees this renewed sense of tranquillity as being the key factor that distinguishes the album from its predecessor, with the change of mood communicating itself immediately to the listener:

> Death Of A Ladies' Man *is like listening to a music box with the lid off, so all the music is going up into the ceiling. On* Recent Songs, *Leonard put the lid back on again. Once he's put the lid back on his music, he's gone back to being a private, intimate singer-songwriter. It's a return to that intimacy, that chamber-like quality: closed room; curtains; phone off the hook; glass of red wine.*[128]

But apart from the distinct absence of firearms and paranoia in the studio, there was something else going on. Following the death and departure that characterised 1978, and the toxic screeds that filled his most recent book, Cohen's new pieces had a gentle, almost resigned flavour. Life may not be perfect, he had reasoned, but rage only makes things worse.

He had been reading widely and deeply in many traditions; for example, the Persian Sufi poets Attar and Rumi, who influenced the first track, 'The Guests'. It's a laid-back admission of his need for love, not lust, with backing vocals provided by Jennifer Warnes, who had sung in concert with Cohen as far back as 1972, but was now recording with him for the first time. Theirs would be a long and fruitful association.

'The Window' carries on this investigation of the shared territory between carnal and spiritual love; once more we're in the world of Stephen Dedalus, in Joyce's *Portrait Of The Artist*, moving towards a healthy balance between the sacred and the profane. Cohen is in seducer mode, but he's trying to convert a woman, not copulate. Intriguingly, much of the religious imagery here has a Christian flavour; he's John the Baptist rather than Don Juan. The spiritual content includes his best joke on the album, a reference to the notion that the Word of God (Logos) acquired substantive form in the person of Jesus (John 1: 14):

Oh bless the continuous stutter
Of the word being made into flesh

Although, in that context, might the implication of a speech impediment be counted as blasphemy?

The most personal song on the album is 'Came So Far For Beauty'. The 'beauty' that Cohen has been seeking is left to hover in a state of ambiguity: it seems to be a woman for whom he has sacrificed everything, but it might just as well stand for a spiritual or even an aesthetic quest. The worrying thing for Cohen's fans is that the mysterious journey appears to have had a deleterious effect on his art, leaving his "masterpiece unsigned". His songs and other writings are generally believed to have been created in response to the events and experiences of his life; but could his unsettled nature, his long-term inability to stay in one place, with one woman, with one religion be the reason that that epochal Great Work – his *Ulysses*, his *Waste Land*, his 'Like A Rolling Stone' – has so far eluded his grasp?

Roshi and his teaching continued to exert a strong, yet benign influence, and the final track 'Ballad Of The Absent Mare', is based on his discussions of an ancient Chinese parable about loss and desire, again preaching acceptance of one's fate. A similar mood of composed resignation (with an enticing side order of quintessentially Zen paradox) haunts the historical sob-story that is 'The Traitor', as Cohen later elucidated:

It was about the feeling we have of betraying a mission that we
were mandated to fulfil; and being unable to fulfil; and then com-
ing to understand that the real mandate was not to fulfil it. And
that the deeper courage was to stand guiltless in the predicament
in which you find yourself.[129]

But the most profound exposition of Buddhist teaching was tucked away in 'The Smokey Life'. Superficially the most straightforwardly

113

jazzy piece on the album, the immediate assumption is that it's a reference to some smoke-filled cellar where sharp-suited tenorists play flattened fifths; alternatively of course, one could just follow the 'Puff, The Magic Dragon' rule – if in doubt, it's probably about drugs.

Cohen, on the other hand, has never been that obvious. 'The Smokey Life' is really a meditation on the insubstantiality of all around, and the need to let go of material things. "Remember when the scenery started fading," croons Cohen: what we think of as life is no more 'real' than a movie or a stage play. Core to Buddhist doctrines is the idea that everything is impermanent, and that fulfilment can only be attained if we rid ourselves from attachment to the physical, and transcend. Everything else is just smoke.

Originally, the whole album was going to be called *The Smokey Life*, but Cohen had one of his characteristic moments of self-doubt and dissatisfaction. Long discussions with friends, including the ever-loyal Nancy Bacal, stretched over several days, and the best he could come up with was *Recent Songs*. Apart from being dull, it was untrue: 'The Lost Canadian' dated back to 1842, and some of the other songs were several years old as well. In its favour, the title offered a sense of continuity to Cohen's earlier albums. The cover (an amateurish portrait of Cohen, based on a photograph taken by Hazel Field) was pretty ropey, but diehard fans had by now become used to that sort of thing.

The superficialities of title and packaging aside, *Recent Songs* remains an enjoyable album, not least because Cohen appears to be set free of the psychological anguish that had beset him for the past few years. He's not exactly happy – this is, after all, Leonard Cohen we're talking about – but he does appear to have achieved some kind of equilibrium, without emasculating his poetic gifts. Perverse as ever, while punk rock was sinking its quintessentially English teeth into the false sentiment of neo-Hallmark songwriting, Cohen was rediscovering his soppy side:

Who would dare to write songs about swans and roses? I felt for some odd reason like rescuing such imagery from the backs of

*Christmas cards, and returning those symbols, those images, to
a place of honour – if they ever had one. And also to use the shab-
biness and irony of those images to really get something from it, as
an ironic device to rescue their real passionate romance. If they're
successful, they do create resonance and harmonics in the hearts
of the listeners, and a landscape that they recognise as true. It's
grotesque, it's shabby, it's beautiful, but then beyond all
that you're willing to forgive these conceits if you recognise
them as true.*[130]

The critical response was polite. Sales in the United States were all
but non-existent and not a lot better in Canada; once again it was down
to the faithful Europeans to pick up the slack. After celebrating his
45th birthday on Hydra in the company of a buxom Romanian wench
named Michelle (as depicted in the photograph accompanying John
Walsh's 1994 interview in *Mojo*), he repaid the loyalty of his Continental fans with another tour, accompanied by most of the *Recent Songs*
musicians. Film-maker Harry Rasky also came along, with a CBC
crew, making what would be the 1980 movie *The Song Of Leonard Cohen*. The British leg of the tour would form the basis of the live album
Field Commander Cohen, not released until 2001. He followed this
with a short tour of Australia, then returned to Montreal. He wouldn't
release another album for over five years.

CHAPTER SEVENTEEN

Complain, complain, that's all you've done

"I think there's music everywhere... that is the literature of our day, those lyrics, those songs, those rhythms are how people wash the dishes and court each other."
– Leonard Cohen, 1984

Cohen was not idle during his recording hiatus, the longest at this point since his career in music had begun. European fans remained implacably loyal, and he embarked on another tour in 1980, enlivened by plenty of female attention. It was not for nothing that Harry Rasky had described Cohen as "truly the first, great vaginal poet".[131]

Away from work, he settled uneasily into the role of weekend father, not helped by protracted custody negotiations with Suzanne, who had taken Adam and Lorca to live in France. His trips there became more frequent after he had made the acquaintance of a French photographer called Dominique Isserman, who was to be his regular companion for some years. Unlike Marianne and Suzanne, Dominique had her own successful career and her own apartment in Paris; this would be a partnership of equals, although Cohen was just as difficult a partner, just as inconsistent and unwilling to commit as he had been in his previous relationships.

His attention deficit also manifested itself in brave endeavours in new media. In 1980, there was another attempt to adapt his works for the stage, when a musical called *The Leonard Cohen Show* opened in Montreal, with David Blue playing the man himself. Cohen's involvement in the play was minimal, but he was more hands-on with another project. Having oscillated between ambivalence and antipathy over others' attempts to capture him on film (most notably Tony Palmer and Harry Rasky), he conceived a 30-minute work called *I Am*

A Hotel. Originally inspired by Cohen's song 'The Guests', the opening track on *Recent Songs*, it was pitched somewhere in the no man's land between art film and promo video. Its episodic nature, flicking between five pairs of lovers in the King Edward Hotel in Toronto, also owes something to Arthur Schnitzler's play *La Ronde*. Production was fraught with difficulties: the pay-TV network that had originally agreed to show the film folded, and Cohen (who plays a wryly enigmatic character known only as 'The Resident') suddenly decided to embark on an extended retreat at Roshi's base on Mount Baldy just as shooting was due to begin. He had another of his crises of confidence, and asked for the project to be scrapped – when he saw the first edit, he hated it.

He preferred the final cut, which also included performances of 'Chelsea Hotel', 'The Gypsy's Wife', 'Memories' and 'Suzanne', and it was broadcast on CBC in May, 1984. To the surprise even of its makers, the film went on to win the Golden Rose at Montreux, the international TV industry's most prestigious award.

Cohen also collaborated with Lewis Furey, from the *New Skin* sessions, on a rock opera called *Night Magic*, which was eventually released as a film and soundtrack album in 1985. Veering close to autobiography, it concerned a Canadian career on a downward trajectory, although Cohen himself did not appear in the eventual production.

Cohen remained fascinated by religion, and was devoted to Roshi, although he did describe his teachings as "the indecipherable ramblings of an old zen monk".[132] He spent months at a time at Mount Baldy, and also accompanied the master on his travels, including trips to Trappist monasteries. And yet at the same time, he was unwavering in his identification as a religious Jew, happily interrupting his long periods of meditation in order to celebrate the Sabbath and high holidays. He was as likely to be seen reading the Talmud as any Buddhist text.

To commemorate this commitment to the faith of his ancestors, and also to mark his 50th birthday, Cohen brought out a new book of poetry in 1984, a radical departure from his previous writings. *Book Of Mercy* (previous working titles had included *The Name* and *The Shield*) was a collection of 50 modern psalms. The spite and rancour of *Death Of A Lady's Man* was for the most part gone, replaced by a sense of spiritual yearning, a desire for contentment – with only an occasional tetchy outburst. Many of the pieces were composed while Cohen was staying in a trailer in France, on one of his visits to his children. Despite this, they are less intensely personal, less solipsistic than much of his previous poetry. They might even be considered to contain a message of hope for the reader, as he explained in an interview in 1984:

> *I sometimes worried about the indiscretion of the thing. First of all, there's a very good Book of Psalms that we already have, and there's no urgency to produce another one. But it was the only thing I could say, and that confers on it a certain legitimacy. And I know that they could be useful to one or two people here and there.*[133]

Despite the formal and philosophical inspiration for the new works, Cohen's brand of Judaism was bracingly unorthodox, with Christian pioneers such as St Augustine being name-checked alongside the Hebrew patriarchs. In one piece (none has a title, in common with the Biblical Book of Psalms) he rails against "black Hebrew gibberish of pruned grapevines"; in another, he seems to question whether the State of Israel has a right to exist – this from a man who'd flown to Israel during wartime to entertain the troops.

At one point, Cohen intended to make *Book Of Mercy* the basis for his next release, intoning the psalms over a string quartet, under the supervison of Henry Lewy, the producer of *Recent Songs*. The recordings never saw the light of day, although a later project on similar lines, Philip Glass's settings of his *Book Of Longing* poems, would attract critical acclaim when it had its premiere in 2007.

Instead, Cohen decided to stick more closely to the genre he knew best and make a more conventional album. Part of the reason may have been financial; his revenue album sales had never been exceptional, and a globetrotting lifestyle, combined with hefty maintenance payments to Suzanne and the children, had chipped away at his finances.

To oversee the sessions for what would become *Various Positions*, he brought back John Lissauer, who seemed remarkably forgiving after Cohen had dumped their *Songs For Rebecca* project. However, a lot had changed since they'd first worked together a decade before, as Lissauer recalls:

Leonard had discovered the Casio drum machine. He had written a few of his songs (most notably 'Dance Me To The End Of Love') while relying quite heavily on the little rhythm machine, and even though we tried a real drummer, he preferred the quirkiness of 'the box' We did use live musicians for almost the entire album, but that song sort of set the tone.[134]

And this may have been part of the problem. What had characterised the previous collaboration between Cohen and Lissauer, as well as Cohen's last studio album, was a sort of open-minded eclecticism, picking and choosing musical styles at will. Although *Various Positions* includes diversions into a number of different genres – 'The Captain' and 'Heart With No Companion' are overtly countryish; 'If It Be Your Will' is based on a Jewish prayer – the overall sound is a sort of sonic/ electronic mush. The critic Andrew Mueller offers the benign suggestion that the pervasive atmosphere of ham-fisted doodling may be what gives the album its awkward charm:

Maybe the reason that Leonard Cohen got away with the whole synthesiser thing is that when everybody else was doing it, it turned into these huge, massively expensive, overproduced, souped-up arrangements; whereas in a weird way his songs and his records still sounded as lo-fi as they ever had. Instead of hacking away at a guitar he couldn't quite play, he was now plonking and plinking on a keyboard he couldn't quite figure out.[135]

It's a lovely idea, of Cohen as some kind of idiot savant outsider musician like Daniel Johnston or Wesley Willis or Jandek, his technical incompetence less important than some sort of transcendent charm.[136] Unfortunately, it does rather ignore the fact that Cohen's subsequent album – made once he'd worked out how to progress beyond his keyboard's factory settings – would be one of his best ever. It remains the case that on *Various Positions*, the presence of several skilled musicians in the studio, such as guitarist Sid McGinnis, is negated by the overwhelming dominance of the synthesisers and drum machines, which in turn distracts from some strong new songs. Stephen Scobie goes so far as to declare that the album contains at least two of Cohen's five best compositions.[137]

Cohen's meticulous, laborious creative method has certainly maintained quality control on the writing front. He is, as always, particularly good at exploring the common ground between two kinds of love, the spiritual and the carnal. Is the faintly Gallic 'Dance Me To The End Of Love' about his life with the Parisian Dominique Isserman (who directed the accompanying video, Cohen's first) or does it really concern Cohen's fractious relationship with the vengeful deity of the Old Testament, as suggested by his invocation of olive branches, doves and Babylon? "End", in any case, is a deliberately ambiguous word: is he moving towards a purpose, a resolution (as in "the end justifies the means"); or to the point where earthly love stops (presumably, death)? The music, at once sprightly and mournful, in the best French tradition, doesn't offer much help. David Sheppard calls it "part Hasidic lament, part Eurovision Song Contest",[138] which is true, but doesn't help much either.

The ambiguities persist. If the guilt in 'The Law' isn't of the mundane criminal variety (that would surely be too easy), is it sexual guilt, with the persistent adulterer contemplating his blistered heart; or, as Maurice Ratcliff suggests, the pervasive Catholic variety?[139] For all his easygoing charm, and his own imperfections and infidelities, Cohen is at heart a moralist, with a strict sense of order and discipline; the authoritarian remarks he made in the 1990s about putting young people in uniform (see Chapter Twenty) came as a shock to some fans, but many of his songs point to long and thoughtful consideration of what is right and what is wrong. It's not just the law that matters; it's the arm and the hand that inflict punishment.

It could of course be the equally pervasive Jewish sense of guilt that was operating on Cohen's mind. The echoes of his own family history in 'The Night Comes On' – the comforting mother, the wounded father – summon up religion, love, guilt, death; his experiences during the Yom Kippur War; hints of Nazi and Russian oppression of the Jews;

pretty much Leonard By Numbers. Even more explicitly drawing on his Jewish heritage (or so it appears) is 'If It Be Your Will', which is based on the words of the prayer recited during the Day Of Atonement. But is it actually God to whom Cohen is speaking? Or a woman? Or Roshi? Or is it simply another manifestation of Cohen's post-Suzanne Elrod, post-Phil Spector mood of peaceful acceptance?

And then of course there's 'Hallelujah', in which King David the Psalmist – the implied model for Cohen's writing in *Book Of Mercy* – meets King David the Sex Pest, truly a case of an artist unable to live up to the elevated aspirations of his own work. More of that in Appendix I.

Columbia Records was widely criticised for its decision not to release *Various Positions* in the United States; Walter Yetnikoff, then President of CBS, was alleged to have told Cohen: "We know you're great, but we don't know if you're any good." But then CBS wasn't a charity or an endowment for the arts; its overriding interest was the empirical bottom line (the "good" bit) rather than any notional measure of "greatness". And wasn't Cohen's original motive for becoming a recording artist at heart financial? A Cohen studio album hadn't shown up in the American charts for 13 years, and a dispassionate listener would probably guess that *Various Positions* wasn't going to break the trend. Cohen's voice sounds weak and tired, especially when sent alongside the delicious harmonies of Jennifer Warnes. A great song like 'Hallelujah' would be done better later, in other hands and other voices; indeed, Cohen himself would do it better. Even the cover photo – a stubbly, suddenly old-looking Cohen scowling into the lens of a Polaroid camera – was the depiction of a man who just wanted to get it all over and done with.

Passport Records, which released the album in the States, didn't manage to sell more than a few thousand units, and Columbia only took responsibility for US sales when it brought out the CD version in 1990. Even with the major label's marketing machine behind *Various Positions*, it failed to make the Top 50 in the UK. Devoted Leonard worshippers might regard it as heresy, but perhaps Yetnikoff was right after all, and Cohen would have to settle for just being "great".

CHAPTER EIGHTEEN
I ache in the places
where I used to play

*"I tend to spend a lot of time alone but it's usually because
I've gone to the wrong city or lost my phonebook."*
– Leonard Cohen, 1988

Although his new material wasn't selling well enough to satisfy the
likes of Walter Yetnikoff, Cohen was still a major draw on the live circuit, in North America as well as in his European power base. His parlous financial situation was not going to be resolved by proceeds from
the pitiful sales of *Various Positions*, so touring had become an economic necessity as much as a display of gratitude to those fans who'd
stood by him despite the vagaries of fashion.

The first half of 1985, therefore, was taken up by a tour across three
continents, including his first New York gigs in a decade. Money, presumably, was the main reason for an unexpected diversion the following year, when he took a role in *Miami Vice*. Michael Mann's definitively 80s cop show, all powerboats, pastels and sockless loafers, was
building a reputation for casting rock stars in guest roles, often as drug
dealers and other colourful bad guys. Cohen appears to have been cast
as the head of Interpol mainly because he speaks French relatively
well; the best thing that can be said about his performance (most of
which was cut from the final broadcast) is that he was slightly more
convincing than Frank Zappa, if not as amusing as Gene Simmons.
Less embarrassing, but presumably also less rewarding in a monetary
sense, was his involvement with a stage show, *Sincerely, L. Cohen*,
which was produced in New York in 1987.

In fact, the venture into theatre may have been more beneficial to
Cohen's prospects than he had thought, albeit indirectly. Projects such
as *Sincerely, L. Cohen* reminded public and critics alike that despite

falling sales, failing vocal powers and an unhealthy fascination with drum machines, Cohen's chief strength was as a writer of songs that were at once clever and honest and poignant and challenging and often even funny. Although many performers, from Nick Cave to Diana Ross, had recorded Cohen's songs over the years, he had always written them with his own voice in mind. This changed in 1984, following a conversation with the singer Jennifer Warnes.

Warnes had worked as a backing singer for Cohen on and off since the early 1970s, although she'd also had a solo career that followed a similar trajectory to his; critical acclaim, but sales seemingly limited to a small, loyal fan base. This suddenly changed in 1982, when she found herself on top of the *Billboard* charts with the single 'Up Where We Belong', a duet with the veteran British blues shouter Joe Cocker.[140] The track, from the movie *An Officer And A Gentleman* went on to take an Oscar, a Golden Globe, a BAFTA and a Grammy – suddenly, Cohen's blonde buddy was a hot property. The fact that the song was the epitome of 1980s, breast-beating, adult-rock vileness was not particularly relevant; Warnes had worked long and hard, and she deserved the break.

In 1984, after a long, depressing conversation about the AIDS crisis that was ravaging Los Angeles, where both Cohen and Warnes were living at time, Cohen was inspired to write a song that, unusually for him, he completed in a matter of weeks. Transcending the bleak, suffocating subject matter, it dealt with the fact that, even with a death sentence hovering, human love and lust and the desire to connect could never really be defeated. With no recording projects of his own lined up, he gave the new piece – 'Ain't No Cure For Love' – to Warnes, an act that persuaded her to realise a long-held desire to record a whole album of Cohen's songs.

It was not quite the first time that anyone had done this. The New Zealand singer Graeme Allwright had recorded a selection of Cohen songs in French, in 1973; and a redoubtable Polish political troubadour named Maciej Zembaty had already made two albums, using his own translations, and would go on to release another six. But it was a first for the English-speaking world, although it was probably an odd time to embark on such a project. Leonard Cohen looked to be a 60s throw-back, early 70s at best, all but disowned by his record company, disdained by critics who prioritised haircuts over insight.

However, Warnes would not be deterred. As Cohen said of her:

This is a real friend and someone who, in the face I might say of great derision has always supported me. And she had always said to me that she intended to make a record of my songs; I thought this was just an expression of friendship. But she did go to record company after record company and was laughed out of most of the offices.[141]

Eventually, Private Music agreed to back the project, with another long-term collaborator, Roscoe Beck (who had played on *Recent Songs*, and would still be part of Cohen's concert band as bassist and musical director in 2009) acting as producer. The eventual selection of songs spanned almost Cohen's entire career, from the second album ('Bird On The Wire') to new tracks that he had yet to record ('Ain't No Cure For Love', 'First We Take Manhattan' and 'Song Of Bernadette', the last of which he has still not released under his own name). Cohen was a watchful presence during the recording in Los Angeles, amending lyrics as required, although he only appears on one track, 'Joan Of Arc'. Other contributors include the blues guitarist Stevie Ray Vaughan and the arranger Van Dyke Parks, a sometime collaborator with Brian Wilson.

Cohen had wanted to call the album *Jenny Sings Lenny*, but at a late stage it became known as *Famous Blue Raincoat*, with a cartoon bearing the original name tucked inside. Critics, once they'd got over the oddness of the concept, were effusive in their praise; moreover, the record actually sold in respectable quantities, topping the charts in Britain and even penetrating the Billboard lists in the States – something Cohen himself had not managed since the release of *Songs Of Love And Hate*.

Biba Kopf (who in 1980, under the name Chris Bohn, had depicted Cohen's delicate state in the aftermath of the Spector debacle) made the point that it wasn't just the fact that Warnes was a 'better' singer than Cohen that made the album interesting, it was also a matter of context. The very fact that Warnes was a woman effectively reinterpreted the songs by itself, even before she'd opened her mouth:

Ambitious to be sure, Warnes' collection is perhaps too LA-ed to be a totally successful translation of Cohen. But, with her more extensive range, she can take these songs to places where the Cohen monotone is denied entry. And the fact of a woman singing songs ridden with male romanticism affords an intriguing shift in perspective. Cohen's work addresses women in the highest of terms. Even the most fallen is accorded the reverence of a Madonna. While this partly accounts for his large female following, other women dismiss his beat venerations as a variant of woman-as-object, a more literate come-on. Warnes' versions usefully render gender secondary to the songs' expressions of feelings.[142]

The success of *Famous Blue Raincoat* gave Cohen's reputation and career a serious boost just as he needed it. (Warnes, oddly, has never quite lived up to her talent. She did enjoy another chart-topping, award-winning hit in 1987, but again with a bad duet from a Hollywood movie – 'I've Had The Time Of My Life' with Bill Medley, from *Dirty Dancing*.)

But he was not happy. His relationship with Dominique Isserman, which had sustained him through the professional trough of the mid-80s, was coming to an end, albeit on rather more civilised terms than those on which his union with Suzanne Elrod had faltered. His customary bouts of self-doubt and depression, expressed as dissatisfaction with the quality of his work, were exacerbated by the fact that he had elected to take on much of the production work himself. Cohen is a free spirit, but he also responds well to strong, wise figures who can take care of business when his own confidence wanes: Roshi; Irving Layton; Jack McClelland; and in the studio, the likes of Bob Johnston and John Lissauer. Although he had steadfast friends and collaborators on hand such as Warnes and Beck, as well as John Bilezikjian (oud) and violinist Rafi Hakopian, who had brought such delicious textures to *Recent Songs*, this time the buck stopped with Cohen.

An objective observer might have predicted a disaster: the incoherent noise of *Death Of A Ladies' Man* perhaps, laced with the self-pity of *Songs Of Love And Hate*. In the event, *I'm Your Man* was one of the most warmly received albums of Cohen's career and, more surprisingly, one of the funniest and most likeable. The synthesisers that permeated *Various Positions* are still a dominating factor, but Cohen by this time has mastered the technology; they have become real instruments, not novelties or toys. Many listeners have remarked on the debt, conscious or otherwise, that 'First We Take Manhattan' owes to 'It's A Sin' by the Pet Shop Boys, released the previous year; other tracks echo the work of Giorgio Moroder, Kraftwerk and – maybe not entirely coincidentally – Jan Hammer's incidental music for *Miami Vice*.

Indeed, Cohen takes great delight in his cheeky larceny from elsewhere. 'Ain't No Cure For Love' lifts the riff from 'Every Breath You Take', the 1983 smash hit by the Police; 'Jazz Police' (the creative response to an argument with his musicians about their tendency to interpolate unorthodox intervals into his songs) cheerfully rips off the theme from *Star Trek*. 'Take This Waltz' is more respectful in its borrowing, and credits its source; 'Pequeño vals vienés', a poem by Cohen's adolescent poster boy, Federico García Lorca. Cohen had originally written the song two years previously, as his contribution to an album commemorating the 50th anniversary of the poet's murder.

But the key songs top and tail the album. 'First We Take Manhattan', which Jennifer Warnes had first recorded on *Famous Blue Raincoat*, is about the political tensions that were then simmering in Europe; Cohen had played in Poland a few years before, and come into contact with the free trade union Solidarity. He sings in the voice of a political extremist threatening some unspecified violent outrage in response to some equally vague provocation; the only thing we know is the two cities he has in his sights. Cohen's lyrics reflect the mixture of unease and exhilaration that preceded the fall of the Berlin wall, but this is undercut by the surreal lyrics ("the monkey and the plywood violin") and the gloriously melodramatic arrangement.

Cohen saves the best till last: 'Tower of Song' is his personal credo as an artist, invoking the ghost of Hank Williams to allow himself admission to the canon of songwriters. It had taken him months to write, but a sudden rush of inspiration prompted him to finish the song and record it, almost single-handed, over one hectic night. It's honest and touching and witty and self-deprecating ("golden voice", indeed, a phrase that he hams up in concert to the delighted whoops of the faithful), even if some of Cohen's keyboard work is, as David Sheppard so cruelly but fairly puts it, "frankly autistic-sounding";[143] his live solo inspires similarly sardonic applause. One can almost see the eponymous edifice, like a cross between the Tower of Babel and the Brill Building, musicians and songwriters alive and dead in every room: Amy Winehouse and Chuck Berry and Bix Beiderbecke and Franz Schubert shooting the breeze by the coffee machine; Hank Williams hawking up chunks of his own raddled lungs from the window of his penthouse suite; Cohen catching up with his meditation and/or a glass of Château Latour in the basement. In the humble opinion of this author, it is the greatest thing he's ever done.

I'm Your Man breathed fresh life into a career that appeared to have fallen to pieces. Even the cover is excellent, a black-and-white shot of a deadpan Cohen eating a banana, an out-take from a session for *Famous Blue Raincoat*. (The image would later be satirised in the packaging for the tribute album *I'm Your Fan*, which had photos of all the contributors posing with bananas.) While sales in the United States were as weak as ever, it topped the charts in a number of European territories.

The critics loved *I'm Your Man*, judging it to be the glorious fulfilment of a 20-year career that at the same time retained an awareness of contemporary musical trends. David Browne in *Rolling Stone* saluted its (relative) cheerfulness, describing it as "the first Cohen album that can be listened to during the twilight hours".[144] In *Q* magazine, Mark Cooper also sensed that in his mid-50s, Cohen had finally shed some of his adolescent angst:

Nowadays he tempers his world-weary innocence with a touch of cynicism; the voice has grown deeper and slower and he acts like a man who's seen and done it all and is just reporting in from his place on a park bench... Leonard Cohen is simply very good at being Leonard Cohen.[145]

The funny thing was, quite a few other people were having a go at being Leonard Cohen as well.

CHAPTER NINETEEN
And the mountain's going to shout amen

"Everybody likes Leonard Cohen, but everyone thinks he is an old hippy, so they don't want to admit it."
– Emmanuel Telier, *Les Inrockuptibles*, 1991

"You know me, I'm just a journalist of the inner dismal condition."
– Leonard Cohen, Royal Albert Hall, May, 1993

Famous Blue Raincoat was a high-profile vindication of Cohen's gifts as a songwriter, but his material had been popular with other performers for years. The breadth of his influences meant that his appeal extended way beyond the mainstream rock genre; Cohen himself even reported that there had once been plans for Frank Sinatra to record an album of his songs.[146]

However, by the early 1990s, it was no longer the likes of Harry Belafonte, Neil Diamond and Nana Mouskouri who tended to express their flattery of Cohen through imitation; it was the purveyors of that amorphous genre known variously as indie, alternative, post-punk or college rock. He made guest appearances on a few suitably peculiar projects, singing on 'Elvis's Rolls Royce' (1990), by the quirky funk outfit Was Not Was; and offering mumbled narration on 'Eclipse', a track on *Weird Nightmare*, Hal Willner's 1992 tribute to the bassist/composer Charles Mingus. On the latter, he was more than a little out-weirded by the spectral squawks of singer Diamanda Galas.

Cutting-edge performers were also taking on his songs for their own nefarious purposes. Nick Cave had essayed 'Avalanche' on *From Her To Eternity* (1984), the first album he made with his band the Bad Seeds; the recording was much to the songwriter's approval, as he said in a German interview the following year:

129

I've never got over that thrill that someone else has chosen a song and wants to do it. I think Nick Cave's instinct in choosing that song to cover was very good because that's just the kind of song that is made to be torn apart and I like the way he tore it apart. I like the way he went out with it.[147]

Echo and the Bunnymen, the Weather Prophets and the Flying Lizards had also raided his back catalogue; Suzanne Vega and Tanita Tikaram sang his praises. Johnny Cash, an icon of the old school, albeit one warmly embraced by the new breed such as Cave, was also an admirer, and would later tackle 'Bird On The Wire' on his comeback album *American Recordings* (1994), produced by Rick Rubin.

Superficially, Cohen's (unwilling) identification with the hippy-ish, otherwordly world of the early-70s singer-songwriter movement made him an unlikely touchstone for the confrontational, post-punk ethos of indie rock. But he was never really a hippy: as in the case of his contemporary and compatriot Neil Young, there was something gritty and honest that cut through any notions of idealism. He responded to a wildly varied bevy of muses, literary and musical, and could never be compartmentalised into any one genre. As the Australian academic Paul Monk later enumerated his influences:

Erotically, Cohen makes Keats seem as though he had freeze-dried testicles and Byron as though he had no heart. Politically, he breathes the spirit of Isaiah over the world after the Holocaust. His unique lyrical style is a wholly contemporary blend of the Psalms and Federico García Lorca, the Chelsea Hotel, Nashville and the Greek islands, Zen Buddhism and the Song of Songs, Franz Rosenzweig and Bob Dylan.[148]

And the Year Zero nihilism of the original punk movement had become less dominant, it was now permissible to admit a certain fondness for someone who might once have worn flared trousers or addressed another as "man". Neil Young was lauded by many of the grunge bands, in particular Pearl Jam; The Cocteau Twins rehabilitated the late Tim Buckley; even the terminally fey Donovan regained a modicum of credibility when the Happy Mondays declared their admiration (and the singer briefly became his son-in-law).

Cohen's most prominent cheerleader was the Australian Nick Cave, who shared his fascination with the conflicting, competing powers of seething lust and a domineering God; his identification with the Canadian even extended to writing a weirdly good novel, *And The Ass Saw The Angel* (1989). It was inevitable that Cave would be involved in the next manifestation of the alt-rock community's love for all things Leonard.

I'm Your Fan was a project of the French music magazine *Les Inrockuptibles*, inspired by the unlikely affection of Black Francis (aka Frank Black), frontman of the none-more-hip Pixies for the *I'm Your Man* album. The idea was simple: draw up a list of indie innovators, such as the Pixies, James, Lloyd Cole and The House of Love, and ask each one to record a song from Cohen's back catalogue. Within the bounds of the genre, Fevret persuaded an eclectic bunch to contribute; the geographical origins of the project mean that some of the performers, such as Geoffrey Oryema and Jean-Louis Murat, were unfamiliar to many Anglophone listeners, but the French inflections are appropriate to the songs. In cultural terms, Cohen was as much a European songwriter as a North American. That icon of decadence Serge Gainsbourg makes a fleeting contribution, producing Dead Famous People's 'True Love Leaves No Traces'; it would have been fascinating to have the two old rogues, Cohen and Gainsbourg, in a studio together, or just in a bar. Although Cohen would probably have disapproved of Gainsbourg's manners.[149]

The quality of the overall product is variable; REM's take on 'First We Take Manhattan' is particularly disappointing, especially since the track was recorded at a point when the band was transcending its alternative roots and becoming a global sensation. But that's not really such an issue; the point was to see what might come of unlikely combinations, and the presence of a dud or two was a risk worth taking. One interesting pattern emerges. The better-known songs tend to be treated with a degree of reverence: Ian McCulloch of Echo and the Bunnymen does a perfectly serviceable job on 'Hey, That's No Way To Say Goodbye', but he doesn't really add anything to Cohen's original. Contrast this with former Triffids frontman David McComb, who dismembers 'Don't Go Home With Your Hard-On' (a critically reviled throwaway from *Death Of A Ladies' Man*, an album about which Cohen would always express mixed emotions) and fashions a peculiar industrial/techno hybrid that's at worst interesting and, if you're in the mood, rather more fun than the original.

The two best tracks are the last. Nick Cave refashions 'Tower of Song' into a swamp-rock epic, shifting the object of veneration from Hank Williams to Cohen himself. Apparently, Cave and the Bad Seeds made several failed, booze-fuelled attempts to nail the song from beginning to end, then gave up and asked the (sober) engineer to impose some sort of coherence on the skeletal fragments. Bizarrely, it worked, although the full, shambolic session has also surfaced as a bootleg.

The album closes with John Cale's 'Hallelujah'. The original had suffered from the weakness of Cohen's voice, and the muddy, synth-rock arrangements on *Various Positions*. Cale himself is hardly Mahalia Jackson, but he can hit the high notes when required, giving his version a yearning purity that Cohen couldn't hope to match; and his stripped-down instrumentation, nothing but voice and piano, focuses attention on the song. This is where that whole, strange 'Hallelujah' business really starts.

Cohen expressed humility that so many young whippersnappers wanted to pledge allegiance to his cause. "Believe me," he said once the album was released, "any attention I get, I'm grateful for. I never believe anyone when they say that they want to pay tribute to me."[150] Ira Nadel argues that this reflects his awareness of his position within the musical and artistic continuum – effectively, the 'tower of song' that he described:

> *For Leonard, the critical thing is to have those songs played, so that people can listen to them, so if you prefer the way that the McGarrigle sisters do it, or the way Nick Cave does it, or the way Billy Joel does it, fantastic. The important thing is getting the song out to other people. And I think that's one of the great things about Leonard, is this generosity which he sees extending outward over*

time, so when he's no longer able to record or sing any more, he
does have some sense that the music is still being heard. It's like
a kind of library where you know that, after the author has died,
people are still able to go and pull that book off the shelf and enjoy
it. Leonard wants other voices to sound his music.[151]

Cohen had intended to bring out an album of his own in 1991, but he
had other distractions. His son Adam was seriously injured in a car accident in 1990, although he made a full recovery after several months
in hospital. More happily, Cohen embarked upon another relationship,
this time with the Hollywood actress Rebecca De Mornay, who was
25 years younger than the singer; his appearance as her companion at
the Academy Awards ceremony drew as much comment for the May-
September incongruity of the union as it did for the sheer weirdness of
Cohen showing up to an event so defiantly showbizzy.

But it was more than a matter of life getting in the way. Cohen's
artistic process was hampered by a condition that resembled writer's block, but was really something more complex. In a long interview with Christian Fevret, the driving force behind *I'm Your Fan*, he
explained:

My brain, when I write, is completely confused. It struggles at the
bottom of a well, trying to find something that will give the song
permanence in this world. To bring a song into existence seems
difficult. Most successes, however, are simple. But I have not found
a simple way to do things. I keep searching. Just because some-
thing takes a lot of time does not mean that it is not urgent, it is
urgent every minute. That's why this situation is impossible... Per-
fection is much too much a luxury for me. It's at a level much more
urgent than perfection. It is survival. Personally and for my work.
How do you escape the cycle? How can I find a sufficient voice to
give life to these songs? It is a situation where luxury has no place,
where only urgency is concerned.[152]

So fans could perhaps consider themselves lucky that his next album
was only about a year late. But *The Future*, which saw the light of day

in November, 1992, proved to be something of a disappointment. It was created in similar circumstances to those of *I'm Your Man*, with Cohen sharing production duties with a number of others, including long-term engineer Leanne Ungar and current love interest De Mornay. The problem is that many of the songs just aren't strong enough.

It's Cohen's most explicitly political album, informed by the collapse of Communism in Eastern Europe, the horrors of Tiananmen Square, the first Gulf War and the Los Angeles riots of 1992, the last of which he had watched from his balcony. Cohen was a latecomer to politically oriented songwriting. In the 1960s and 1970s, while his contemporaries were marching and strumming in support of numerous righteous causes, Cohen's attentions were focused inwards. In an interview in 1972, he claimed that his meticulous, time-intensive method of writing meant that it was very difficult to create a work in response to a specific social event or crisis:

> *I've never written with the kind of luxury of choice. I've never sat down at my table and said 'there are people starving and there are people who are being tortured and brutalized, I must write a song to redeem them'. My songs have come to me, I've had to scrape them out of my heart. They come in pieces at a time and in showers and fragments and if I can put them together into a song and I have something at the end of the excavation I'm just grateful for having it. It tells me where I am and where I've been. I can't predispose the song to any situation or anything in the political realm, but if I live in the political realm and I'm aware of what is going down, my songs come out of that awareness of ignorance. A lot of my songs come out of ignorance.*[153]

This naïveté and solipsism began to dissolve towards the end of the latter decade, as the grim impasse of his relationship with Suzanne resolved itself, and he also began to pull back from his reliance on drugs. His new-found social awareness was clearly based on his deep knowledge of religious texts, especially the Bible, as demonstrated in an interview to promote *The Future*:

I've been writing about this for a long time. In a song I wrote in 1979 I said these are the final days, these are the final hours, this is the darkness, this is the flood. Y'know – don't wait for the apocalypse, IT'S ALREADY HAPPENED. It's already come down on us, we are in it right now. It's not something that's going to happen outside, this one is inside and it's raging.[154]

It's this sense of turmoil and paranoia and eschatological doom that inhabits the most powerful tracks on the album, which are good enough to stand alongside Cohen's greatest works. 'Democracy' is a Cohen classic, although it takes its initial inspiration from Henry Wadsworth Longfellow's patriotic poem of 1850, 'Sail On, O Ship Of State'. Like 'Hallelujah', it had a difficult, extended birth, with dozens of verses being written and discarded over a period of several years. Cohen had been ambivalent about the anti-authoritarian upsurge that had provoked the disintegration of the Soviet bloc, arguing that Western notions of freedom were not necessarily a perfect fit in places such as Russia; and this had little to do with communism, because totalitarian tendencies had been prevalent in the country well before Lenin's Bolsheviks came to power in 1917. He also felt that, although the people of the United States honestly aspired to democracy, the dominant economic and cultural forces at work in the country conspired to squash any chances that it might be fully realised. The key lines come in the first verse:

It's coming from the feel
That it ain't exactly real,
Or it's real but it ain't exactly there.

How can we identify a phenomenon such as 'democracy' or 'freedom', he asks over a military drum beat,[155] if what we experience is permanently mediated by the opinion-formers of CNN or MTV? As the critic Simon Schama says, comparing it with Longfellow's earnestness, the tone "could scarcely be less rah-rah... The starchy Longfellow anthem gets made over, in the election year of 1992, into a disabused song of possibility."[156]

The deceptively jaunty title track is also strong, Cohen in hellfire preacher mode, although some of his points of reference – "crack and anal sex" – are not usually the subject of Sunday morning sermons, and were ignominiously beeped from the versions released to radio and TV. How St Paul might have felt about joining a rogue's gallery including the likes of Stalin, Charlie Manson and the Berlin Wall is also one to ponder. Despite the gratuitous nastiness that pervades the song, Cohen does actually have a positive message tucked away in there: "love's the only engine of survival."

And love is the key to the wryly bluesy 'Anthem', a song of modest hope, drawing on Kabbalistic sources, enhanced – and given ecumenical appeal – by the lungs of the Los Angeles Mass Choir. Even by Cohen's elephantine standards of gestation, this one was a long time coming; it had taken a decade to compose, having been recorded and rejected for his previous two albums. In 1999, Adrienne Clarkson (who had given Cohen significant exposure on Canadian television in the mid-1960s, just as his music career was starting) quoted from the song when she was invested as Governor-General of Canada: "There is a crack, a crack in everything / That's how the light gets in." Only through our imperfections do we appreciate our own humanity.

But three very good songs with strong, confrontational lyrics is an EP, not an LP (a format that still existed, just about, in 1992). Considering how much emotional effort Cohen put into the writing, much of it is throwaway stuff; not exactly bad, but pretty inessential. Actually, make that three and a half good songs. 'Closing Time' has some fabulously mordant lyrics about how people will still need to drink and dance and fuck even as the end of the world approaches;[157] but it's let down by its identity as yet another jaunty hoedown. It's as if Cohen still feels an obligation to placate his Montreal contemporaries who used to come and hear the Buckskin Boys play square dances in 1954.

There are two cover versions: a soul song, 'Be For Real' on which, David Sheppard suggests, Cohen sounds "not unlike Barry White";[158] and Irving Berlin's standard 'Always', to which he adds blues inflections and some pretty superfluous additional lyrics. The gentle noodling of the album's closer, 'Tacoma Trailer', seems to be inspired by the sequencing of Cale's 'Hallelujah' at the end of *I'm Your Fan*. Unfortunately, Cohen didn't bother to write a real song to enhance the sense of gentle comedown; in fact, he didn't bother to show up, leaving matters in the hands of two session musicians, Bill Ginn from the band Passenger, and Steve Croes.

Or perhaps it's as well that he didn't sing. His voice had become a real weak link, its moody authenticity no longer enough to compensate for its cracked tunelessness. The cover is rather mediocre as well, resembling the sort of tattoo an accountant might get to celebrate her divorce. *The Future* was really not the sort of offering that might appeal to fans of REM or the Pixies whose curiosity had been whetted by *I'm Your Fan*. As Edwin Pouncey observed in the *NME*:

> *Hardcore Leonard Cohen admirers will, no doubt, adore this with a passion. Those who have yet to be introduced to the most reclusive and personal of artists may find* The Future *a bit of a shock.*[159]

The *Rolling Stone* review was more placatory, rightly arguing that much of Cohen's lyric writing was forthright, eloquent, and brave: "A more troubling, more vexing image of human failure has not been written,"[160] wrote Christian Wright.

Perhaps this troubling nature was the trouble. It was a period of growing optimism, especially among Americans. Communism had been defeated; Saddam Hussein had been driven back to Kuwait; the release of the album came three weeks after Bill Clinton, pride of the baby boomers, had been elected to the Presidency. In the same year, the historian Francis Fukuyama had published *The End Of History And The Third Man*, which declared that political ideology was, if not dead, then pretty much irrelevant, and US-style liberal democracy was the inevitable model for human society. As Anthony DeCurtis described it:

> *Particularly in the United States, there was a kind of go-go atmosphere in the 90s. There was this sense that everything is getting better, money's around, we're going into the new millennium, we're riding high and suddenly this album* The Future *comes along:*

"I've seen the future, baby: it is murder." He was looking at a dif-
ferent thread running through... The apocalyptic element
of what millenarianism is, and finding underneath all that pumped-
up hoopla, finding the dread underneath it; I think that's what
The Future *is about. And again, it just hit a perfect mark because*
it was something that was out there and submerged.[161]

Too submerged, perhaps: the album sold miserably in the United
States, although fans in New York and elsewhere packed out Cohen's
live appearances. *The Future* was perhaps ahead of its time; five years
later, the English band Radiohead would release *OK Computer*, which
offered a similar menu of millenarian dread, to critical rapture and
huge sales.

In 1993, Cohen brought out a new book, a 'Greatest Hits' of sorts.
Stranger Music contained most, but not all of his published poems and
song lyrics, going back to *Let Us Compare Mythologies* in 1956. In an
interview to publicise it, he made an attempt to characterise his state
of mind, and at the same time hinted at the reason for his inability to
hold down relationships (De Mornay by this stage having slipped off
the radar):

It's just having the rug pulled out from under you and not being
able to locate yourself and reaching out very needily for another
heart, for a caress, for an affirmation or whatever it is; just a kind
of deep neediness. And then a kind of manly withdrawal from that
neediness and an attempt to reform yourself so you can exist in a
landscape that's blowing up around you.[162]

Stranger Music, far better than *The Future*, offered an excellent introduction to any newcomers, many of whom had little idea that he had
an identity outside the music business. Hardcore Cohen junkies, however, objected to some of the apparently arbitrary omissions, and to the
author's obsessive rewriting of his own texts; a factor that was partly
to blame for the fact that the book was three years late. But they were
by now used to his peculiar sense of timekeeping.

CHAPTER TWENTY
The bad monk

"I've always been drawn by the voluptuousness of austerity."
– Leonard Cohen, 1994

Interviewed in 1992, Cohen was philosophical about his advancing years, and claimed to be happier, personally and professionally than he had been in decades:

> *There is a wisdom appropriate to each age of man, and the early wisdoms all embrace notions of glorious finality, of burning beautifully – not a bad idea... But after a certain point in life, the allure of all that fades. Now that I'm in advanced middle-age I've discovered a certain buoyancy. Life weighs heavily upon one's shoulders, but then you find that, with a certain kind of shrug, it will just lift off for a moment or two.*[163]

And yet that happiness, that release from the depression that had plagued him for most of his adult life, still wasn't enough. The combination with his other pastimes, chemical and carnal, could not be sustained: he later claimed that he abandoned the anti-depressant Prozac because of the deleterious effect it had on his sex drive.[164]

Instead, he needed the sort of sustenance that sex and drugs and critical acclaim and the adoration of indie-rock icons couldn't bring. The myth has it that for a nine-year period, including most of the 1990s, Leonard Cohen was apart from the rest of the world, ensconced in Roshi's hideaway on Mount Baldy. This wasn't quite true; between the end of 1992 and 2001 he made a number of public appearances, conducted several interviews and continued to write poetry and music.

What he didn't do between those dates was to release any studio albums. For most of the time, his main residential address was at the monastery, where he lived in an austere, two-room cabin, with few creature comforts (although he was permitted to bring his keyboard). While at Mount Baldy he would rise at three in the morning for a day mostly composed of meditation, although the lifestyle was not entirely about self-denial; Roshi's fondness for an occasional drop of the hard stuff set the standard for an acceptance of pleasure in moderation. Cohen travelled fairly widely at this time, but much of his movement was on Zen business, accompanying Roshi on visits to Buddhist and other religious centres around the world. This may not fit with the conventional perception of monasticism, but as Cohen explained in 1988, the purpose of the meditation and discipline he enjoyed and endured on the mountain was to help him to engage with reality, not to escape from it:

> *It keeps the mind fit. It cools me out and gets me closer to myself. I cut right down on smoking and start eating right. I could go to a health farm I suppose but there you wouldn't get a chance to bang nails and carry boulders. Buddhist meditation frees you from God and frees you from religion. You can experience complete at-homeness in this world.*[165]

As discussed earlier (see Chapter Eleven), there was nothing unusual about Western entertainers becoming involved with Eastern religions. Buddhism was especially popular in the 1990s, partly because of public interest in the teachings of the Dalai Lama and the persecution of his Tibetan followers. Stars such as Richard Gere, the Beastie Boys, Tina Turner and Sharon Stone, as well as Cohen's fellow Canadians Alanis Morissette and kd lang, gave publicity to various schools of thought, some rather more rigorous than others. Kurt Cobain of Nirvana also claimed to be following the tenets of Buddhism, for what good it did him: he committed suicide in April, 1994.[166]

But Cohen's practice was more committed than most. Despite his fondness for various fleshly diversions, he had never led a particularly ostentatious lifestyle; his record sales wouldn't allow it, for a start. In some ways, the monastery reminded him of the companionable simplicity that prevailed at the Jewish summer camps where he worked in the 1950s, and subsequently recreated in *The Favourite Game*:

It's a monastic situation, like an old boy-scout camp. It's Roman-esque with stone walls. It's a nice life. We get up at three in the morning and shovel our way through the snow to the meditation hall. I love it man. Everything's perfect. It couldn't be worse.[167]

In 1996, the French director Armelle Brusq shot a documentary about Cohen's life on Mount Baldy, released as *Leonard Cohen: Spring 96*. Made on video, it interspersed scenes depicting the rigorous ritual of the monastery, as described above, with touching banalities, such as Cohen pottering around in his saggy long johns and helping Roshi unpack his suitcase. It also demonstrates the relative freedom that he had: tinkering on his synthesiser in his room (playing an early version of 'A Thousand Kisses Deep' which would appear on *Ten New Songs* in 2001); popping into his favourite Jewish deli in Los Angeles; smoking; eating ice cream. There's a great deal of Cohen – sporting the regulation monastic skinhead haircut – musing to camera; of particular interest is his consideration of the equivalence between his art and the practice of *zazen*, the form of meditation that was central to life on Mount Baldy:

I've always liked music... I had whatever few materials I had, but mostly it was chaos and desolation. It was just to organise something with what I had. A little melody, a chord, just pieces of bone and rag, a few pieces put together. And at a certain point they breathe, that mess, that formless pool of slime and despair. Even if it's about that, even if the song is about those matters, it still becomes a universe of its own. You can sing it, you can communicate it, you can inhabit it. It strengthens you to do that kind of work, but you have to dive into it. Just the same way with zazen. Things arise that are very, very disturbing. And there's no way around it, there's no way over it, there's no way under it, there's no way to the side of it, there's no way of forgetting it. You have to sit in the very bonfire of that distress and you sit till you're burned away and it's ashes and it's gone. And it's the same way with writing. Some kind of itch. Some sense of unbearable disorder in your own life.[168]

141

On August 9 of the same year, Cohen underwent ordination, taking the monastic name Jikan, variously translated as 'at ease', 'the silent one' and 'one who brings silence'; although even this question provoked intense debate among devotees who hadn't had a new studio album to dissect for four years.[169]

However, the faithful were allowed a few new releases over the rest of the decade, and Cohen made himself available for a modest round of interviews to promote them. His second live album appeared in 1994, to be known variously as *Cohen Live, Live In Concert* and *Leonard Cohen Live In Concert*. The cover artwork is equally confused; the album is encased in what is possibly the lousiest sleeve in the long and depressing history of Cohen wrappers. All typewriter fonts and blurry photocopies, it's as if an elderly lady had been asked to concoct a poster for her great-nephew's punk rock band, her sole knowledge of punk coming from a cursory glance at a club scene in a mid-1980s John Hughes movie.

Fortunately, the content makes up for the visual train-wreck. It gives an excellent flavour of his live shows at the time (the tracks came from 1988 and 1993), although there's an odd focus on the early period of his recording career, with the majority of the tracks featured having been written before 1974. Thankfully, the arrangements tend to dispense with the monolithic synthesisers of his recent recorded output, delivering a sound more akin to *New Skin* and *Recent Songs*. Bob Metzger on guitar and violinist Bob Furgo are particularly strong.

The album also documents Cohen's tendency to rework and reinvent his own back catalogue (a process he also extended to his written work, as demonstrated in *Stranger Music*). For example, 'Hallelujah' – represented here in a version from a performance in 1988, just four years after the studio version – is radically rewritten, with most of the Biblical references excised. 'Bird On The Wire', from a Toronto concert in 1993, also acquires a new verse.

In his review of the album, Andy Gill identified what was so attractive about Cohen's persona as he approached his seventh decade:

There are still substantial undercurrents of gloom in Cohen's later work, but they're tempered by a weary, wry wit, a hollow laughter which renders the pessimism not just bearable but actively enjoyable: this is the voice of experience, gently mocking the idealism of youthful innocence without dismissing it entirely.[170]

The grim existentialism of the early *Songs...* albums had not exactly been softened, but tempered, relaxed. The old man seemed happy within himself, in a way that the awkward bard at the Isle of Wight never really could be. Maybe this Buddhism business wasn't such a bad idea.

The problem with the Mark II Cohen, all laconic charm and wry *bons mots*, was that it could sometimes be expressed in an alarming lack of quality control. *The Future* had exhibited this tendency; when it was good, it was very, very good, and when it wasn't... meh.

The flaws in the next album to bear Cohen's name, however, couldn't be laid at his door. *Tower Of Song* was another tribute album, aimed at a more mainstream audience than *I'm Your Fan*. It was conceived as a 60th birthday present from his manager, Kelley Lynch, although, with a sense of urgency that seems to attend many Cohen-related projects, it came out almost in time for his 61st. The liner notes are the work of Tom Robbins, author of the novel *Even Cowgirls Get The Blues*. They begin:

He was rowed down from the north in a leather skiff manned by a crew of trolls. His fur cape was caked with candle wax, his brow stained blue by wine – though the latter was seldom noticed due to the fox mask he wore at-all times. A quill in his teeth, a solitary teardrop a-squirm in his palm, he was the young poet prince of Montreal, handsome, immaculate, searching for sturdier doors to nail his poignant verses on...

...and then get worse.

Which rather sets the tone for the rest of the album, sadly. It's not all bad: Willie Nelson gives a sombre, heartfelt rendition of 'Bird On The Wire', and long-term Cohen fan Suzanne Vega does a decent job on 'Story Of Isaac', but much of the rest exhibits the mawkish earnestness of post-Band Aid adult pop. Sometime Eagle Don Henley ('Everybody Knows'), Bono of U2 ('Hallelujah') and Elton John ('I'm Your Man') are particularly grating. Cohen had appeared on Elton's 1993 album *Duets*, contributing to a version of Ray Charles's 'Born To Lose', with equivalently uninspired results. That said, Cohen declared that Billy Joel's rendition of 'Light As The Breeze' was better than his own version on *The Future* ("That's the song I really meant."[171]) so who are we to argue? Lynch apparently asked Phil Collins to contribute, but he was too busy. Perhaps we should be grateful for such small mercies.

Cohen expressed his gratitude for the album (Lynch would later give him rather less cause to be so grateful) and declared that "I can play it in my jeep without fear".[172] Perhaps unwittingly, this rather summed up the overall quality of *Tower Of Song*; it's music for people who want to listen to Cohen in a safe, sterile environment, in their SUVs as they pick their kids up from school.

Fortunately there was a proper, non-jeep-friendly Cohen on the horizon, in the form of another compilation. *More Best Of Leonard Cohen* (a grammatical and stylistic abomination of a title if there ever was one) is packed with good stuff, although the selection of tracks is restricted to releases from the past decade, exhibiting again Cohen's tendency to revisionism. While the first *Greatest Hits* album contained nothing released after 1974, the new compilation has nothing from before 1988. Three studio albums – *Death Of A Ladies' Man*, *Recent Songs* and *Various Positions* – are written out of the approved history, which is a great shame for the casual listener interested in tracing the development of Cohen's style. The late 70s and early 80s saw Cohen's transition from anguished, self-obsessed poet to wry, eloquent observer, from Ladies' Man to Lady's Man; what critic Sylvie Simmons identified as "a switch from poet to raconteur, from the sparse bedroom bard beloved of the lonely and literate to a slow, dry, deadpan rapper in a big, tough world."[173] A leap from *New Skin For The Old Ceremony* to *I'm Your Man* – a period of 14 years – suggests two very different performers, different writers, different people, even.

Within those bounds, *More Best Of...* is a good round-up of Cohen's last three albums, with the strongest tracks from *I'm Your Man* and

Before The Storm

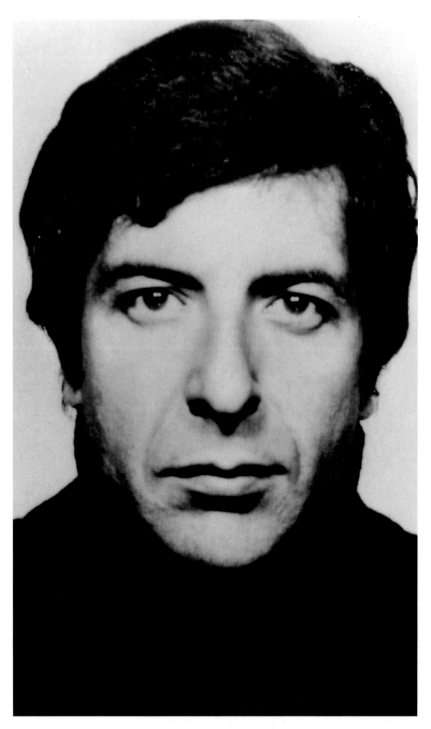

Bard of the Bed-Sitting Room

With Joni Mitchell

In the Thick Of It

The Many Faces of....

Top **With Moses Neimer at poet Irving Layton's funeral**
Bottom **Garcia Lorca**

LEONARD COHEN

FIRST WE TAKE MANHATTAN

LEONARD COHEN FESTIVAL

Heights Arts Society presents its 2007

September 7–21
Visual Arts Display
Curated by Phil Dietz
City Hall, Admission FREE

September 21
Birthday Party
Featuring Sheri-D Wilson
Supported with poetry reading and open-mic'
Meyer Horowitz Theatre, Students' Union Building, University of Alberta at 8PM

September 22
LEONARD COHEN NIGHT
Featuring Crystal Plamondon, Jarret Evans, and Ida Vanderkloot
with musical director Kit Johnson and choir producer Karen Shmirsky
Meyer Horowitz Theatre, Students' Union Building, University of Alberta at 8PM

Tickets at Tix on the Square. Phone 780-420-1757. Admission $25

A Multi-Day Celebration of the Arts inspired by the works of Leonard Cohen. For more info visit www.leonardcohenrights.org

RD
EN
OUR 2009

The Australian - AU
en remains an artist
of impeccable class"
– January 2009

er Evening News - UK
e, soul-stirring event,
surely destined to be
mbered as one of the
at shows of the year"
– June 2008

he Dominion Post - NZ
how I have ever seen"
– January 2009

ER 15 YEARS

ROYAL ALBERT HALL
General Manager: FRANK J. MUNDY

Sunday, 10 May, 1970
at 7.30 p.m.   Doors open at 7

LEONARD COHEN

ARENA   C   20/-

ROW   13   Enter by
SEAT   2   Door No.   2

TO BE RETAINED

LEONARD
COHEN

I'M YOUR MAN

The Gaze

REAL | SATURDAY, OCTOBER 25, 2003 | QUEBEC'S OLDEST DAILY | SINCE 1778

A COMPANION FOR LENNIE

Leonard Cohen, poet, author, lover, songwriter, singer, Zen student and, now, Companion of
Canada, has a bow of greeting for Governor-General Adrienne Clarkson as he receives his honour.
Clarkson, in an effort to make the investiture more of a family affair, moved the ceremony from her
the Château Laurier. Among the 49 other recipients were actor Kiefer Sutherland, there with his
Douglas, former Ontario NDP leader Stephen Lewis, carrying his grandson, and Guy Saint-Pierre,

NONS DE ROUTE

Elle lui a redonné souffle et inspiration alors qu'il était
en plein doute. Il lui a dédié I'm Your Man. La photographe
Dominique Issermann revient en images sur sa
fructueuse rencontre avec
cette semaine en France.

BK 105   ROW   W   SEAT 147

LEVEL 1
ENTRANCE H

AEG LIVE PRESENTS
LEONARD COHEN
WORLD TOUR
THE O2, LONDON, SE10
DOORS 6:30PM
THU 17-JUL-08
PRICE   60.00 S/C   6.75   TOTAL 66.75

The O2
www.theo2.co.uk

Lenny's Ladies

With Ajani Thomas

With Dominique Isserma

With Rebecca De Mornay

With Marianne Ihlen on Hydra (plus one unkno

Suzanne Elrod with Lorca and Adam Cohen

Nico

The '80s look

Early 1990s

Receiving the 'Companion of the Order of Canada' from
Governor General Adrienne Clarkson in 2003.

On tour 2008 & 2009

On tour 2008 & 2009

Thank you and goodnight

The Future and a representative selection from *Cohen Live*. Following the exploitative orthodoxy of the record business in the 1990s, there are also two previously unreleased tracks, so that diehard Cohen completists who already had the last three albums would be forced to shell out again. (*Greatest Hits* doesn't follow this pattern, which would have shocked the hippyish sensibilities of Cohen's fans in the 1970s.)

The two new pieces are interesting, if not essential. Oddly, they mirror the closing sequence of *The Future*, following a rhythm-and-blues stomper with an avant-garde experiment. 'Never Any Good' mixes religious and sensual imagery in the pursuit of an apology that the lover/narrator may not mean. 'The Great Event', like 'Tacoma Trailer', is a studio-based experiment in which Cohen's involvement as performer is minimal. A robotic, female voice announces that she will play Beethoven's Moonlight Sonata backwards,[174] an act that will "reverse the effects of the world's mad plunge into suffering". The looming apocalypse at which Cohen hinted in 'Closing Time' (from *The Future*) is replaced by a sense of redemption and salvation. And yet, at the same time, the track is eerie and unsettling. It's reminiscent of Radiohead's 'Fitter Happier', on the *OK Computer* album, which was also released in 1997, and at the same time strangely filmic, echoing the troubling dream sequences in the works of David Lynch.

Lynch didn't come calling during the 1990s, sadly, although Cohen's songs did accompany the films of a number of other dark and dangerous directors. In 1994, fellow Canadian Atom Egoyan used 'Everybody Knows' in the disturbing *Exotica*, set in a Toronto strip club; in the same year, Oliver Stone gave him even more exposure, putting three tracks from *The Future* on his hyper-violent satire *Natural Born Killers*, which had been written but then disowned by Quentin Tarantino. The last film was a particularly good match for the Cohen of this period. He had developed some trenchant views on law and (dis)order, which might have startled some of his fey followers in the 1960s, not to mention his Buddhist friends in the 1990s:

They should put the boys and girls into uniform. There should be universal North American conscription again. It's us against drugs. If you don't understand that, you're gonna lose.[175]

Even though Cohen made sparse appearances in the media during the 1990s, his devoted admirers, especially those in Europe, kept the flame burning. Chief among them was a Finnish auditor named Jarkko Arjatsalo, who began a website called The Leonard Cohen Files in 1995, now the largest online resource in the world; despite his isolation, Cohen himself took advantage of Mount Baldy's new dial-up internet connection and began contributing poems and drawings to the site, many of which would appear in his next poetry volume, *Book Of Longing.* And in 2008, it would be Jarkko who first published news of the itinerary for Cohen's comeback tour, ahead of the music press and mainstream media.

In fact, for all his re-invention as 'the silent one', when Cohen finally released a new studio album, after a gap of nine years, it felt as if he'd never really been away.

CHAPTER TWENTY-ONE
Live my life in Babylon

"I tuned the old banjo."
– 'Boogie Street

In her review of Cohen's 1997 compilation album, Sylvie Simmons contemplated the changes that time and age and cigarettes had wrought on Cohen's voice, and the effect that had had on his performing style:

Somewhere during the 22 years between the two Best Of *collections, Cohen's voice has dropped way down past his nicotined lungs and settled somewhere south of his boots. It's worn-in, battered, more than a bit dissipated, but still sensual, suiting a new despair that's less existential, more worldly-wise.*[176]

Essentially, although Cohen's voice remained distinctive and eminently suited to the tone and content of his own words, he could no longer 'sing' in any conventional sense (the sceptics, however, would argue that this had always been the case). In 2001, a couple of new releases gave listeners the chance to compare the two sounds.

Field Commander Cohen was based on recordings from concerts in London and Brighton on his 1979 tour. Many of the musicians were from the *Recent Songs* sessions, probably the most technically gifted outfit that Cohen worked with, and while they are inevitably at their strongest on the four tracks from that album, reinventions such as a bluesy 'Bird On The Wire' are a little less successful. But it also documents a time when Cohen's voice was as good as it ever was, gruff but flexible, in total command, our "favourite singing millionaire", as the title track has it.

One of the backing singers on that tour, alongside Jennifer Warnes, was Sharon Robinson, who 22 years later had a key role in Cohen's next album. In fact, it's probably better to define *Ten New Songs* as a joint project between Cohen and Robinson, rather similar in that respect to *Death Of A Ladies' Man*. Fortunately, there was less anguish this time, and fewer guns.

The album was created in unusual circumstances, only made possible by modern digital recording technology. Cohen sent Robinson some very basic demos he'd made in his sparsely furnished cabin on Mount Baldy; she worked on the melodies and sampled instrumentals, before returning the expanded versions to Cohen. This back-and-forth process continued, aiming for a contrast between Cohen's voice, barely singing, often barely above a hoarse whisper, and Robinson's lush synthesised sounds and multi-part harmonies. The end result was unlike anything Cohen had done before, although it was clearly his own work.

Aside from the new technology, much of the difference was down to a subtle change in Cohen's spiritual direction. In 1998 he gave an interview about his life on Mount Baldy and he expressed, if not dissatisfaction, then a sort of rueful insubordination:

> *It's a rigorous life, but kind of interesting for the freaks that are up there... I don't like it very much. Nobody really likes it. I don't think any monk really likes it... the life is designed to overthrow you. There are moments in the day, in the week, in the year when it's worthwhile, when this study, this investigation of the self is the most important and the most urgent thing in your life. A lot of the time you just feel you'd just like to go down the hill and light a cigarette and have a drink at a bar. Which you can't do any more.*[177]

As had so often been the case, he felt like a change of scenery. Towards the end of the last millennium, he had spent some time with the guru Ramesh Balsekar in Mumbai. Balsekar's philosophy distinguished action from the individual – doings from the doer – and did a great deal to relieve Cohen's anxiety about his periods of writer's block and the long and frustrating paths his songs often took until they were good enough for public consumption. Now, he was more relaxed. If a song was going to come, it was going to come. As he explained it:

*If it is your destiny to be this labourer called a writer, then you
know that you've got to work every day, but you also know that
you're not going to get it every day. You have to be prepared but
you really don't command the enterprise.*[178]

There's definitely something relaxed and passive about the *Ten New
Songs* that he and Robinson released. Most drift by in at a slow-to-me-
dium tempo, nodding more than a little to the adult, sophisticated side
of modern R&B. The lyrics, unusually, are simple and heartfelt. He's
no longer making abstruse references to Persian poets or medieval Tal-
mudic scholars, but to Robert Frost, the sort of thing that gets covered
in American high schools. In 'A Thousand Kisses Deep', for example,
the couplet:

*And maybe I had miles to drive,
And promises to keep*

is almost a verbal sample of Frost's 'Stopping By Woods On A
Snowy Evening'. Compared with his last studio album, *The Future*,
this is hardly esoteric, challenging stuff.

Love, as ever, is the theme, of woman or of God or both. And yet now
Cohen is too old to be a pursuer of love – or maybe, under the influence
of Balsekar, he does not feel the need to chase too hard. As he croons
in 'You Have Loved Enough':

*I am not the one who loves –
It's love that chooses me.*

It will come in its own time. Don't push too hard. Critics were happy to see Cohen finally at one with himself, and probably relieved that
he had another album in him after such a persistent drought. This may
have led them to overestimate the ultimate value of the piece. Steven
Chean's review for *Rolling Stone* is an example of this:

Cohen returns, the undisputed landlord of those dark, damaged places. Ten New Songs *manages to sustain loss's fragile beauty like never before and might just be the Cohen's most exquisite ode yet to the midnight hour.*[179]

In fact, it's almost *too* exquisite. The multiple layers of samples and voices don't so much highlight the ravaged beauty of Cohen's voice as muffle it. The album is well made, with an open, welcoming sound, a complete reversal from the snarling harshness of *The Future*. As Cohen described it:

There's a sense of relaxation in the tunes that comes through, there's a kind of pulse, an invitation to get into it – a groove. A lot of people have danced to it... well, actually, one person. And she was an executive of Sony in France, and she's a trained dancer.[180]

It also helps that Cohen's ability to create a great song has never deserted him: check out The Handsome Family's rendition of 'A Thousand Kisses Deep' with Linda Thompson, on the *Leonard Cohen: I'm Your Man* film. Many of the lyrics have a simple eloquence, although occasionally it's too simple. For example, here's Cohen speaking in 2008 about the inspiration behind the song 'Boogie Street':

There is a Boogie Street in Singapore [actually Bugis Street]*, or there used to be... By day it's a place of shops and booths with a lot of bootleg records – I asked one of the vendors if he had any Leonard Cohen records and he came out with an entire box of my catalogue, much more thorough than most of the stores that I'd been to and a dollar apiece, reasonably priced I thought. At night it transformed into this alarming and beautiful sexual marketplace where there were male and female prostitutes, transvestites, extremely attractive people offering to satisfy all the fantasies of their numerous customers. So Boogie Street became a symbol of commerce and desire.*[181]

Which sounds like just the sort of place in which Cohen might find some glorious material. But aside from a passing mention of 'maps of blood and flesh', the song 'Boogie Street' hovers six feet above the grimy sidewalk, not wanting to get its stanzas dirty, never quite engaging with the commerce or the desire. Cohen isn't the only one, of course; Bugis Street itself was redeveloped and cleaned up in the 1980s, and is now just another shopping destination.

The lyrics do offer a bit of grit here and there, despite the unctuousness of their musical surroundings. 'My Secret Life' tells of a man who can only escape from his dull, downtrodden existence through fantasy; a Walter Mitty/Reggie Perrin for the new millennium; the damaged ideologue of 'First We Take Manhattan' who's given up his wicked ways and now works for an insurance company. And Robert Christgau has identified in the closing track, 'The Land Of Plenty', a premonition of the response to the 9/11 attacks, although any song with "courage" and "truth" came in handy during that time.[182]

Ultimately, though, *Ten New Songs* is Cohen Made Safe, Cohen As Muzak. The people who bought *Tower Of Song* to enjoy in their jeeps can half-listen to this album bubbling away in the background when they next host a dinner party. And Cohen deserves rather more than that.

CHAPTER TWENTY-TWO
Exceptionally kind in my old age

"And the heart must pause to breathe
And love itself have rest."
– Byron, 'We'll Go No More A-Roving'

Canada had always been quietly proud of Leonard Cohen, despite his frequent absences and his sometimes querulous attitude to the city of his birth. In 2003 he was awarded the rank of Companion of the Order of Canada by Governor-General Adrienne Clarkson, who as a CBC journalist had interviewed him nearly four decades before.

It would have been a neat culmination to a glorious career: the globe-trotting, speed-guzzling, gun-loving, womanising Zen Jew, B.A. *(McGill)* ambling in his seventieth year towards the embrace of his indulgent nation. But Cohen had work to do, an album to make.

The working process behind *Dear Heather* was similar to that used for *Ten New Songs*, with digital files being passed between the collaborators. In addition to Cohen, Sharon Robinson and engineer Leanne Ungar, these now included the singer and pianist Anjani Thomas, who was by this point his romantic partner. There are similarities between the two albums, with synths and samples predominating over 'real' instruments, but the sound is very different, with Robinson's lush layering of tones and voices replaced by skeletal instrumentation. Much of the album sounds like a demo, rather than a finished release. The title track, for example, seems to borrow its backing track from a 1970s TV advertisement for a Bontempi home organ – which isn't necessarily a bad thing, just a very strange thing.

The other noticeable change is in the state of Cohen's voice. Three years before it had sounded quite rough; on *Dear Heather* it resembles the croak of a man dying of thirst or worse, somewhere between Tom Waits and Lee Marvin in his role as Ben Rumson in the movie *Paint Your Wagon* (1969), which spawned the brilliantly unmusical single

'Wand'rin Star', a chart-topping hit in Britain the following year. He has abandoned even the pretence of singing, intoning his words where appropriate, stepping back with some relief to let Robinson and Thomas handle much of the musical stuff. The final track, a live performance of 'Tennessee Waltz' from 1985, demonstrates the precipitous decline (or, if you prefer, the idiosyncratic maturing) that had taken place over 19 years.

'Tennessee Waltz' (written in 1947 by Redd Stewart and Pee Wee King, and subsequently recorded by a diverse selection of performers including Patti Page, Otis Redding, Emmylou Harris and Tom Jones) is a golden oldie from Cohen's adolescence, and much of the other material looks backwards. 'The Faith' resuscitates the backing track from 'The Lost Canadian (Un Canadien Errant)' on *Recent Songs*, from 1979; 'To A Teacher' is a tribute to his absent poetic mentor AM Klein, and is based on a piece from *The Spice-Box Of Earth* (1961); the line "a long pain ending without a song to prove it" expresses compassion for a talent cut short by mental illness (Klein died in 1972). Cohen seems particularly interested to examine the influences on his parallel career in verse: 'Villanelle For Our Time' is a poem by another mentor, FR Scott, and was recorded at Mount Baldy in 1999. 'Go No More A-Roving' is older still, being based on a poem by George Gordon, Lord Byron originally written in 1817. It's interesting that Cohen waited so long to approach the legend of Byron, whose persona as seducer, substance abuser and frequenter of war zones shares many elements with his own (although Byron only lived to the age of 36).[183]

The only time *Dear Heather* stirs itself from nostalgic reverie is on 'On That Day', which contemplates the events of September 11, 2001, three years before and still resonant. It's an interesting piece because it avoids the earnest breast-beating that infected many musical responses to the attacks and their aftermath; for example, Paul McCartney's 'Freedom' and Toby Keith's 'Courtesy Of The Red, White & Blue (The Angry American)'. As Alexis Petridis put it in his review of the album:

His inability to hold a tune means he sounds indifferent during 'On That Day', his response to 9/11 and its aftermath, yet it fits perfectly because his response to 9/11 is dolefully puzzled: "Some people

*say it's what we deserve/ some people say they hate us of old/
I wouldn't know, I'm just holding the fort.*"[184]

Cohen's Zen-inflected detachment releases him from the rage and
sorrow that others felt. And even 'On That Day' contains a gentle reminder of his earlier career, as he takes out the trusty Jew's harp that
defined the sound of his second album.

Dear Heather is an interesting album; it's inconsistent, but that also
means that it's spared from the slightly cloying uniformity of sound
that marred *Ten New Songs*. Once again, as is so often the case in
the history of Cohen's recorded output, the album sleeve is an absolute shocker, resembling nothing so much as the packaging for a range
of feminine hygiene products from about 1986, decorated with the
Chinese symbol for his monastic name, 'Jikan'. Cohen has nobody to
blame for this, as it's based on one of his own drawings.

Reviewers were impressed by Cohen's continuing ability and desire
to reinvent himself, and his brave decision to dispense with extraneous
studio trickery. But the sheer decrepitude of his voice, which makes
him sound much older than 70, and the retrospective tone of many of
the songs, surely suggests a mood of closure, of coming to terms with
an ending. As Robert Christgau put it: "Not only do I like the guy, I'm
Old enough to identify with him. But I doubt I'll ever be Old enough
to identify with this".[185]

Cohen might have taken such well-meant joshing as a hint that he
ought to put his feet up and enjoy the fruits of a well-earned vacation. But suddenly, that wasn't an option. The strange tale of what happened to Leonard Cohen's fortune will probably never be told to the
satisfaction of everyone involved. It's a financial Mexican stand-off, a
three-way bout of he said/she said, involving law suits, countersuits,
threats, disappearing e-mails, tax bills, legal bills, a SWAT team, dark
rumours of insanity and a hint of tantric sex just to keep things exciting. The best and clearest account came in an article Katherine Macklem wrote for the Canadian magazine *Maclean's* in 2005,[186] although
even that piece left several question marks trailing behind it, almost
certainly for legal reasons.

The bare bones are these. Cohen's long-term manager Marty Machat died in 1988, and his assistant Kelley Lynch took over the reins. All apparently went smoothly for many years, including long periods that Cohen spent in seclusion – but not creative inactivity – at Roshi's monastery on Mount Baldy. In 1997, with her encouragement, he sold his music publishing company to Sony (by then, the owners of his record label, Columbia), a deal that would offer a number of large payments over the next few years, enough to create a comfortable pension. Much of this money was placed in a trust fund, managed by Neal Greenberg, an investment advisor based in Los Angeles.

Cohen only became aware that something had gone wrong in 2004, after a chance encounter between his daughter Lorca, at that point running a furniture store in LA, and the boyfriend of one of Lynch's employees; the latter mentioned that it might be advisable for Cohen to look more closely at the state of his finances. Lorca alerted her father, who discovered unexplained transfers of funds from his account to Lynch. He immediately fired her, but it took several months, and the expensive attentions of a team of forensic accountants, to discover that over 8 million dollars had been removed from his funds. After a writing and recording career spanning nearly five decades, his assets now amounted to about $150,000.

Greenberg became involved when it was suggested that he should have taken more care over his client's interests; concerned about the threat to his reputation, he sued Cohen, claiming that he had warned him many times about his shrinking funds. Cohen denied that he had received these communications, and attention shifted back to Kelley Lynch who had, it was alleged, intercepted many of Greenberg's e-mails.

That was when things got really bizarre, and were further complicated by the belated revelation that Cohen and Lynch had also had a sexual relationship in about 1990. Now, she responded to the allegations with a torrent of e-mails that led many to question her sanity; at various times she accused Cohen of sending a squad of armed police to arrest her, and invited Greenberg to sample the delights of tantric sex in her company. Friends grew concerned at her behaviour, and she even lost custody of her son. Meanwhile, Greenberg had claimed that Cohen and his lawyer Robert Kory were offering to drop claims against Lynch, if she helped them retrieve the missing funds from Greenberg's insurers.

Cohen tried to remain above the fray but, aside from the parlous financial situation in which he found himself, he was in a scenario where he had to make decisions. Never the most confrontational of men, his time with Roshi and Balsekar had imbued him with a benevolent sense of passivity. Stuff happened, as it always would – usually the best course was to let it. In the event, a Los Angeles court made an award in Cohen's favour in 2006, but Lynch did not respond to a subpoena, and the money was not forthcoming. Cohen stated that he didn't want to punish Lynch, but simply wanted to find out where the hell his money had disappeared to, and retrieve as much of it as he could. As he put it:

> *I didn't really experience it as a betrayal. I don't know why. I don't know whether it's because I had good teachers or good parents or good genes. Maybe it will hit me one of these days.*[187]

But just letting things be was no longer an option; not only were legal and accountancy bills eating away at his massively depleted savings, there was also a seven-figure tax bill to be addressed. From the perspective of the Internal Revenue Service, he had earned the money, even if it had subsequently vanished. It was a troubling time for Cohen and those close to him, forcing him to spend most of his time on the tedious minutiae of business that he'd previously avoided:

> *I was spending enormous amounts of time in lawyers' offices, tax specialists' offices, accountants' offices, detectives' offices. In fact, I was spending all my time in offices, and I had to say to myself at a certain point, "If God wants to bore you to death, I guess that's His business."*[188]

This was not the way things were meant to happen. No matter what Christgau and his kind might have wanted, Cohen had to keep working.

CHAPTER TWENTY-THREE
It's been hell, it's been swell

"You wouldn't worry about whether you were as good as Ray Charles or Edith Piaf"
–'You'd Sing Too' (2006)

Dear Heather was dedicated to Cohen's book publisher Jack Mc-Clelland, who died in 2004, having remained loyal despite his client's erratic sales and cavalier attitude to deadlines. Another of Cohen's long-time champions, Irving Layton, died early in 2006, his energy and irascible wit already stilled by Alzheimer's disease; Byron's 'Go No More A-Roving', on the same album, had been a poignant tip of the hat to the old rogue.

The man who had lost his father at the age of nine had always needed gurus, mentors, and now, one by one, they were falling away. Yet Roshi remained a constant presence, reaching his one hundredth birthday in 2007. Cohen's devotion to the Mount Baldy brand of Zen had ebbed and flowed over the years – when he came down from the mountain, he renamed his publishing company 'Bad Monk' in self-mocking acknowledgment of his own limited adherence to the rules – but he remained devoted to the old man himself, building the sort of relationship he'd never been able to enjoy with his own father. He had realised, after many years of self-discipline and self-examination, that it wasn't actually Roshi's teachings that brought him fulfilment, as he explained in an interview in 2006:

I wasn't really interested in Buddhism. I had a religion of my own which was perfectly serviceable. I wasn't an enthusiast for the dogma or the Buddhist scriptures. What I was there for was to be in the company of Joshu Sasaki Roshi, who was the central figure of that monastery... He had these two qualities I observed: He was at ease with himself and was at ease with others. And very few peo-

157

*ple really achieve that. I wasn't so interested in any spiritual edu-
cation. What I was interested in was feeling better. That system is
designed to overthrow a 20-year-old. And I always spent several
months of every year with Roshi, often as his secretary and finally
as his cook. I left because it just seemed appropriate. I was about
65. It was just too rigorous.*[189]

And it was those lessons in achieving ease that seemed to have paid
off in his response to the quagmire in which he found himself. Just as,
back in 1966, he had essayed to solve his financial difficulties by making music, that's what he did 40 years later.

Blue Alert, however, was not billed as a Leonard Cohen record. He
produced and arranged it, and wrote the lyrics, but his collaborator/
lover Anjani Thomas was the featured singer and composer. To an extent, though, this was a natural progression from *Ten New Songs* and
Dear Heather, which had seen Cohen's own rusty pipes tucked away
in a corner where they couldn't do too much harm. Anjani supposedly
thought she was recording demos for a new Cohen album, but her boyfriend had other ideas.

It was still very much a Cohenesque record, if not a Cohen record,
with John Lissauer, who had first worked with him 32 years previously, providing instrumental and production services. Anjani reprised
the song 'Nightingale', which had first appeared on *Dear Heather*, two
years previously; it carried a dedication to another colleague, the singer and actor Carl Anderson, best known for playing Judas in the film
of *Jesus Christ Superstar*, who had succumbed to leukaemia in 2004.
Also, 'The Mist', like 'True Love Leaves No Traces', was a rework-
ing of 'As The Mist Leaves No Scar', a Cohen poem only two years
younger than Anjani herself. And some of the lyrics are vintage LC.
The last track, 'Thanks For The Dance' is witty and poignant, with
a dash of personal resonance – there's a hint of a failed pregnancy in
there – written for a woman contemplating a lover who may be a little
past his prime:

*Thanks for the dance,
I'm sorry you're tired...*

Try to look inspired.

Inspiration, to be fair, was something Cohen didn't lack these days. One project particularly close to his heart was a Canadian documentary called *This Beggar's Description* (2005), directed by Pierre Tétrault, about his brother (and Cohen's friend) Philip Tétrault. Philip is a talented writer from Montreal, whose potential has never been realised because of his bouts of schizophrenia, which have provoked periods in jail, in hospital and on the streets. Cohen's songs adorn the soundtrack, and he makes a couple of appearances in the film, including one hilarious scene on a park bench where the two poets discuss Kris Kristofferson, dead Quebec politicians and losing toes to frostbite. It highlights Cohen's warmth, something that gets submerged beneath his persona as a brooding philosopher of the human heart; he doesn't see Philip as a madman or a drunk or even particularly as a writer. He's just some guy it's fun to hang out with, sip a little V8 and eat tortilla chips.

He even found the time to bring out a new volume of poetry, his first entirely new book since 1984. That said, *Book Of Longing* had spent several years in gestation, to the extent that self-appointed comedians in publishing were referring to it as the *Book Of Prolonging*. Many of the poems were brief and insubstantial, prompting the literary critic John Walsh (who had written a long piece about Cohen As Musician in 1994) to decide that he was "not a great poet, perhaps, but a good, bittersweet light versifier."[190] The poet's tendency to decorate his works with line drawings probably didn't help matters, making the book look and feel somehow less than serious. The pictures were actually exhibited at a gallery in Manchester, England, in 2007, despite the fact that Cohen himself doesn't care for pictures on his own walls.[191] The spleen of previous pieces was now supplanted by a whimsical melancholy as the poet remembered his lost friends; the review on the Popmatters website sneered that "It's as if Cohen is composing a Canadian Book of the Dead."[192]

In 2007, the minimalist composer Philip Glass used the poems as the basis for a song cycle, also called *Book Of Longing*, for which Cohen himself recited his own lines at the premiere and for the recorded version. Glass was better known for his operas such as *Einstein On*

The Beach and movie soundtracks, especially *Koyaanisquatsi*, but this wasn't the first time he'd attempted to incorporate pop lyrics into his work; *Songs From Liquid Days* (1986) had made similar use of the words of Paul Simon and Suzanne Vega. Glass's stripped-down, repetitive motifs provide an intriguing setting for Cohen's words (there are interesting comparisons to be made with the skeletal synthesisers of *Dear Heather*) and the whole project does make one wonder what direction Cohen's work might have taken if his 1984 string quartet project with Henry Lewy (see Chapter Seventeen) had reached fruition.

Meanwhile, the wave of adulation for Cohen from other musicians, younger and older, refused to abate. Part of this was expressed in the 'Hallelujah' meme, which had given this previously overlooked album track the status of a left-field karaoke classic. But others were creating more extensive testaments to his popularity; one particularly touching tribute came from Judy Collins, who brought out an album compiling her many Cohen cover versions to mark his 70th birthday.

Meanwhile, Hal Willner, the American producer who specialised in multi-artist tribute albums and concerts to offbeat musical innovators such as Thelonious Monk, Kurt Weill and Charles Mingus (the latter featuring Cohen) staged a series of Cohen-themed events under the 'Came So Far For Beauty' banner, with the first taking place in Brighton in 2003. The shifting line-up included Nick Cave, Rufus and Martha Wainwright, Lou Reed, Laurie Anderson, Beth Orton, Jarvis Cocker, Mary Margaret O'Hara, the Handsome Family and Kate and Anna McGarrigle, offering interpretations of the Cohen songbook that went from the respectful to the outrageous. Cave and Cocker's rendition of 'Don't Go Home With Your Hard-On' in Brighton was especially startling. The leg in Sydney, Australia was filmed by Lian Lunson as *Leonard Cohen: I'm Your Man*. Highlights there included Cave turning 'I'm Your Man' into the sort of thing that would have gone down a storm in Las Vegas in the early 1960s if the Ratpack had consumed something a little less legal than Scotch; and The Handsome Family triumphantly reclaiming 'A Thousand Kisses Deep' from the synths and samples of *Ten New Songs*. The film version added a studio-bound collaboration in New York between Cohen and U2 on 'Tow-

er Of Song', that was a little tepid, but infinitely preferable to the griev-
ous bodily harm that Bono had previously inflicted on 'Hallelujah'.

Also expressing a love of Cohen in their own strange way was the
Australian gypsy fusion outfit Monsieur Camembert, whose fondness
for Cohen's work extended into a full-blown live show and double album. But band leader Yaron Hallis explained that the appeal lay beyond the strength of the individual songs:

> *I wanted a show where we could explore the extent of his bril-
> liance, not only in the songs and the beautiful melodies, but also
> in the spoken bits. Virtually every time he opened his mouth in the
> last 50 years he has been brilliant. Whether he's talking to some-
> one in a cafe over a cup of coffee, or introducing one of his songs
> on stage, his turn of phrase is such that at times it's almost impos-
> sible to distinguish between what's poetry and what's something
> that he just said off the cuff.[193]*

It was clear that Hallis wasn't the only person keen to enjoy Cohen
in person, not just through the medium of his work. It was delightful
to see Nick Cave and Martha Wainwright sinking their teeth into the
songs, but there was a loyal constituency that wanted an encounter
with the man, not the fans.

Moreover, the music business was changing, as it became increasingly difficult for performers to guarantee a high income from recorded music. It was now so easy to download music files from the internet
that legitimate sales of CDs and other media were suffering badly. The
decades-old financial model, by which an act would record an album,
then play live gigs (often barely breaking even) to raise its profile, had
been shot to pieces. Major stars such as Madonna and Paul McCartney were signing innovative contracts, which meant they derived a far
higher percentage of their incomes from touring, with the album now
more an advertisement for the gigs, rather than the other way around.

Quirky books of poetry and collaborations with avant-garde composers were not going to resolve Cohen's troubles. For the first time
in 15 years, he had to go out on the road and play live concerts; an environment that the fans had always enjoyed rather more than he had.

TWENTY-FOUR

We're busted in
the blinding lights

"You always have a feeling in a hotel room that you're on the lam."
– Leonard Cohen, 1965

"While he eats a very healthy diet, like a Zen Buddhist would, every now and again we discover he's slipped out the back door and gone to McDonald's to buy a Filet-O-Fish."
– Charley Webb, backing singer, 2008

From the early 1970s onwards, for about 20 years, Leonard Cohen's professional life seemed to fit into a specific, roughly predictable mould. An album would be released; reviews would be mixed; sales would be a little disappointing, but solid enough to ensure that he wasn't dropped by his label; he would then embark on a long tour where his fans, especially those in Europe, would bestow upon him all the love that nobody else in the industry could seem to muster. Sometimes – especially in the early tours with the band known as The Army – the performances would teeter on the verge of violence and chaos; later they were attended by the more conventional lifestyle choices of booze, drugs and sex.

But in 2008, Cohen hadn't toured for 15 years. His last couple of studio albums had not exactly redefined the face of rock and roll; the die-hard fans, as ever, bought them and enjoyed them, but they had failed to impinge much on the wider public consciousness. Moreover, much of the world was teetering on the brink of the biggest economic recession since the late 1920s. If people were really going to spend money, surely it would be on more upbeat modes of entertainment. Was there any appetite to see and hear Leonard Cohen run through his sardonic, downbeat schtick? Was he even up to it? His time on Mount Baldy had improved his mental and physical discipline – but he was 73 years old.

In recent years, a number of veteran performers had confounded the cynics and achieved critical and commercial success on the live circuit. Brian Wilson of the Beach Boys had toured to massive acclaim with shows based around his *Pet Sounds* and *Smile* albums; Paul McCartney and the Rolling Stones remained serious crowd-pullers; The Police overcame their mutual loathing to get back on stage together; and there was of course, still Bob Dylan and his never-ending tour, revisiting and reinventing his oeuvre for diehards and newcomers alike. Meanwhile, Johnny Cash had faced down any number of physical challenges to record a series of primal, stripped-down albums that matched or even surpassed his classics from the 50s and 60s. However, Cohen was older than any of them (Cash having died in 2003, at the age of 71). It was not unknown for jazz or blues stars to keep going at such an advanced age, but with a few exceptions – Chuck Berry springs to mind – rocking into one's eighth decade was unknown territory.

On the other hand, he needed the money. In January, Cohen announced that he would begin a set of Canadian dates in Fredericton, New Brunswick, on May 11.

His confidence was boosted, if such a thing were necessary, in March, when he was finally inducted into the Rock and Roll Hall of Fame, alongside a deliciously eclectic cohort of fellow worthies: Madonna; John Cougar Mellencamp; the Ventures; and the Dave Clark Five. Lou Reed, his old buddy from the New York days, introduced him; Cohen, dapper in a dinner jacket, made a characteristically self-effacing speech that upended the notoriously messianic acclamation of Bruce Springsteen by his future manager:

This is a very unlikely occasion for me. It is not a distinction that I coveted or even dared dream about... So I'm reminded of the prophetic statement of Jon Landau in the early Seventies: I have seen the future of rock and roll and it is not Leonard Cohen.[194]

And then it was time to get busy. He spent the summer touring Canada and Europe, with stops at some of the major festivals, including the

Montreal, Montreux and Nice jazz festivals (were the Jazz Police providing security, one wonders?), Benicassim in Spain, the Big Chill in Ledbury, UK and a set at the Glastonbury Festival.

Any misgivings Cohen or those close to him may have had about returning to the road were soon forgotten. He had a well-drilled band including such stalwarts as Sharon Robinson, Roscoe Beck and Bob Metzger, alongside newer friends including the Spanish multi-instrumentalist Javier Mas (perhaps a nod to Cohen's doomed flamenco tutor?) and the Webb sisters as backing singers. The audiences and reviewers were entranced, and several tranches of new dates were added, stretching well into the following year. His manager Robert Kory, the lawyer who supported him in the legal tussles with Lynch and Greenberg, explained that the concerts were planned to build gradually, and to accommodate the needs of a septuagenarian:

> As we were initially putting the tour together, and he looked at the routing, with Glastonbury and the O2 Arena and Edinburgh, this wide range of stadiums. He said to me, 'What have you gotten me into?' But in planning this tour, he set out a series of conditions and I said, Leonard, this is a no compromise tour, we will do it exactly the way you want to do it or we won't do it. So every element of the tour is articulating his vision, from three months of rehearsals with the band and doing 20 warm-up dates in these little towns in the Maritimes. From the very first concert, in a little 900-seat theatre, it was clear he had complete command and the band was just stunning. And we evolved to larger and larger venues, 900, 1,200, 12,000, and so playing for 90,000 people at Glastonbury sort of fitted right in. This is fuelled on silence. And deep rest – we have a closed backstage, no interviews – and providing a level of support that enables him to just do those performances night after night. Fortunately there are curfews in most places, or he'd sing more.[195]

Another reason Cohen managed to withstand the rigours of life on the road was that he had shed many of the bad habits that had propped him up for so much of his adult life. He'd never indulged in the sort of touring Bacchanalia enjoyed by bands such as the Rolling Stones and Led Zeppelin; he was more likely to throw a copy of Yeats's poetry out of the window than a TV set. But he'd drunk, he'd taken drugs and he certainly hadn't been averse to the attention of attractive women; as Arthur Smith said of him, "He's not just an inspiration to the poet in oneself, he's an inspiration to the pisshead in oneself."[196] Even when he was a monk, he'd sneaked the occasional cigarette, and shared Roshi's fondness for wine and spirits.[197] But it was a new, clean-living Cohen who took to the stages of the world. Giving up tobacco hadn't quite given him his voice back, but it did allow him to tackle some of the higher registers. And while his last tour had been buoyed by three bottles of Château Latour a night – *before* he went on stage – this time around he was almost teetotal:

I find I can't even drink a glass of wine. It interferes with my mood. On Friday night I'll have a glass of wine with my family when we celebrate the Sabbath. A sip or two. Occasionally I'll take hard liquor. I can take a whiskey or a vodka. But I can't drink wine the way I used to. I regret it in some ways. Bob Metzger and I used to drink a lot together on tour. I don't know why that is. It just doesn't go down well any more... I lost my taste for it. Just like cigarettes.[198]

Indeed, Cohen's only indulgence appeared to be his choice of headwear. At every gig, he sported a natty fedora, a style that band members and then audiences began to emulate.

Autumn saw a return to Europe, followed by performances in Australia and New Zealand. Then, in February, 2009, he played his first New York concert since the early 1990s, at the Beacon Theatre, followed by a full North American itinerary. Early 2009 saw the release of Cohen's fourth live album, called simply *Live In London*. Recorded on July 17 the previous year, in the cavernous expanse of the O2 Arena in east London (a space he described at the concert as "a place just the other side of intimacy"), it captured perfectly the sense of occasion. He stands proud on the cover, clutching his guitar, as if to announce that the days of mumbling over synthesisers are gone; he's singing again.

He and you and I, and the hundreds of thousands of people who were turning out to hear an elderly man in a smart suit and hat croak his way through four decades' worth of songs about women and God and regret and hotel rooms, are ugly, but by God, we still have the music. The tour may have been forced on Cohen by financial necessity but, as one review put it, "fans came together to celebrate rather than commiserate."[199]

And yet it was more than a celebration; it was a vindication. The executives who'd failed to back his endeavours, the succession of critics who'd made the same dumb joke that every Cohen album should come with a free razorblade – they were all wrong. It was also sweet revenge against the people he had trusted, who had let him down. As one devoted fan at the Dublin gig said: "All the buzz was that he had to tour because his manager had run off with his money. Well, thank you, madam, I'm glad you did..."[200] And what made the situation sweeter was that he was too much of a gentleman to sneer at their idiocy and mendacity. Even when touring didn't go smoothly – for example, the cancellation of a proposed Palestinian concert amid demands for a cultural boycott of Israel – it was a sign that he mattered. There had been a time when nobody would even have noticed whether he was playing or not.

Cohen, like Cash before him, was not just back; in the eyes of many, he was bigger and better than ever before. This was an Indian summer (and winter and on to the next summer and on for as long as the fedora can stand it) that we could all enjoy.

NOTES

[1] *The Fourth, The Fifth, The Minor Fall* (BBC Radio 2, November 1, 2008). In addition to her admiration for his writing, Ms Williams recently prefaced a live rendition of 'Hallelujah' thus: "I'd really, really, really like to shag Leonard Cohen, but I know his heart just couldn't take it."

[2] Paul Williams, 'Leonard Cohen: The Romantic in a Ragpicker's Trade', *Crawdaddy*, March, 1975.

[3] *Ladies and Gentlemen. . . Mr Leonard Cohen* (Dir: Donald Brittain, Don Owen, National Film Board of Canada, 1965) Although surely no artist is totally devoid of arrogance; to consider one's work fit to be viewed by others demonstrates a degree of conceit at least. But Cohen probably comes close, or at least we'd like to think so.

[4] Harry Rasky, *The Song of Leonard Cohen: Portrait of a Poet, a Friendship and a Film* (Oakville, Ontario: Mosaic, 2001), p. 99.

[5] Ira B. Nadel, *Various Positions: A Life of Leonard Cohen* (Toronto: Random House, 1996; revised edition, University of Texas Press, 2007), p 3.

[6] Jian Ghomeishi, 'I'm blessed with a certain amnesia', *The Guardian*, July 10, 2009. The amnesia line is one that Cohen has used and reused in recent years, like a secular mantra. Maybe he gets a little closer to nirvana each time he says it.

[7] Sylvie Simmons, 'Travelling Light', *Mojo*, December, 2008.

[8] Susan Lumsden, 'Leonard Cohen Wants the Unconditional Leadership of the World', *Weekend Magazine*, September 12, 1970; quoted in Nadel, p. 24.

[9] *Ladies and Gentlemen... Mr Leonard Cohen* (1965).

[10] *Leonard Cohen: I'm Your Man* (Dir: Lian Lunson, Lionsgate Films, 2006). Shelley made the remark in the conclusion to his 'Defence Of Poetry' (1819).

[11] Klein was unable to become involved with *CIV/n* as, like Pound, he had been confined to a psychiatric institution. Thanks to Stephen Scobie for alerting me to the Klein-Cohen continuum.

[12] Adrian Deevoy, 'Porridge? Lozenge? Syringe?', *Q*, November, 1991.

[13] Sylvie Simmons, 'Travelling light', *Mojo*, December, 2008.

[14] Ruth R Wisse, 'My Life Without Leonard Cohen', *Commentary*, October 1, 1995. Wisse was a student journalist, and had been in charge of the sales effort for *Let Us Compare Mythologies*.

[15] Northrop Frye, *University of Toronto Quarterly*, April, 1957. Reprinted in Jean O'Grady, David Staines (eds), *Northrop Frye on Canada* (Toronto: University of Toronto Press, 2003), p. 165.

[16] Allen Donaldson, *The Fiddlehead*, November, 1956.

[17] *Songs From The Life Of Leonard Cohen* (BBCtv, 1988).

[18] *Leonard Cohen Under Review, 1934-1977* (Sexy Intellectual, 2007).

[19] John Walsh, 'Research, you understand...', *Mojo*, September, 1994.

[20] *Take 30* (CBC tv, May 23, 1966).

[21] Pico Iyer, 'Leonard Cohen Unplugged', *Buzz* (Los Angeles), April, 1998.

[22] According to Cohen, as an advisor to the Minister of Tourism: see Christian Fevret, 'Comme un guerrier', *Les Inrockuptibles*, August 21, 1991. Michael X's planned revolution collapsed into petty infighting back in Trinidad, and in 1975 he was hanged for the murder of two associates, one of them the daughter of a British Member of Parliament.

[23] *Ladies And Gentlemen. . . Leonard Cohen* (1965)

[24] Radio interview with Kari Hesthamar for NRK, Norway (2005).

[25] John Walsh, 'Research, you understand...', *Mojo*, September, 1994.

[26] Sylvie Simmons, 'Travelling Light', *Mojo*, December, 2008.

[27] John Walsh, 'Research, you understand...', *Mojo*, September, 1994.

[28] *Ladies And Gentlemen... Mr Leonard Cohen* (1965)

[29] *Leonard Cohen: The Classic Interviews* (Chrome Dreams, 2009).

[30] 'The LRC 100 (Part One)', *Literary Review of Canada*, January/February, 2006.

[31] David Bromige, 'The Lean and the Luscious', *Canadian Literature*, Autumn 1961.

[32] Nadel, p. 101.

[33] *Take 30* (CBC, May 23, 1966).

[34] Nadel, p. 89.

[35] *Youth Special* (CBC tv, November 12, 1963).

36 Letter to McClelland, quoted in Nadel, p. 88. When the book was adapted as a movie in 2003, 'Lawrence' became 'Leo', narrowing the gap between art and life even more.

37 TF Rigelhof, 'The Favourite Game', *Globe and Mail (Toronto)*, January 22, 2000.

38 Around the time of Cohen's 70th birthday, the Canadian radio host Paul Kennedy began a campaign to have him nominated for this honour. See John Mullan, 'The Nobel art of Cohen,' *The Guardian*, April 20, 2005.

39 *Ladies And Gentlemen. . . Mr Leonard Cohen* (1965).

40 Milton Wilson, 'Letters in Canada: 1964 Poetry', *University of Toronto Quarterly*, July 1965.

41 Jon Ruddy, 'Is the World (or Anybody) Ready for Leonard Cohen', *Maclean's*, October 1, 1966.

42 Linda Hutcheon, *The Canadian Postmodern: A Study of Contemporary English-Canadian Fiction* (Don Mills, Ontario: Oxford University Press, 1988), p. 22.

43 Robert Fulford, 'Leonard Cohen's Nightmare Novel', *Toronto Star*, April 26, 1966.

44 John Wain, *New York Review Of Books*, April 24, 1966.

45 *This Hour Has Seven Days* (CBC, May 1, 1966).

46 Leonard Cohen, note to Chinese edition of *Beautiful Losers* (Nanjing: Yilin Press, 2000).

47 William Ruhlmann, 'The Stranger Music of Leonard Cohen', *Goldmine*, February 19, 1993.

48 *Take 30 Show* (CBC, May 23, 1966).

49 See Ian MacDonald, *Revolution In The Head: The Beatles' Records And The Sixties* (London: Pimlico, 1995), pp. 296-299.

50 Simon Reynolds, 'From the Velvets to the void', *The Guardian*, March 16, 2007.

51 Phil Alexander, 'Poet Cornered', *Mojo*, December, 2008.

52 Jon Ruddy, 'Is the World (or Anybody) Ready for Leonard Cohen', *Maclean's*, October 1, 1966.

53 *Songs From The Life Of Leonard Cohen* (BBCtv, 1988).

54 Buffy Sainte-Marie, 'Leonard Cohen: His Songs', *Sing Out!*, August/September, 1967.

[55] *Songs From The Life Of Leonard Cohen* (BBCtv, 1988).

[56] For example, David Sheppard, *Leonard Cohen (Kill Your Idols series)* (London: Unanimous, 2000), p. 26.

[57] Interview with the author, May 2009. A radio interview with Cohen and Hammond in 1986, not long before Hammond's death, managed to avoid any mention of Simon whatsoever: *The John Hammond Years*, BBC Radio 2, September 20, 1986.

[58] Harvey Kubernik, 'Leonard Cohen', *Melody Maker*, March 6, 1976.

[59] Brian D Johnson, 'Hallelujah!', *Uncut*, December, 2008.

[60] *Arthur Smith Sings Leonard Cohen* (BBC Radio 4, February 5, 2004). The veteran Smith has also created shows fashioned around Dante's *Inferno* and the music of Andy Williams; one wonders where Cohen stands within that particular creative continuum.

[61] Rasky, p. 98. Verdal herself subsequently said that she was already separated from Armand when the events that inspired the song happened; and that later, once he had become more successful as a musician, Cohen suggested something more intimate, which she declined: *You Probably Think This Song Is About You* (BBC Radio 4, June 23, 1998).

[62] Nadel, pp. 282-285. Cohen was still telling the 'snowstorm' story to journalists as late as 2005.

[63] *The John Hammond Years*, BBC Radio 2, September 20, 1986.

[64] Arthur Schmidt, *Rolling Stone*, March 9, 1968. No, I don't know what a flaming shit is either.

[65] Donal Henahan, 'Alienated Young Man Creates Some Sad Music', *New York Times*, January 28, 1968. Henahan also referred to the album's uneasy combination of "*weltschmerz* and soft rock".

[66] Aidan Day, 'Dylan at sixty', *Prospect*, April, 2001; see also Appendix II.

[67] *The Velvet Underground And Nico* (1967) was, despite the credit to Andy Warhol, for the most part produced by Tom Wilson, who had previously worked on some of Dylan's key early albums.

[68] *Leonard Cohen Under Review, 1934-1977* (2007).

[69] William Kloman, 'I've Been On The Outlaw Scene Since 15', *New York Times*, January 28, 1968.

[70] *Leonard Cohen Under Review, 1934-1977* (Sexy Intellectual, 2007).

[71] Surely there's a whole alternative history waiting to be written about how Cohen's career might have turned out if he'd remained a devotee of L Ron Hubbard. The line "Did you ever go clear?" from 'Famous Blue Raincoat' on *Songs Of Love And Hate* (1971) may be a reference to a stage in Scientology practice; 'clear' is a state of freedom from harmful influences, roughly equivalent to Buddhist nirvana.

[72] Nadel, p.194. Cohen would give this background detail in his introduction when he performed it in concert in the early 1970s; it's in the preamble on the *Live Songs* version (1973).

[73] Rasky, p. 84.

[74] Sheppard, p. 67.

[75] John Walsh, 'Research, you understand...', *Mojo*, September, 1994.

[76] Doug Beardsley, 'On First Looking into Leonard Cohen', in Stephen Scobie (ed.), *Intricate Preparations: Writing Leonard Cohen* (Toronto: ECW, 2000), p. 8.

[77] Maurice Ratcliff, *The Complete Guide to the Music of Leonard Cohen* (London: Omnibus, 1999), p. 24.

[78] *Leonard Cohen: I'm Your Man* (2006).

[79] Nadel, p. 169.

[80] *Songs From The Life Of Leonard Cohen* (BBCtv, 1988).

[81] Sylvie Simmons, 'Travelling Light', *Mojo*, December, 2008.

[82] 'Leonard Cohen: A Sad Poet Gets Happy', *Toronto Star*, June 30, 1973.

[83] Cultural historians disagree over the point at which the 1960s really died; alternative suggestions include the Manson killings, the death of Jimi Hendrix, and the use of the Beatles' song 'Revolution' in a Nike ad (in 1987).

[84] Billy Walker, *Sounds*, October 23, 1971.

[85] Judith Fitzgerald, 'The Dancer And His Cain', *Essays On Canadian Writing*, Winter, 1999.

[86] Ratcliff, p. 35. 'Gloomy Sunday' has been performed by such notorious auto-destructives as Billy Mackenzie of the Associates, Rozz Williams of Christian Death (both of whom killed themselves), Billie Holiday and Serge Gainsbourg. The composer Reszo Seress committed suicide by jumping from a window in 1968.

[87] Arthur Schmidt, *Rolling Stone*, September 2, 1971.

[88] Tony Wilson, 'Behind The Enigma', March 25, 1972.

[89] Allan Jones, 'Stop me if you've heard this one before', *Uncut*, December, 2008.

[90] Brian D Johnson, 'Hallelujah!', *Uncut*, December, 2008.

[91] Sheppard, p. 72.

[92] Sylvie Simmons, 'Travelling Light', *Mojo*, December, 2008.

[93] Jack Hafferkamp, 'Ladies and Gents, Leonard Cohen', *Rolling Stone*, February 4, 1971.

[94] George Woodcock, *Odysseus Ever Returning* (Toronto: McClelland & Stewart, 1970), p. 109. How delightfully undiplomatic of McClelland to allow one of his authors to suggest that another had rather gone off the boil.

[95] Paul Saltzmann, 'Famous Last Words from Leonard Cohen (The poet's final interview, he hopes), *Maclean's*, June, 1972.

[96] Rasky, p. 66.

[97] Nadel, pp. 196-198.

[98] Rasky, p. 88.

[99] Robin Pike, 'September 15th 1974', *ZigZag*, October, 1974.

[100] Interview with the author, May, 2009.

[101] Nadel, p. 201.

[102] Joplin recorded Kristofferson's 'Me And Bobby McGee' in 1970, a few days before she died of a heroin overdose in Los Angeles, becoming a charter member of 'that stupid club' of rock stars who died at the age of 27; other members include Brian Jones, Jimi Hendrix, Jim Morrison and Kurt Cobain.

[103] Sheppard, p. 113.

[104] The critic Johnny Rogan also identifies a correlation between Cohen's enumeration of causes of death in 'Who By Fire' and Dorothy Parker's poem 'Résumé' (aka 'You Might As Well Live') in which she ticks off the drawbacks of various means of suicide. See *Leonard Cohen Under Review, 1934-1977* (2007).

[105] *How The Heart Approaches What It Yearns*, interview with John McKenna (RTE, May 9, 1988).

[106] Ratcliff, p. 41.

[107] Paul Nelson, 'Loners and Other Strangers', *Rolling Stone*, February 27, 1975.

[108] Bob Woffinden, *NME*, September 21, 1974.

[109] Allan Jones, 'Stop me if you've heard this one before', *Uncut*, December, 2008.

[110] Steve Turner, 'Depressing? Who? Me?', *NME*, June 29, 1974.

[111] Harvey Kubernik, 'What Happened When Phil Spector Met Leonard Cohen?', *LA Phonograph*, January, 1978.

[112] *Leonard Cohen: The Classic Interviews* (Chrome Dreams, 2009).

[113] Christian Fevret, 'Comme un guerrier', *Les Inrockuptibles*, August 21, 1991.

[114] Cliff Jones, 'Heavy Cohen', *Rock CD*, December, 1992.

[115] Blakely had performed a similar role for Bob Dylan in his recent live shows, and soon after working with Cohen and Spector would have a prominent role on the controversial 'Hurricane' from his 1978 album *Desire*.

[116] Ratcliff, p. 53.

[117] I'm thinking Cohen and Suzanne as Brad and Janet, Spector as Frank N. Furter, Bob Dylan as Riff-Raff, maybe Roshi as Dr Scott?

[118] Paul Nelson, 'Leonard Cohen's Doo-Wop Nightmare', *Rolling Stone*, February 9, 1978.

[119] Sandy Robertson, 'Leonard Cohen: Death of a Ladies' Man', *Sounds*, November 26, 1977.

[120] Stephen Godfrey, 'A New Artistic Twist for Pied Piper Poet', *Globe and Mail (Toronto)*, March 1, 1980.

[121] Chris Bohn, 'Haunted By Spector', *Melody Maker*, January 5, 1980.

[122] *Leonard Cohen: I'm Your Man* (2006).

[123] Karl Dallas, 'Cohen Down the Road', *Melody Maker*, May 22, 1976.

[124] Mark Rowland, 'Leonard Cohen's Nervous Breakthrough', *Musician*, July, 1988.

[125] Interview with the author, May, 2009.

[126] Rasky, p. 109.

[127] Sylvie Simmons, 'Travelling Light', *Mojo*, December, 2008.

[128] *Leonard Cohen Under Review, 1978-2006* (Sexy Intellectual, 2007).

[129] *Leonard Cohen: I'm Your Man* (2006).

[130] Chris Bohn, 'Haunted By Spector', *Melody Maker*, January 5, 1980.

[131] Rasky, p. 19.

[132] Letter to the *Hollywood Reporter*, October 25, 1993; quoted in Nadel, p. 232.

[133] *Leonard Cohen: The Classic Interviews* (Chrome Dreams, 2009).

[134] Interview with the author, May 2009.

[135] *Leonard Cohen Under Review, 1978-2006* (2007).

[136] For more on outsiders such as Johnston, see Irwin Chusid, *Songs In The Key Of Z: The Curious Universe Of Outsider Music* (London: Cherry Red, 2000).

[137] 'Hallelujah' and 'If It Be Your Will'; interview with the author, June 2009.

[138] Sheppard, p. 80.

[139] Ratcliff, pp. 71-72.

[140] It is compulsory to refer to the fact that Cocker is "a former gas-fitter from Sheffield" and "no relation to Jarvis". It's in the rulebook for music writers. You just *have* to mention one or the other, if not both. I think you lose your licence if you don't. Incidentally, he's done some interesting cover versions of Cohen songs over the years.

[141] *Songs from the Life of Leonard Cohen* (BBC, 1988).

[142] Biba Kopf, 'Lenny Sings *Jenny Sings Lenny*', *NME*, March 14, 1987.

[143] Sheppard, p. 84.

[144] David Browne, 'Leonard Cohen: *I'm Your Man*', *Rolling Stone*, June 16, 1988.

[145] Mark Cooper, 'Leonard Cohen: *I'm Your Man*', *Q*, March, 1988.

[146] Biba Kopf, 'Lenny Sings *Jenny Sings Lenny*', *NME*, March 14, 1987. If this really was a serious consideration, it wouldn't have been as weird as it seemed: in 1969, Sinatra released *A Man Alone*, a collection of songs by Rod McKuen, another poet-turned-song-

writer. See Richard Havers, *Sinatra* (London: Dorling-Kindersley, 2004), pp. 311-313.

[147] *Leonard Cohen: The Classic Interviews* (Chrome Dreams, 2009).

[148] Paul Monk, 'Under The Spell Of Stranger Music: Leonard Cohen's Lyrical Judaism', *Australian Financial Review*, June 8, 2001.

[149] It was Gainsbourg who in 1986, during a French TV show hosted by Michel Drucker, let it be known that he wanted to "*ferrk*" fellow guest Whitney Houston.

[150] Adrian Deevoy, 'Porridge? Lozenge? Syringe?', *Q*, November, 1991.

[151] *Leonard Cohen Under Review, 1978-2006* (2007). Despite the plaudits of Messrs Christgau and Cohen, this is the only time in this book that 'Billy Joel' and 'fantastic' will appear in the same sentence.

[152] Christian Fevret, 'Comme un guerrier', *Les Inrockuptibles*, August 21, 1991.

[153] Billy Walker, 'Complexities and Mr Cohen', *Sounds*, March 4, 1972.

[154] Gavin Martin, 'Hello! I Must Be Cohen', *NME*, January 9, 1993.

[155] Or maybe not so military: the opening scenes of Armelle Brusq's documentary *Leonard Cohen; Spring 96* show Cohen and his fellow monks marching in strict rhythm to their 3am prayer obligations; the sound of their feet echoes the martial tempo of Vinnie Colaiuta's percussion.

[156] Simon Schama, 'The high priest of minimalism', *The Guardian*, June 28, 2009.

[157] I still maintain, with no supporting evidence whatsoever, that 'Closing Time' is an unacknowledged influence on the greatest Canadian film of all time, Don McKellar's *Last Night* (1998), which depicts Torontonians contemplating an imminent, unexplained apocalypse.

[158] Sheppard, p. 85.

[159] Edwin Pouncey, *NME*, 'Future Shocking', November 28, 1992.

[160] Christian Wright, 'Leonard Cohen: *The Future*', *Rolling Stone*, January 7, 1993.

[161] *Leonard Cohen Under Review, 1978-2006* (2007).

[162] *Leonard Cohen: The Classic Interviews* (Chrome Dreams, 2009).

[163] Alan Jackson, 'Growing Old Passionately', *The Observer* (London), November 22, 1992.

[164] Nick Paton Walsh, 'I never discuss my mistresses or my tailors', *The Observer* (London), October 14, 2001.

[165] Steve Turner, 'Leonard Cohen: The Profits Of Doom', *Q*, April 1988.

[166] Cobain made an ambiguous reference to Cohen ("Give me a Leonard Cohen afterworld") in his song 'Pennyroyal Tea', from the album *In Utero* (1993).

[167] John Walsh, 'Research, you understand...', *Mojo*, September, 1994.

[168] *Leonard Cohen: Spring 96* (Dir: Armelle Brusq, Lieurac Productions, 1997)

[169] Cohen himself clarified the matter – to an extent – in a post on leonardcohenforum.com in 2005: "Interesting. I never suggested that Jikan meant 'The Silent One', that somehow got into the air and was taken up by journalists – whenever I've been asked I've given Roshi's bad English translation which is something like: 'ordinary silence, normal silence, just ok everything don't sweat it silence'. Roshi always got pissed off when people wanted to explore the deep meanings of the names he'd given them – new versions of their self-importance. He wasn't trying to honour you with some poetic revelation of your adorable nature that he had discerned, he was just trying to give you a name that he could remember and he has his own private associational method. I won't go into the matter, but Jikan was someone in his own life that he knew very well." (author's punctuation)

[170] Andy Gill, 'Leonard Cohen: *Cohen Live*', *Mojo*, August, 1994.

[171] *Leonard Cohen: I'm Your Man* (2006).

[172] Ratcliff, p. 129.

[173] Sylvie Simmons, 'Leonard Cohen: *More Best Of*', *Mojo*, November, 1997.

[174] The Beethoven reference may be inspired by John Lennon's remark that 'Because', from The Beatles' *Abbey Road* (1969) was essentially the Moonlight played backwards. See MacDonald, p. 291.

[175] John Walsh, 'Research, you understand...', *Mojo*, September, 1994.

[176] Sylvie Simmons, 'Leonard Cohen: *More Best Of*', *Mojo*, November, 1997.

[177] *Leonard Cohen: The Classic Interviews* (2009).

[178] *Leonard Cohen: I'm Your Man* (2006).

[179] Steven Chean, 'Leonard Cohen: *Ten New Songs*', *Rolling Stone*, October 9, 2001.

[180] Nick Paton Walsh, 'I never discuss my mistresses or my tailors', *The Observer* (London), October 14, 2001.

[181] Sylvie Simmons, 'Travelling light', *Mojo*, December, 2008.

[182] *Leonard Cohen Under Review, 1978-2006* (2007). *Ten New Songs* was recorded before the attacks, but released exactly four weeks afterwards. On his next album, Cohen would address 9/11, albeit obliquely.

[183] An article by Karen Schoemer in the *New York Times* of November 29, 1992, described him as 'Leonard Cohen, the Lord Byron of Rock-and-Roll'.

[184] Alexis Petridis, 'Leonard Cohen: *Dear Heather*', *The Guardian*, October 22, 2004.

[185] Robert Christgau, 'Sonic Refuges', *Village Voice*, November 2, 2004.

[186] Katherine Macklem, 'Leonard Cohen goes broke', *Maclean's*, August 22, 2005.

[187] Phoebe Hoban, 'Zen, Lawsuits, and Poetry: Why is Leonard Cohen so downright content these days?', *New York Magazine*, May 22, 2006.

[188] Simon Houpt, 'Coffee and candour with Cohen', *Globe and Mail* (Toronto), February, 27, 2009.

[189] Robin D Schatz, 'Leonard Cohen Talks About Book of Longing, Monk's Life, Fame', bloomberg.com, June 5, 2006.

[190] John Walsh, 'Naked truths from the bard of Mount Baldy', *The Independent* (London), October 27, 2006.

[191] Christopher Goodwin, 'Reasons to be cheerful', *The Times* (London), July 1, 2007.

[192] Gerry Donaghy, 'Book of Longing', popmatters.com, May 25, 2006.

[193] John Shand, 'Monsieur Camembert', *Sydney Morning Herald*, June 22, 2007.

[194] 'Madonna, Mellencamp, Cohen Honored at Emotional Rock and Roll Hall of Fame Induction', *Rolling Stone*, March 11, 2008.

[195] Sylvie Simmons, 'Travelling light', *Mojo*, December, 2008.

[196] *What Leonard Cohen Did For Me* (BBC4, September 2, 2005).

[197] While in the monastery, Cohen usually got up half an hour earlier than the prescribed 3 A.M. rising time, although the motivation was not so much an excess of monastic zeal, more the fact that he needed coffee and cigarettes to make it through the rituals. See Nick Paton Walsh, 'I never discuss my mistresses or my tailors', *The Observer* (London), October 14, 2001.

[198] Brian D Johnson, 'Hallelujah!', *Uncut*, December, 2008.

[199] Dan Cairns, 'Leonard Cohen: *Live In London*', *The Times* (London), March 29, 2009.

[200] Michael Bonner, Nick Hasted and John Lewis, 'Come On Friends, Let's Go...', *Uncut*, December, 2008.

CONCLUSION
End of my life in art

"While silence blossoms like tumours on our lips"
– 'Poem' (1956)

"Tennessee Williams said: 'Life is a fairly well-written play, except for the third act.' I'm maybe at the third act, where you have the benefit of the experience of the first two acts. But how it ends is no-body's business and is generally accompanied by some disagreeable circumstances."
– Leonard Cohen, 2001

So, how good is Leonard Cohen? No, that was Walter Yetnikoff's question, the one he used to justify Columbia's refusal to release *Various Positions* in the States. But in this case, it's the wrong question.

Rewind, erase.

So, how *great* is Leonard Cohen? Maybe it's a stupid thing to ask. I mean, can you put an empirical value on greatness? Do you give marks out of ten, or stars out of five, or a Christgau-style academic grade for greatness? And then of course there's the argument that it doesn't matter what anybody thinks anyway; that nobody's opinion is any more important than anyone else's; and if someone prefers Shakira or 50 Cent or Mario Lanza or Wesley Willis or Alexandra Burke or Jason Castro or the Dave Clark Five to Leonard Cohen, then that's perfectly OK, and there's no point arguing about it. It's all just an opinion, isn't it, and we should just enjoy what we enjoy, right?

I rather guess that people who think that way won't be reading this book. In fact, part of me rather guesses that people who think that way don't read very many books of any description. So this is between you and me, the people who care.

Again, how great is Leonard Cohen? I'd say, as a lyricist in the American songwriting tradition, when he's firing on all cylinders, he's up there with Bob Dylan and Smokey Robinson and Hal David, even with Cole Porter and Lorenz Hart. His deft wordplay can weave Biblical references and expressions of carnal longing into images that are immediately resonant with the lives of his listeners. Part of this is of course down to the seriousness with which he applies himself to the task at hand, his meticulous, time-consuming method of writing an rewriting poems and songs until he is completely satisfied; a method that can sometimes take him years. As far back as 1971, he was identifying himself more as a craftsman than as an artist:

I don't see it so much as creativity as work and if you just lose the taste of the real command of a certain kind of work. I suppose it's like the workers who do the high building work, if you lose your nerve for it it's no great disgrace, it means you can't do that any more and I think that there are other honourable kinds of work that I think I could find. I think one of the things has wiped so many people out who do other kinds of work, like factory work, is that they're not involved in the perfection, they don't have a standard of excellence and I think if a man doesn't have a standard of excellence his work becomes meaningless. I feel that you're interviewing me with a kind of idea of what a good interview is – a standard of excellence – and I'm enjoying it. If you were completely indifferent, I know that your whole heart is not totally involved in what's going down here, but you're working with a certain kind of skill that is acceptable and when that level and acceptability really declines then it's time to get out of it.[1]

But heartfelt, serious commitment to one's work is surely not enough on its own. Cohen is also extremely well read, at least by the standards of modern popular songwriters. He comes from an age before the intellectual depredations of declining attention spans, the cultural dominance of television, Google and Wikipedia. He was brought up in a system that assumed there was a defined canon of texts with which educated men and women would be familiar, and that one's own work should be written and read with reference to that canon. Who else in 2004 would begin an album with a Byron poem?

And yet his undoubted cleverness is never off-putting. He's at once clever and real:

> *Well my friends are gone and my hair is grey.*
> *I ache in the places where I used to play.*
> *And I'm crazy for love but I'm not coming on.*
> *I'm just paying my rent everyday in the Tower of Song.*

Now, that's as good a depiction of the middle-aged hipster as I've ever read. And it's funny too. In his 2000 stage show, the British comedian Arthur Smith described the lugubrious Canuck as "the greatest comedian of the 20th century... His humour is of a higher order, so high that he has never actually got a laugh."[2] It's certainly true that his persona as Cohen the Clown, especially on his early albums, can be submerged by a pervading air of melancholia; a situation that's exacerbated by sparse arrangements and his sometimes monotonous vocals. David Sheppard suggests that this may account for his disproportionate popularity in countries where English isn't a first language; even if you don't really understand what he's saying, he just *sounds* bloody miserable.[3] In which case, a huge chunk of his most devoted demographic loves him thanks to a fundamental misunderstanding.

Because, grim as some of his songs can be, the man's laconic wit just won't stay in the box for long. Cohen's definitely scrapping for a place among the 100 Greatest North American Comedians; maybe not quite Richard Pryor or Lenny Bruce, but Denis Leary should really be looking over his shoulder when Cohen starts his between-song schtick: "I was 60 years old the last time I stood on a stage – just a kid with a crazy dream..."[4] Or just check out the footage of one of his poetry recitals in the 1965 documentary *Ladies And Gentlemen... Mr Leonard Cohen*, in which the audience roars with laughter as he embarks on bizarre, neo-jazz riffs about performing in mental hospitals, and offers up the notion that all hair removed from the human body should be stored safely for future contemplation: "a man should be able to go into one of these hair asylums and review his own life."[5] It's like a prototype for Eddie Izzard, but without the frocks.

His interviews are also excellent value, although he often treats them as one-on-one performances, re-using and re-working old lines the way he rewrote 'Hallelujah' and 'Democracy'. As has been pointed out more than once, he has described the heart as "sizzling like a shish kebab" in interviews in 1977, 1988, 1997 and 2001.[6] And he'll probably do it again, although his fans will doubtless complain that they preferred the original version.

Witty words aside, he's also underrated as a tunesmith. His music is rarely complex or sophisticated – he leaves that to well-chosen producers and arrangers – but he's got an instinct for insistent hooks and minor-key melancholy. The acoustic guitar figures that herald many of his earlier songs, often influenced by flamenco techniques, are instant earworms. This unorthodox musical facility, according to Robert Christgau, is almost as central to his appeal as his lauded wordplay:

One reason he was arresting was that, however he came upon it, he had a musical knack; and you don't have to understand musical technique very well to know that a good melody is where you find it... He definitely had a talent for it, and in my mind it was the melodies as well as all the rest of the stuff that made it happen.[7]

Ah yes, the doubters will always ask, but what about that voice? These days, of course, nobody needs to be a technically brilliant singer if they want to be successful. Bob Dylan, Lou Reed, Mark E Smith, Morrissey, Tom Waits, Marianne Faithfull, Billy Bragg; all performers whose vocal imperfections infuriate the technical purists, but create a captivating, instantly recognisable sound to their songs. That said, Leonard Cohen takes things to another level, especially in the last couple of decades. For the first dozen years or so of his musical career, he offered a croaky croon that sort of worked because, hell, he was Leonard Cohen and that's how these songs are supposed to sound. Thereafter, either the hard living finally got to his throat, or maybe he just gave up trying. Colleagues such as Jennifer Warnes and Sharon Robinson took an increasingly prominent role, so that on many tracks on his two studio albums of the 2000s, Cohen offered little more than a low-down *sprechgesang* (talk-song) while the proper singers got on with the proper singing.

And yet, affecting and successful as Warnes (and Jeff Buckley and Nick Cave and kd lang and Judy Collins and Monsieur Camembert and … even Billy Joel) may be at interpreting the Cohen oeuvre, there's still something quintessentially *Lenny* about plenty of his own takes. In many ways, it's because of his technical imperfections that his renditions succeed; so many of his lyrics deal with the narrator's own insecurity and insignificance in the face of God or a woman or history or Hank Williams that it would seem incongruous to have a great, strong voice attempting them. He's a damaged man with a damaged voice singing broken Hallelujahs to a damaged world. As the critic Biba Kopf realised when contemplating *Famous Blue Raincoat*, the first English-language album solely devoted to cover versions of Cohen songs:

With Cohen, song and voice seem inseparable. Not only are writer and subject matter intimately entwined – the musicality of his language rhymes perfectly with the undervalued musicality of his vocal's blackened volcanic power. [8]

The voice has certainly changed over the decades – as is often the case with volcanoes – but the subjects with which Cohen deals have remained fairly consistent. Inevitably, for someone operating within the context of Western popular song, many of his lyrics deal with love; but the depth of his analysis and interpretation leaves the corny platitudes of most ordinary love songs way behind.

Yes, he deals with the love of men for women; but the women appear as martyrs and tempters, adulterers and saints, the real women he encounters (the Suzannes, Marianne, Nico, those two teenagers in Edmonton) becoming blurred in his words and our minds with the archetypes and icons of his imagination. He mythologises the relationship between the sexes; indeed, his naïve idealisation was one of his key motivations for becoming a writer in the first place:

I thought that all women were poets. I thought that all women inhabited this highly charged landscape that poetry seemed to arise from. It seemed to be the natural language of women and it seemed to me that if you wanted to address women... you had to do it with this highly charged language.[9]

It is this fevered mythology that can make a distinction between Cohen's love songs and his hymns a tricky task. As one critic put it: "Cohen does not reduce religion to sex. He reduces sex to religion."[10] One reason for his lack of greater commercial success is that he interrogates the sexual instinct that lies at the heart of so much modern music. You can still feel it in his songs, but you have to think about it as well, an intellectual leap that plenty of people are simply not prepared to take.

There is also a deep thread of solipsism in his love lyrics, in that, instead of focusing on the woman he loves, his attention is on the love itself, the transaction, with himself as the protagonist. It's all about Leonard. Consider this couplet, from 'Take This Longing', on *New Skin For The Old Ceremony*: "Your body like a searchlight. / My poverty revealed." As with all straight, male writers of the erotic, from the author of The Song Of Solomon to the director of some cheap porn flick, he is entranced by the textures and contours of the female form, its quintessential difference from his own too-solid, too-sullied flesh. Feminists might complain that he objectifies women, constantly subjecting them to the tyranny of the male gaze. But to Cohen, the most exciting thing – perhaps even the sexiest thing – about the woman is what she reveals about him; he's the one who's been illuminated.

It's inevitable at this point that we should draw together the threads of Cohen's own love life, although this line of enquiry is inevitably fraught with difficulties. Among the ranks of poets and musicians there are dozens, hundreds of men – Carlo Gesualdo, Byron, Ted Hughes, Jerry Lee Lewis, Ike Turner, Phil Spector – whose relationships with women might be thought to leave something to be desired; indeed, many of them are known to have exhibited behaviour that would make Cohen look like a modern saint in comparison. However, if we condemned all art on the basis of its creators' bad behaviour, then we'd have about three short stories and a watercolour left.

The two long relationships Cohen enjoyed in the 1960s and 70s were in many ways structured in his favour: Marianne Ihlen and then Suzanne Elrod would offer the anchor of domestic comfort while Cohen wandered the world, being An Artist, indulging himself in any number of short-term, casual entanglements, trying in his way to be free. But there was a clear, pre-feminist double standard at work here, in that any hint that Cohen's number one girl might want to stray from the road of fidelity would be treated as an act of betrayal. In 'Paper-Thin Hotel', Cohen's reaction to the end of his relationship with Suzanne is presented as her in the act of cheating on him; an interesting perspective, to say the least. But the adultery is on the other side of the flimsy wall. Once again, the focus is not on her enjoyment, but on his perception of her enjoyment, the emotions he feels, the epiphany he undergoes as he listens:

I was not seized by jealousy at all
In fact a burden lifted from my soul
I heard that love was out of my control
A heavy burden lifted from my soul

Well that's all right then, Leonard, just so long as you feel better about the whole thing. To be fair, in recent years his attitudes have matured greatly, and he has been scrupulously honest about his own failings, in his work and in conversation; here he is in 1996, from the sanctuary of Mount Baldy:

I was very poor at relationships. I wasn't good at it. I wasn't good
at marriage, and I wasn't good at husbandhood or fatherhood.
I struggled along, and I did my best. I continue to do my best.[11]

And it must be remembered that for all his countercultural trappings, Cohen was born in 1934, and brought up in a world where the traditional roles of the sexes – man as hunter, provider, and sower of seeds; woman as nurturer, cleaner and turner of blind eyes – were deeply ingrained. When feminism became a serious political and intellectual force in the Western world, in the early 1970s, he was already nearly 40. It's often forgotten that, for all the talk of love and peace and freedom among the hippies and flower children, there was often an unspoken assumption that the 'chicks' should still do the dishes; Black Panthers leader Stokely Carmichael once suggested that the best position for women in the revolution was "prone". Indeed, this sort of Neanderthal sexism and hypocrisy was a key motivator to the nascent women's liberation movement, as women realised that the reality of free love was that it was only free to men.

And since the break-up with Suzanne Elrod, Cohen's perspective on and interaction with women, in his work and in his life, has matured greatly. His subsequent serious relationships have been with confident, autonomous women with their own lives and careers, who don't rely on him as the sole breadwinner: photographer Dominique Isserman; actress Rebecca De Mornay; musician Anjani Thomas. In contrast with Marianne and Suzanne, all have played roles – beyond muse and star of album sleeve – in his work. He's also placed great trust in other women he's collaborated with, such as Jennifer Warnes, Sharon Robinson, Leanne Ungar, Perla Batalla, Julie Christensen, the Webb twins and – considerably less happily – Kelley Lynch. Openness and willingness to undergo change has characterised his music and his spiritual life, and this seems to have permeated his relationships; although one suspects that he wasn't being entirely serious when he fielded a question about whether he'd ever had a gay experience:

No, because I have had intimate relationships with men all my life and I still do have. I've seen men as beautiful, I've felt sexual stirrings towards men so I don't think I've missed out. Maybe I have, maybe it's time to look into it. Maybe not, maybe I've left it too late. Maybe I'll not be able to get anybody.[12]

As to Cohen's own analysis of his fatherhood skills, it would seem that his ties with his two children is certainly no worse than that of many fathers who, because of a failed marriage, live apart from their offspring during their formative years. His relationship with them as adults – Adam is a musician, Lorca runs an antique shop in Los Angeles – appears to be warm and loving, and both have spent time living with him. Neither has exhibited the sort of troubled behaviour that seems so often to afflict the spawn of celebrities. Only slightly at a tangent, Cohen has long been a nurturer of abandoned or otherwise needy animals: as a child, he tended to a rescued pigeon, among several other creatures;[13] Rufus Wainwright reports that when he first met Cohen, the great man was in his kitchen in Los Angeles, wearing only his underwear, chewing salami to feed to a bird that had fallen from its nest.[14]

What is clear is that, leaving the matter of sexuality and fledglings aside, the deepest, most lasting relationship Cohen has ever enjoyed has been with a man, in the enigmatic person of Joshu Sasaki Roshi. There is a long tradition of musicians and other artists becoming enthralled by specific individuals who, to a greater or lesser extent take over their lives and works. These are often religious and spiritual leaders, as with the many and various gurus to whom musicians of the 1960s pledged allegiance, but there have been pairings in other contexts; one thinks of John Lennon and Yoko Ono, or Brian Wilson and the controversial psychotherapist Dr Eugene Landy, who eventually began to receive songwriting and production credits on his client's records.

Cohen's relationship with Roshi is rather different. Having been brought up in an observant Jewish household, with strong rabbinical traditions on both sides, he could see the extent to which intellectual and spiritual power might be combined and deployed, in a manner that brought comfort to the disciple but also demanded an unusual degree of obedience. And as an artist, most specifically as a rock star, he realised that he shared some of these traits, or at least had the potential to use them; a gift that he'd enjoyed since his farcical adolescent escapades with the household staff, as he explained to Armelle Brusq around the time he became ordained as a monk:

I've always had a great suspicion of charismatic holy men. I think it's very, very dangerous to hook up in a certain way with these guys. A lot of them are just head hunters. They know how to do it. The content of their presentation is that they know how to do

*it, they know how to gather people around them, that's what their
gig is. They make you think something important is going on and
you're hooked. I was always suspicious of them because I was able
to do it in my own small way... It's just a kind of gift. It's like hyp-
nosis. I was a very good hypnotist when I was young.*[15]

His hard-won realisation some years later that *zazen* was not actually for him makes his fond personal relationship with Roshi – which
has continued since he left the monastery – seem even more special. In
Brusq's documentary, we see him dutifully going through the rigours
and rituals of his life on Mount Baldy; but this is juxtaposed with footage of Cohen and the old teacher together that is touching in its down-
to-earth normality, even banality. Although Cohen clearly respects
Roshi as a teacher, the dynamic on display is more like that of someone tending solicitously to the needs and comforts of an elderly parent
– Roshi would have been approaching 90 years of age at the time the
film was shot, and he reached his 102nd birthday in April, 2009. Cohen
may have identified himself as being a poor husband and father but,
despite his peripatetic lifestyle and his sometimes awkward relationship with his mother, he did at least try to take his responsibilities as a
son seriously. Now, as is so often the case, when parents age, the roles
of the relationship are reversed, and Cohen finds himself in possession
of a new, rather unlikely persona; that of a solicitous mother figure.

So Roshi is no longer Cohen's guru, if he ever was. But if Cohen's
relationship with Roshi does not define his spiritual and religious identity, what does? The fact remains that, despite his childhood fascination with Catholicism, his flirtations with Scientology and the *I Ching*,
and his long association with the practice of Zen Buddhism, Cohen is,
always was, and probably always will be a Jew. Perhaps he cannot be
considered a particularly good Jew, not at least by the rigorous standards of his parents' orthodox faith. The sex and drugs in which he indulged for many years aren't usually a part of the package; he doesn't
appear to take the dietary laws particularly seriously, although he has
been seen frequenting Jewish restaurants; his political standpoint with
regard to the State of Israel is ambivalent, to say the least. In recent
years he has begun adhering to the traditional injunction that male

Jews must keep their heads covered; although his fedora is as much a sartorial affectation and a protective carapace (his once dense mop of black curls having been replaced by a thinning white thatch) as a mark of pious affiliation. And he has long maintained the tradition of lighting the candles for the Sabbath meal on a Friday night, if possible with members of his family. But he is settled in his identity, still fascinated by other religions and forms of enlightenment, but no longer feeling the need to try them on for size. His rapport with God (or G-d, as he now writes it, following the Jewish tradition that the deity's name is too sacred to be uttered in full) may not be one of cognac and wisecracks, but he seems pleased enough to be there. When he was a monk, he was a bad monk; now he is a bad Jew, but a Jew nonetheless.

Perversely, it may actually be Cohen's experience of Eastern philosophies that has helped him to this point of acquiescence. Just as he has accepted the fact of his financial misfortunes with a degree of calm and equanimity that has baffled many observers, the teachings of Roshi on Mount Baldy and Balsekar in Mumbai have enabled him to accept what life deals out, good, bad and indifferent. He was born into a certain family, which brought with it a specific religion and ethnicity and culture, and that is how it is. On the other hand, as early as 1974 he was tempering his support for Judaism with the acknowledgement of its imperfection in practice:

I've never disguised the fact that I'm Jewish and in any crisis in Israel I would be there. I was there in the last war and I would be there in another war. I am committed to the survival of the Jewish people. I have a lot of quarrels inside that camp with Jewish leadership and Jewish values and that sort of thing.[16]

That said, it is possible to identify a process of mellowing and maturation in Cohen's perspective on his own Jewishness. Consider the seething rage that permeates his early poems, especially those contained in *Flowers For Hitler*; the "blindfold of skin", a nightmare image from the concentration camps; the grim fascination with men such as Eichmann, and the Führer himself ("Cadres of SS waken in our minds"). But then skip forwards to the psalms of *Book Of Mercy*; there is still sadness in there, but he is acknowledging the beauty of the Jewish cultural tradition, rather than indulging in grim, black humour about the agonies suffered by his people. Or of course, 'Hallelujah', where the complex tropes of the Old Testament exist as a metaphor for the pain we all suffer, rather than a focus for the collective sadness of one race, one religion, one people. In recent years, specific Jewish references have become less common in his writing, although 'By The Rivers Dark' (from *Ten New Songs*) does include repeated references to the tradition of Babylon, where the Jewish people lived in exile in the 6th century BC; a trauma depicted in the prophetic books of the Bible that fascinated Cohen in his youth.

Which brings us, if not neatly, then with a degree of serendipitous relevance, to a crucial question about Cohen: where does he come from? What is it that makes his songs what they are? The Jewish elements in his background are of course significant, but there is a long and noble and well-documented tradition of Jewish musicians in the history of popular music, from the days of Irving Berlin, George Gershwin and Al Jolson through to Phil Spector, Bob Dylan, Burt Bacharach and Carole King and on to the less expected adherents of the faith, including Joey Ramone, the Beastie Boys and Lenny Kravitz.

Less documented is the presence of Canadians in the rock tradition, especially because so many of them, like Cohen, find that to operate at the highest levels of the business, they have to relocate to New York or Los Angeles. And since to many fans (including, it has to be said, quite a few Americans), Canadian accents are all but indistinguishable from those in the United States, many musicians from north of the 49th parallel become absorbed into a sort of homogeneous Story of American Rock, in a way that their British or Australian counterparts don't. Performers such as Bryan Adams, The Band, kd lang, Avril Lavigne, Joni Mitchell, Rush, Shania Twain or Neil Young may never have explicitly pretended or claimed to be Americans, but it can sometimes be difficult to extrapolate what makes them different. Many of their musical influences, for a start, would have been pretty much the same as those of the contemporaries across the border; the young Cohen was a fan of Hank Williams, Frankie Laine, Josh White and Ray Charles, none of them compatriots of his.

He is clearly different from most rock performers, but is his difference quintessentially one of Candian-ness? Indeed, is there such a thing? Stephen Scobie chooses his words with care:

I have no easy answers, except for answers that caricature Americans in ways I would object to if they were used to caricature Canadians. Thus, I might venture that Canadians are more tolerant of ambiguity than Americans are, and that it is this capacity for ambiguity that puts Americans off. When Adrienne Clarkson was installed as Governor-General of Canada, she quoted "There is a crack in everything / That's how the light gets in." I can't conceive of any American President, even Obama, using that quote. Nor will you see any American marching band playing "Democracy is coming / To the USA." I think 'Democracy' is a great song, but it really is about the USA, not about Canada, and it is a song of sceptical reflection about the national self, which is not a great American pastime. No American would think of a National Anthem as an occasion for ironic self-reflection.[17]

But then Scobie is a Canadian, and an academic to boot. US citizen Jennifer Warnes might be relied upon to offer a more objective, more creative – and less political – view:

It's because he dares to talk about sorrow. Americans in general – not the Europeans – Americans like to be [sings] *"Keep your sunny side up!" Put on your smile and come out swinging no matter how ruined you've been. And Leonard will say, "Look at the shreds of my heart, you pulled out my heart with a pair of prongs,"* [sic] *acknowledging that the whole act of living contains immense amounts of sorrow and hopelessness and despair – and also passion and high hopes and deep love.*[18]

Such generalisations might help to tell part of the story, and indeed go some way to explain why Cohen's commercial clout in the United States has been so negligible, when compared with the esteem in which he's held elsewhere in the world; it's not so much his specific

Canadian-ness as his un-American-ness that alienates him from the mainstream. But it's surely not the whole story. The Canadian rocker Bryan Adams is perfectly capable of the sort of upbeat, clean-cut earnestness that supposedly hits the collective G-spot in the Land of the Free. Conversely, someone like Lou Reed, who inducted Cohen into the Rock and Roll Hall of Fame, is just one of dozens of American songwriters who join him on the dark side of the street.

But it's not just that Cohen is Canadian; it's also that he's from Quebec. His status, as an English-speaking Jew in an overwhelmingly French-speaking, Catholic province that is in turn marooned in an Anglophone continent means that he is profoundly aware of the nature of isolation, of otherness. He accepts his Canadian identity, but refuses to be bound to it, understanding the oddity of his own situation, as he explained in an interview in 1972:

It's my native land, my homeland, all the feelings one feels for one's homeland...very tender feelings about it. I don't like hearing it being criticised. I like to hear it praised. I return often and I live there part of every year... I think we're very lucky it's not a first-rate power and that it's... I don't know, it's my homeland, what can I say? And it's not even Canada, it's Montreal. Not even Montreal, it's a few streets.[19]

The fact that he then chose to exile himself, variously to London, Hydra, New York, Nashville and Los Angeles has only heightened that sense and self-image of being set apart from the norm.

Paul Monk has tied this rootless lifestyle, and Cohen's tangential relationship with the mainstream of modern music, to his ethnic, religious and cultural background, as if he (consciously or not) fulfills the medieval, anti-Semitic archetype of the Wandering Jew, condemned to travel the Earth until the Second Coming in punishment for the heinous sin of mocking Christ on the way to his crucifixion:

The Jew is, from of old, the perennial 'stranger' in the world – leaving Ur, leaving Egypt, exiled to Babylon, dispersed across the face of the world, hunted to death by the goyim. *At several levels of experience and active metaphor, this is the temper of Cohen's whole body of work.*[20]

Yet at the same time, Cohen fulfills a different, more modern archetype – the neurotic outsider of 19th century romanticism and 20th century existentialism: Dostoevsky's Underground Man; Kafka's Josef K; Eliot's J. Alfred Prufrock; Orwell's Winston Smith; Camus's Meursault; Salinger's Holden Caulfield; Kerouac's Dean Moriarty; his own Lawrence Breavman; the damaged nobodies who people the absurd theatrical landscapes of Pinter and Ionesco and Beckett.[21] This sociocultural trend was brought to the centre of public debate in 1956, by the British author Colin Wilson in his book *The Outsider*, prompting thousands more young people to don black polo-necks and expressions of studied melancholy; it was a hugely important precursor to the anti-establishment youth movements of the 1960s. But Cohen – who of course published his own first book in the same year that Wilson's appeared – managed to out-outside the outsiders: he was too square for the beatniks; too apolitical for the folkies; too grumpy for many of the love-and-peace-and-flowers crowd at the Isle of Wight Festival in 1970, where he performed while on barbiturates rather than their preferred herbal relaxants. (Cohen admitted to talking to the flowers on Hydra, but he never felt the urge to wear any in his hair.) Beyond his peculiar knots of devotees in Granada and Gothenburg and Gdansk, it was not until the 1980s that he found himself in a club that actually wanted him a member, when he was adopted as a sort of honorary uncle by the better-read, better-dressed arm of the alternative rock movement. Nick Cave, who has recorded and performed several of Cohen's songs, explained the startling effect that hearing his early work had on an awkward, introverted youth growing up unhappily in a deeply conservative provincial town in early 1970s Australia:

There was that album of his, Songs of Love and Hate, *and in a small town like Wangaratta, when someone finds this record and you play it, it's like something that's been created on the moon, emotionally... The thing with Leonard Cohen was he really seemed to be the first person to approach a song really poetically and*

spend time. There's a real slowness to the way he works and it
takes a long time for his songs to form. They're really high art.[22]

Some critics – those few canonical conservatives who still maintain
that there must be a distinction between high art and low art, between
culture and anarchy – might choose to take issue with Cave's last sentence. There's still a hard core of book-lovers who believe that the rock
'n' roll circus destroyed the literary career of someone who could have
been one of the truly great poet and novelists of our age. At the same
time, pop fundamentalists might see him as too arcane, too difficult,
too thoughtful to be a pop star in the strictest sense of the word; his
working methods, in which a song might take a decade before it's recorded, and then still need fine-tuning, are the ponderous antithesis
of pop, even of its more grown-up siblings such as rock or folk. He's
stranded between two banks of the river, not quite erudite enough for
art, and yet not vulgar enough, whatever Robert Christgau might argue, for pop. Has he found, in the words of AM Klein, "a new function
for the déclassé craft"? Or has he just debased poetry, and turned his
craft to the purpose of making lots of cash? Which, in an act of quintessentially un-poetic justice, has been taken away from him...

Whichever bank might be his natural home, he's surely proved himself worthy of being taken seriously, however; and that necessitates
placing him in some sort of artistic context. It is of course possible to
pick out specific influences on specific works of Cohen: bits of folk,
blues and country music; Yeats and Lorca; Judaism and Zen; the conflicts and complexities, some of them self-imposed, of his own event-
ful life. He's crafted a public persona that's shifted subtly over the
years, as Rufus Wainwright has argued:

He's managed to be true to himself but also change. He's had sev-
eral incarnations: he's gone from this Jewish intellectual folk sing-
er onto this kind of ladies' man, Greek islands kind of look, to this
dark messenger of death – to Barry White.[23]

Like any performer, like any person, he finds himself moving with
the times; it's just that the move he decides upon isn't necessarily the

same one that everybody else is making. And this charming idiosyncrasy is, in part, what isolated him for so long; he is beyond the conventional family trees of post-war American music, off in a small shrub of his own, in the least favoured corner of the garden. Despite his claims to be influenced by Hank Williams and García Lorca, he is *sui generis*, a true original, a stranger both in his own strange land and in everybody else's.

And if we're not sure where he comes from, we sure as hell don't know where he's going next. In the preface to his collection of essays, *Intricate Preparations*, Stephen Scobie tries to provoke Cohen into activity through the power of wish-fulfilment alone:

> *On two previous occasions... I lamented the non-appearance of long-promised Cohen books; in both cases, the books appeared before the ink on my words was dry. Third time lucky; perhaps this rash statement will produce the long-awaited* Book Of Longing.[24]

Scobie was indeed lucky, although for his last wish to come good, he had to wait another six years. So I hope I might be permitted to indulge myself a little. For a start I'd like Cohen to produce at least one more book. Perhaps not poetry; as the lukewarm critical response to the eventual appearance of *The Book of Longing* proved, he seems to have retreated into the realm of trite pleasantries in that medium. Maybe an autobiography: although there will always be the question over his ability to mythologise and misremember, as the changing stories of his songs' interpretations show. If such a book ever does appear, it may turn out to be something like Dylan's *Chronicles*, fragmentary, chronologically eccentric; intriguing but not necessarily as factually informative as the trainspotters might wish.

So some new fiction might be preferable; although, if we are still following the parallel of James Joyce, there's the risk that a third published novel would be as unfathomable as the Irishman's *Finnegans Wake*, a narrative so stylistically bizarre that several Joyce scholars admit that they've never finished it properly. Perhaps a book of short stories, then, please, Mr Cohen. That would be nice, and probably more manageable for our 21st century, bite-sized-attention-span culture.

It would also be intriguing to see something of Cohen in curator mode. Since 1993, the Southbank Centre in London has held its annual Meltdown Festival, in which a musician chooses a varied selection of his/her favourite acts to play in the arts complex by the Thames. Previous curators include self-confessed Cohen fans such as Nick Cave, Jarvis Cocker and Laurie Anderson, as well as performers with stylistic similarities and eccentric reputations, such as Scott Walker and Robert Wyatt. What, one wonders, would a Cohen Meltdown sound like? Another model might be Bob Dylan's *Theme Time Radio Hour*, broadcast since 2006; in it, Dylan plays a decidedly eclectic spread of tunes from folk to rap, linked by a theme, and the part-time DJ's idiosyncratic ramblings.

But, despite all his other hats (the fedora only being the latest), Cohen's place in popular culture is assured above all by his status as a musician. He is still writing songs, and says he has enough for a new album; several of them inevitably deal with his thoughts about his own mortality,[25] and others may be based on his most recently published poetry. Rumoured titles for as yet unreleased tracks include 'Book Of Longing', 'The Darkness', 'Lullaby' and 'Puppets', although whether any of these survive his rigorous creative process remains to be seen. But as I write this, Cohen is scheduled to be touring well into November 2009, if not beyond, some time after the book is due to go to press; so any potential studio work will presumably have to be held off until then. As he says himself, "There's a record there, if I ever get off the road."[26]

Which is of course frustrating for the fans, but does give time for the imagination to work a little. So, might I be permitted one last pull of the wishbone? Just as Johnny Cash went into the studio with Rick Rubin towards the end of his life and recorded a succession of stripped-down albums that raged against the dying of the light, maybe Cohen could do something similar (but probably without quite so much rage). No synthesisers or drum machines this time; a sympathetic producer (a Johnston or a Lissauer, Mr Spector being indisposed); a tight bunch of musical collaborators; and a good mixture of songs, old Cohen (maybe revisiting some of the *Various Positions* songs), new Cohen, and a few unlikely covers – it would be fun to hear the man essaying songs by

Cave, Wainwright, Buckley, REM, U2 and others who have paid homage to him, as well as some of his early influences like Hank Williams and Ray Charles.

But this would need to be a Cohen album, not a meshing of lovely female voices with Leonard growling counterpoint from the sidelines. Yes, Cohen's vocal capabilities have suffered over the years, although it's fair to say the decline has been from bad to worse; as Christgau suggests, "Leonard Cohen has had No Voice since he began recording at 33."[27] By the time of Cash's last recordings with Rubin, his voice was weak and tremulous, but crucially, it was still definitively Johnny Cash. A new Cohen album would need to be similarly warts-and-all, similarly exposed for our contemplation.

But of course, that's just my wish list. Leonard Cohen, as has long been the case, will do just what he bloody well wants to do.

197

APPENDIX I
The Baffled King Composing

"The heavens declare the glory of God: and the firmament sh-eweth his handywork."
– Psalm 19

"Onions have layers. Ogres have layers. Onions have layers. You get it? We both have layers."
– *Shrek* (2001)

"What in life does not deserve celebrating?"
– Adrian Veidt, *Watchmen* (2009)

So, what's so special about 'Hallelujah' anyway? How has a song from one of his least successful albums, recorded during what was probably the lowest point in his career, wriggled out from obscurity and transcended the rest of his work, usurping the likes of 'Suzanne' and 'Bird On The Wire'? It's become the Leonard Cohen song that's loved even by people who don't like Leonard Cohen – even by people who may never have heard of Leonard Cohen.

Because, let's be honest here, Leonard Cohen has never been huge, and that's not just a snarky dig at his height. Although many of his themes are universal, his choice of language and perspective can be off-putting for the casual listener or reader. Add to that the idiosyn-cratic qualities of his singing voice, and you've got someone appar-ently destined for niche status. That said, it's quite possible to build a respectable musical career with a relatively small number of fans, pro-vided those fans are committed.

Two examples come to mind. The first is the Velvet Underground, the New York avant-garde rock band that once featured the husky vo-cal skills of Cohen's sometime crush Nico. As Roxy Music noisenik/ ambient pioneer Brian Eno is alleged to have said, only a few hundred people bought the first Velvets album when it came out in 1967, but every single one of them went on to form a band. It's an exaggeration, but as with all the best exaggerations, there's a germ of truth nestling inside. The Velvets laid the groundwork for punk, Goth, New Romantic, industrial and emo, not to mention a good chunk of glam rock and heavy metal. Most of what we now regard as 'indie' or 'alternative rock' would have been impossible without the Velvets; there are millions of people who have never knowingly heard a Velvet Underground song, but hear their sound and attitude filtered through several layers of influence until it comes out as Franz Ferdinand or the Kings of Leon or My Chemical Romance.

The other is the Grateful Dead. Leader Jerry Garcia once explained the appeal of the psychedelic boogie band thus: "Our audience is like people who like licorice. Not everybody likes licorice, but the people who like licorice *really* like licorice." There's definitely an element of Cohen in there; the elements in his music that turn off 93% of listeners – the droning voice, the fascination with lust and death and religion, the refusal to engage properly with current musical fashions, the bad album covers, the hats – are what really capture the attention and affection of the other seven per cent.

In terms of his place in popular culture, Cohen can be seen as a fusion of the Velvets and the Dead: his influence outweighs the size of his fan base, and those people who appreciate him tend to verge on the obsessive side of fandom. But of course, he doesn't sound anything like either band; and any attempt to compare him with another performer will instead bring us round to the looming presence of Bob Dylan. The similarities are obvious: a fascination with the power and mystery of the English language; a self-consciously crafted bohemian persona; a profoundly unorthodox Judaism, and the associated tendency towards cherry-picking from other religious traditions; a respect for country music, without ever quite embracing the genre whole-heartedly; a technically ropy singing voice. None of these tends to endear a performer to the average fan of popular music, if such a person exists.

And yet Dylan, alongside Elvis Presley, the Beatles and a few others, is widely regarded as one of the building blocks of rock's DNA. People who can't stand him could probably hum at least half a dozen of his songs – something you probably couldn't say for Cohen.

One reason for the discrepancy is that Dylan was lucky in the acts that chose to record his songs. Peter, Paul and Mary, Joan Baez, the Byrds, Manfred Mann and Jimi Hendrix (and, more recently, Adele, the White Stripes and Ronan Keating) have given his work a radio-friendly sheen that his own versions rarely achieved. Of course, part of Cohen's initial success was down to the sponsorship of Judy Collins, who recorded his songs before he did; and Jennifer Warnes' *Famous Blue Raincoat* album surely won a few new admirers to his cause.

But even when respected artists lined up to pay tribute to Cohen (as on the *I'm Your Fan* and *Tower of Song* albums) there was still the distinct feeling that this was about musicians saluting one of their own: as with the Velvet Underground, Cohen only made sense to those who knew their way around a fretboard.

And then, around the turn of century, a strange phenomenon occurred, centred around his song 'Hallelujah'.

A quick recap: 'Hallelujah' first saw the light of day on the *Various Positions* album, released in 1984, although Cohen had been working on the song for (depending on which story he's telling, and to whom) several months or several years. The album was not a huge critical or commercial success when it first came out, and Columbia didn't even bother to release it in the United States. John Lissauer, who produced it, believes that it's this secret status, as "one of the great undiscovered, should-have-been-a-hit records"[28] that set the foundations for the subsequent success of 'Hallelujah' in the hands of other performers; because Cohen's original version remained obscure, there was no fixed idea of how it should sound. When you come to record 'Hallelujah', you don't have the spectre of a definitive take, a this-is-how-it-should-be-done rendition. Cohen taped it first, but it's not really 'his'. You don't have a Cohen song, you have a song.

There may be an element of retrospective wishful thinking on Lissauer's part, as well as a justifiable desire to offer the finger to the idiots at the record company. But the *Various Positions* version of 'Hallelujah' was still a work in progress, and it's not certain that it would have achieved the same level of success if Cohen hadn't kept tweaking it. By Hallowe'en, 1988, when he performed it in Austin, Texas (the version heard on the 1994 live album), much of the religious imagery had been replaced by the secular and the sensuous, the references to David and Samson giving way to an agnostic "Maybe there's a God above", and only the last verse – "the Lord of Song" remaining intact. Despite this, the song's hymn-like qualities were still present. This wasn't just another love song.

And there it remained, a song for Cohen fans; one more nugget of lugubrious erudition for them to contemplate and share with likeminded obsessives over a bottle of wine. Bob Dylan was an early adopter, and performed the song in concert in 1988; but Dylan's critical and commercial standing in 1988 was fairly low, that being the year of *Down in the Groove* and the first Travelling Wilburys album.

Then, in 1991, John Cale decided to record a new version of 'Hallelujah' for the forthcoming *I'm Your Fan* project. Cale had been a founder member of the Velvet Underground, and had subsequently earned respect as a performer, songwriter and most significantly, for his production work on early albums by the Stooges, Patti Smith, Squeeze and the Happy Mondays. In fact, he'd come within one degree of separation from Cohen in 1972, via Jennifer Warnes, when he went behind the console for her album *Jennifer*. As such (and in common with many of the other performers on *I'm Your Fan*, such as Nick Cave and the Pixies) Cale was an acquired taste. His fan base was devoted and substantial enough to ensure that he could make a decent living from his music; but not so large that he could ever hope for his own private jet or mink-lined swimming pool.

Aware that Cohen had subjected the song to a process of continuous revision over the years, even after having recorded it, Cale asked him for a definitive version. Cohen, still unsure whether such a thing existed, responded by faxing dozens of verses to him, some of which he'd never performed himself, leaving Cale to pick out the ones he liked the most. The resulting version replaced Cohen's quickly dated synthesisers with a restrained piano accompaniment; and while his voice was hardly a thing of heart-stopping beauty, it was closer to a conventional technical definition of "good singing" than the song's author (or Dylan) had previously managed. He repeated the trick on a live album the following year.

The *I'm Your Fan* album sold relatively well, and consolidated Cohen's position as a muse for the 1990s generation of alternative rockers; 'Hallelujah' was generally regarded as a highlight, by contrast with some tracks that probably sounded better as interesting concepts than they did in the banal light of reality. But it was a version of the song released in 1994 that pushed 'Hallelujah' into the mainstream, or at least as far into the mainstream as Cohen had penetrated to that point. Jeff Buckley's father Tim had been a contemporary of Cohen's as a singer-songwriter in the late 1960s and early 1970s, before his drug-related death in 1975. Jeff inherited not just his songwriting skills, but his ethereal, almost androgynous voice which, when applied to 'Hallelujah', utterly transformed the song. In Buckley's rendition it retained its own spiritual connotations, but his love for the vocal acrobatics of qawwali singers such as Nusrat Fateh Ali Khan, and an echoey, almost sitar-like guitar introduction shifted the song's emotional centre eastwards. In subsequent live version, he incorporated lines from The Smiths' 'I Know It's Over', adding to the mournful weirdness of his rendition, and taking it even further away from the essential sobriety and restraint that characterised Cohen's original recording.

The emotional resonance of Buckley's 'Hallelujah', the sixth track on his album *Grace*, was enhanced by the singer's accidental drowning in 1997. Under normal circumstances, Buckley's success would have ring-fenced the song for a generation, making it off-limits to any other singer who might wish to record it.

But as far as performers were concerned, there was something uniquely compelling about 'Hallelujah'. It was as if the music business had stepped back to the age of songwriters such as Irving Berlin and Cole Porter, when a successful song would be recorded by all the major performers, and the notion of an 'original version' was bestowed with far less cultural significance than it usually is today. In Andrew Mueller's words, "It has turned into the singer's equivalent of something like *Hamlet* or *Macbeth*; everybody wants to have a lash at it if they want to be taken seriously."[29]

Not that they all succeed in that mission, of course. Bono's version on *Tower of Song* was half-hearted, although not quite the most embarrassing contribution to that sorry project. But the floodgates really opened when Cale's 10-year-old version was used on the soundtrack of the hugely successful animated movie *Shrek* (2001). It seemed to be an unlikely marriage; Cale's recording had previously appeared in Julian Schnabel's *Basquiat* (1996), a biopic of the troubled New York artist, which seemed to be a better fit. However the presence of some of the other performers (Eels, the Proclaimers) suggest that the tale of the grumpy, flatulent ogre wasn't solely aimed at the pre-teen market, and the song suited the sometimes melancholy tone of the story.

For convoluted contractual reasons, it was Rufus Wainwright, another spawn of the 1970s singer-songwriter set (son of Loudon Wainwright III and Kate McGarrigle), who performed the song on the spin-off album, using an arrangement almost identical to Cale's. The momentum began to build. The British indie band Starsailor (named after a Tim Buckley album) released a live recording as a b-side in 2002;[30] Allison Crowe cut a powerful version on her 2003 album *Tidings*, alongside other spiritually-inclined standards; the following year her fellow Canadian chanteuse kd lang included an excellent rendition on *Hymns of the 49th Parallel*, which also included 'Bird On The Wire', as well as songs by other Canadian songwriters such as Neil Young and Joni Mitchell. Sheryl Crow, Regina Spektor and Brandi Carlile offered their own interpretations; Fall Out Boy incorporated the chorus into their song 'Hum Hallelujah'. Also of note was the version by Algerian artist Khalida Azzouza, who stressed the cultural universality of the song by performing it in Arabic.

With everyone having a go, it was inevitable that some attempts would be more successful than others. About Bon Jovi's live version, performed on the 'Lost Horizon' tour, the less said the better. The same goes for the football-themed adaptation, in which a fan of Middlesbrough FC refashioned the song to pay tribute ("but you don't really play the long ball, do ya?") to Australian striker Mark Viduka, in a manner that Weird Al Yankovic might consider to be a little heavy handed. Classical crossover singers such as Aled Jones and Katherine Jenkins treated the song as if it were a hymn, which is appropriate on one level – it's got that spiritual/secular/singalong hybrid appeal, like 'Over The Rainbow' or 'You'll Never Walk Alone' – but one does rather wonder if Jones and Jenkins really *get* Cohen as such.

Following on from *Shrek*, it seemed that movies and TV shows of every genre felt the need to include one version or another, most often Buckley's, emoting in the background: political epic *The West Wing*; Austrian satire *The Edukators*; failed airport show *LAX*; arms trade thriller *Lord Of War*; forensic franchise *CSI: NY*; medical misanthropy classic *House, MD*; fashion comedy *Ugly Betty*; British hospital soap *Holby City*; Sapphic titillation *The L Word*; arithmetical crimebusting caper *Numb3rs*; sci-fi chiller *The Dead Zone* (in which it was sung by the show's star – and onetime John Hughes geek – Anthony Michael Hall); and airbrushed teen saga *The OC* (which used Buckley, but also gave coverage to Imogen Heap's atmospheric *a cappella* version). And as an apparent nod of thanks to their comrade from 1973, the Israeli defence force radio station still plays the song at 2 AM every Sunday.

In an effort to differentiate their uses of the song, some directors even went back to the source and resuscitated Cohen's version. One example is Zack Snyder, who used 'Hallelujah' in a sex scene between Nite Owl II (Patrick Wilson) and Silk Spectre II (Malin Akerman), characters in his 2009 adaptation of the graphic novel *Watchmen* – although his explanation doesn't sound particularly complimentary to Cohen:

> *Well, I originally had a different version of 'Hallelujah' on that scene – it was the version by Alison Krauss, and it was really beautiful. Too beautiful, as it turned out, because when I showed it to my buddies, they were like, "Wow, you really mean this, this love scene." So I was like, okay, that didn't work. But with the Leonard Cohen, in that moment, it's a little sadder of a song, it's a little bit more twisted, it's a little more broken, which expresses to me what's going on in that scene, between those two characters.*[31]

At least Snyder had cottoned on to the fact that the song is about rather more than miserable, teenagers with unfeasibly great skin. But, twisted or otherwise, how did this one song, plucked from Cohen's whole oeuvre, suddenly become such an aural cliché? In 2007, Michael Barthel presented a paper about the conundrum to the Experience Music Project in Seattle, Washington:

*What's fascinating about all this is not simply the song's ubiquity
on TV dramas – it's that it's used in the exact same way every time.
Songs can be used sincerely, ironically, as background shading,
as subtle comment, as product placement. But 'Hallelujah' always
appears as people are being sad, quietly sitting and staring into
space or ostentatiously crying, and always as a way of tying together the sadness of different characters in different places... The
way 'Hallelujah' is being used here is the auditory equivalent of
a silent film actress pressing the back of her hand to her forehead
to express despair – emotional shorthand. It's sometimes called a
needledrop, and it's an element of visual grammar that signals the
mood of the scene loudly and unmistakably... But it doesn't work
if it's too explicit. That theatrical gesture of hand to forehead has
no obvious connection to the emotion of despair, and neither does
'Hallelujah'. It gets used in scenes more obviously soundtracked
with songs called, say, 'We Are In a Hospital And Everyone is Dying Or Facing Difficult Choices'. But that would be too explicitly
about sadness, whereas the chorus of Cohen's song was designed
to apply to a range of emotions – the different Hallelujahs. It can
both reinforce and counterpoint.*[32]

The visuals reinforced the music, so that even if viewers/listeners
didn't quite get all the nuances of Cohen's writing about chairs and
hair, it was drilled into them that 'Hallelujah' = 'sad'. A melancholy
reaction became instinctive. This would come in useful when the next
wave of 'Hallelujah' cover versions appeared. Despite Cohen's occasional expressions of fondness for the tackier avenues of popular
culture (such as his passion for the Twist in London during the early
1960s), one can't imagine that he'd have much time for the numerous
reality and talent shows that defaced television around the world at the
beginning of the 21st century. However, it was this phenomenon that
helped to bring his works to an unprecedentedly wide audience.

It began, modestly and indirectly, in Norway, a country where Cohen had long enjoyed the sort of adulation for the most part denied to
him in the English-speaking world. Two successful contestants, Kurt

Nilsen and Alejandro Fuentes, from the *Norwegian Idol* TV talent show formed a band called the New Guitar Buddies, and their acoustic version of 'Hallelujah' topped their country's charts in January 2007. A meme began, a suggestion that the work of this lugubrious, sometimes bleakly pessimistic poet might be appropriate fodder for the phone-voting sofa generation: Jason Castro's version (from the 2008 season of *American Idol*), briefly topped the iTunes singles chart, also prompting renewed download sales for Jeff Buckley's version; the winner of the Dutch version of the *The X Factor*, Lisa Hordlijk, performed the song in the finale, and took it to the top of the charts in the Netherlands.

Hallelujahmania really took hold in Britain in late 2008, where the song was the centrepiece for the final of *The X Factor*, which featured competing versions by a boyband, JLS, and soul singer Alexandra Burke.[33] The solo act triumphed, with a faux-gospel arrangement that was at least vaguely relevant to Cohen's spiritual intent, although Burke's lung-busting bellow was a little less contemplative than the author might have preferred. The show's success propelled the recording to the top of the UK singles charts. In response, a tongue-in-cheek campaign by 'real music' purists dragged Buckley's version to number two, and even brought Cohen's original stumbling into the Top 40, the first time he'd achieved such an accolade in four decades of recording. 'Hallelujah' received the Musicnotes Song of the Year Award for the best-selling sheet music of 2008, 24 years after it had first been released.

So what is it about this song that equally enthuses avant-garde rockers, gay torch singers, AOR breast-beaters, bedroom strummers and the sort of people who brought Leona Lewis, Clay Aiken, Kelly Clarkson and Susan Boyle into our lucky lives? Musically, it's not all that complex, although in terms of meaning it's far from accessible, especially to those without a reasonable knowledge of the Old Testament. And even then, Cohen's references seem a little incoherent. We begin with the future King David, "a cunning player on an harp" (I Samuel 16: 16-23); then pitch forwards to David's pursuit of the bathing Bathsheba (II Samuel 11), although the latter isn't the straightforward tale of lechery that it appears, as David arranges for the death of Bathsheba's inconvenient husband, Uriah. And then, chronologically speaking, we skip back several generations; the haircut reference is clearly to the legend of Samson (Judges 16), whose strength, contained in his lush tresses, was lost when he became ensnared in the charms of the faithless Delilah. The narrative position changes back and forth between the first ("I") and second ("you") person; and that's before we acknowledge the additional complication that there are several distinct versions of the song, using different combinations of verses, in different orders.

This is something unusual in modern songs; it's far more common in folk music, which is often transmitted orally, resulting in variations in phrasing and order. Every time a singer decides to perform 'Hallelujah', there's a choice of what to include and what to leave out, a scenario that can be exhilarating but not a little frightening. The English singer Kathryn Williams comes from a folk tradition, but even she felt a little unnerved when she first performed the song:

It's so weird, because I've got maybe 15 or 20 songs of his that I prefer to listen to but the first time I sang it to myself at home – I don't really sing other people's songs much – it was a very strange feeling. It wasn't like singing any other song. It's like a journey. Each verse I did, I closed my eyes and I was in this room. I imagined myself going through it and then you do the "Hallelujah!" and then you're back into the next room. It was like a journey for me. And now I've been singing it for 10 years. It's still different every time I sing it. I suppose it's like a hymn, in the way that people can sing that all their lives; and it's written by someone, but no-one thinks about the person it's written by. They all sing it and take what they want from it.[34]

The journey that Williams mentions, the sense of throwing oneself into a work of art and relying on a combination of choice and chance to navigate one's way through it, is an unusual concept in popular song. It has something in common with the aleatoric or chance music developed by avant-garde composers such as Boulez, Cage and Stockhausen in the mid-20th century, and later employed to an extent by Brian Eno on some of David Bowie's 'Berlin' albums in the 1970s. A better analogy might be the world of computer games and interactive entertainment, where players move from zone to zone; or of experimental novels such as BS Johnson's *The Unfortunates* (1973) and Georges Perec's *Life: A User's Manual* (1978), in which the chapters can be read in many different orders, delegating control from the writer to the reader; in a way, turning the reader into an author of sorts.

Clearly, this flexibility, this potential to refashion and exert control, albeit with the implicit authority of the original writer, is a major part of what makes 'Hallelujah' an appealing, if slightly unnerving challenge to singers and producers. When they first approach it, they have to make decisions not just about tempo or instrumentation, but about the content itself; everybody is faced with the same dilemma that John Cale confronted, as verse after verse spewed out of his fax machine. John Lissauer, who should know, acclaims it as "just one of those songs that seems to inspire others to wrap themselves around it."[35] But they have to do rather more than that; they have to decide what it says, what it means. Because of Cohen's prior reputation as a poet, there's a tendency to treat his song lyrics with the forensic thoroughness usually employed by literary critics. A few other songwriters (Bob Dylan, inevitably, being the most notable victim) fall prey to this treatment, but Cohen doesn't help his case by turning poems into lyrics, and also publishing lyrics in the midst of collections of poetry.

Not that song lyrics shouldn't be smart and profound and oblique and challenging and packed with Biblical references, of course. Songs are allowed to be clever and poetry can often be crass and banal. But, on balance, the songwriter doesn't need to strive for *meaning* in quite the same way that the poet must. "Awopbopaloobopalopbamboom" is gibberish on the printed page, to the extent that no two people can agree even on how it's spelled. But when Little Richard bellows it at the start of 'Tutti Frutti', it communicates lust and abandon and the rapture of being young in a manner that transcends conventional language.

'Hallelujah' – the word, for the moment, not the song – fulfils a similar role. It's a Hebrew word that literally means 'Praise God', and is particularly associated with the Book of Psalms. In Jewish and Christian usage, it's generally an expression of joy, sometimes relief, and has long been incorporated into hymns and other religious works; for example, the chorus from Handel's *Messiah* oratorio of 1742, and Julia Ward Howe's 'Battle Hymn of the Republic' (1861). In more recent times it's been used by secular songwriters as diverse as the Krautrock pioneers Can (as 'Halleluwah'), Manchester bad boys the Happy Mondays, the 1979 Eurovision Song Contest winners Milk and Honey, and Cohen's own idol Ray Charles ('Hallelujah I Love Her So', released as a single in 1956). It transcends languages and cultures and genres.

But like Little Richard's ecstatic shriek, many of the people who use it with such abandon don't really know what it means. Or, more accurately, they have an idea of its meaning – perhaps a sort of non-specific expression of happiness – but can't necessarily articulate it in dictionary-friendly terms. Cohen himself, as is often the case, has been wary of ascribing too much specific meaning to his work, but in an interview in 1988 he did attempt to explain what the word itself – again, as distinct from the song – meant to him:

Finally, there's no conflict between things, finally, everything is reconciled but not where we live. This world is full of conflicts and full of things that cannot be reconciled but there are moments when we can transcend the dualistic system and reconcile and embrace the whole mess and that's what I mean by 'Hallelujah'. That regardless of what the impossibility of the situation is, there is a moment when you open your mouth and you throw open your arms and you embrace the thing and you just say "Hallelujah! Blessed is the name." And you can't reconcile it in any other way except in that position of total surrender, total affirmation.[36]

It's all about connotation, implication, nuance, a hotline to the listener's subsconscious; perhaps that involves surrender to God, or love, or whatever floats your own spiritual boat, but also surrender to the ineffable power of language itself. Guy Garvey, Cohen devotee and frontman for the British indie band Elbow, presented a radio show about the song in 2008, and explained that his understanding came not from his musical background, but from his Catholic upbringing:

One of the things I didn't realise I do as a songwriter is to employ mantra a lot, and a big part of why this song works like it does is this most ancient of mantras, which moves around, but once you've said it, you're not thinking about the words any more, as much as what your voice is doing. It's almost the breathing that becomes more important to me.[37]

This is a crucial point – the separation of words from their meaning – that unites all the religious traditions that have fascinated Cohen over the years. Many Jews have only a loose grasp of Hebrew, and rely on phonetic transliterations to take part in ceremonies, chanting words as sounds rather than signifiers; for hundreds of years, the Catholic Mass was celebrated only in Latin, leaving a substantial majority of worshippers unaware of its literal meaning; and Buddhist rites are often conducted in Sanskrit or Pali, ancient languages known only to monks and scholars. Many Muslims too, are far from fluent in Arabic, despite the fact that it is the language of the Qur'an, and that only the Arabic text can be regarded as the revealed word of Allah. As far as ordinary participants are concerned, what specific meaning there might be in the rituals is implicit, emotional, perhaps not liable to articulation by mere mortals. Sometimes this can be a conscious decision to protect the mysteries of the religion from the uneducated, the lower orders.

Which leads into problematic territory, where we ask whether some performers of some genres of music are to be classed as priests, while others are merely supplicants. Surely the likes of Cale and lang and Williams have pondered the meaning of the words: but is it presumptuous to wonder whether a performer such as Alexandra Burke – who recorded the song because she was told to, so she could win a talent show and have a Christmas number one and a recording contract, and good luck to her – really interrogated what Cohen was getting at? And if she had done, would she still have gone through with the performance? After all, whatever version you get hold of, it's not the sort of song that anyone might want played at a wedding, provided you've listened properly to the words.[38] As the journalist Bryan Appleyard argued, before the whole talent show phenomenon added yet another layer to the song:

The aesthetic trick at the heart of this is the undermining of the word Hallelujah. *It means praise to the Lord but it is, basically, just a musical sound, like* la la la *or* yeah, yeah, yeah. *Describing the chord structure in those three lines in the first verse makes the words, sort of literally, into the music. Similarly, the chorus, which consists simply of the repetition of the word, is pure song in which the words and music are inseparable. And it is a pure pop song or contemporary hymn – a catchy uplifting tune and a comforting word. It has almost a sing-along quality. The words become the happy tune, the tune gets into your head and, once there, reveals itself as a serpent. For what you will actually be singing along to is arid sex, destroyed imagination, misogyny and emotional violence.*[39]

Because, although 'Hallelujah' relies so much on resonance and atmosphere, the hymnal communality of the word that forms its title, it's still in English, and the lyrics do still mean something. The problem comes when someone attempts to squeeze the words into a particular religious framework, to co-opt Cohen's language to one faith or another. Here, for example, is a Catholic theologian musing on the lyrics:

For Cohen, our destiny now is no different, yet we sing from a context of fallenness. If sinfulness precluded praise, then we would live in spiritual silence. Thankfully it does not. The "broken Hallelujah" on earth conveys praise of God's glory now as the "holy Hallelujah" will in heaven.[40]

Except that Cohen is not looking to redemption in heaven; he acknowledges his spiritual brokenness – which can be expressed in Christian terms as original sin – but the intervention of God or Christ or Church won't make things better right now. All he can do is to confront his plight, here on earth.

The references to David and Samson, to God and "some pilgrim" may not stand up to close textual analysis, especially from Biblical scholars, but what they do add is a certain religious sensibility. Anybody with even the vaguest memories of the Old Testament, or who has seen a couple of those Technicolor Bible epics from the 40s and 50s, will know what he's getting at. The exhortation on the original sheet music to play "in a gospel style" confirms the spiritual intent, however superficial. Yet at the same time, the love, the lips and the tying to chairs add a distinct flavour of profanity to the sacred – a bit of Mary Magdalene or the Song of Solomon, Hedy Lamarr trying to seduce Victor Mature. And then, provided you're listening to the right version, the two become tangled together in a sweaty embrace:

I remember when I moved in you,
and the holy dove was moving too...

In this couplet, in which the carnal union is imbued with holiness in a manner that would have delighted DH Lawrence, Cohen encapsulates the creative tension that has been at the heart of Western popular music for the past 50 or 60 years: between sex and God; between love and fear; between lust and redemption. It's not the Devil who has all the best tunes, or Jehovah; the best tunes are the ones that happen when they fight it out; when, as Cohen himself suggested in *The Favourite Game*, the Chinese mystics have a chance of getting laid. Listen to Aretha Franklin[41] and Little Richard and Al Green and Jerry Lee Lewis and Marvin Gaye; the conflict between the holy and the secular, between the gospel and the brothel is the bedrock of what we call, in its loosest, broadest sense, popular music. It's the attitude at the heart of the blues, that even when life seems unbearable, we can still find something to celebrate, even if it's nothing more than our own endurance, our own survival. It may be a triumph of hope over experience, but at least it's a triumph. In Greg Kot's words:

The narrative explores how the erotic becomes political, how relationships are defined not by trust but by conquest, and how lovers become trophies to be discarded. And, somehow, the survivors hope it will be different next time. The broken Hallelujah is life itself.[42]

And 'Hallelujah' captures that, not with a faux-gospel call and response (although some of the talent show versions have come perilously close to that), but with the wry contemplation of the flawed but ultimately redeemed whiskey priest in Graham Greene's *The Power And The Glory*; a lapsed rabbi, a bad monk. In his own, weird way, Cohen has written a classic of soul music.

But even this isn't quite enough to explain the fascination. OK, 'Hallelujah' is about sex and it's about God, and that's lovely. But there's something else going on here. Cohen is also drawing attention to the very structure of the music: not simply the "secret chord" and the "Lord of Song", but also the way Cohen describes the tune as he plays it ("the fourth, the fifth" and so on). The most obvious precedent is Cole Porter's 'Ev'ry Time We Say Goodbye' (1944), in which the lyrics tracking "the change from major to minor" also comment on the chords. But there are implicit nods also to a tradition of meta-songwriting, songwriting about itself, songwriting that jettisons any artifice or illusion and just says "Hey, would you look at this song I'm writing?"[43] Some critics have mocked the rhyme scheme in later revisions of the song, the verses that end with "knew ya", "do ya", "outdrew ya" and so on, because it seems heavy handed, repeatedly drawing attention to the craft – rather than the art – of the writing process, the act of making words fit. But that's the whole point; songs don't simply fall out of the sky fully formed, and Cohen makes an effort to remind us of the fact.

And perhaps this is why respected, credible songwriters such as Cale, Buckley, Wainwright and lang have been prepared to put aside their own compositions and inhabit Cohen's words for a few minutes. He speaks of a process that they must recognise, the meticulous partnering of melody and meaning that seems so straightforward ("it goes like this") but really isn't. 'Hallelujah' is about the love of life and the fear of death – which is why fans of all tastes respond to it, because those are themes that occur in nearly every genre – but above all it's about the weird majesty of music itself. The "blaze of light in every word" suggests the Word of God, the notion prevalent in many religions that the Supreme Being reveals himself via certain sacred texts, but also the power that the songwriter – or any kind of writer or artist – possesses. It's not just the Almighty who creates, after all.

This validation of their craft goes some way to explain why musicians of all styles find something in it to make their own. Even those strange people on the talent shows, although that may have been a kind of tipping point. Just as guitar shops had long put up notices forbidding the performances of 'Stairway To Heaven' and 'Smoke On The Water', so bars and coffee houses that hosted open-mike nights started to realise that even a song as open to such multiple interpretations as 'Hallelujah' can suffer the deadening effects of over-familiarity. An article in *Paste* magazine in 2009 placed it at the top of a list of songs that should be rested, if only temporarily, ahead even of Lynyrd Skynyrd's 'Freebird', 'Wonderwall' by Oasis and 'One' by U2;[44] there's even a Facebook group to protest at its ubiquity. Where once it might have summoned up images of anguished, emo-ish boy-men whose great cheekbones can't protect them from the real problems of life, now the cold and broken Hallelujah just makes us think of Simon Cowell and his expensive grin.

And that's a feeling that the author of the song would appear to share. As the weary Cohen put it, after Zack Snyder has co-opted his voice to accompany moving images of rutting superheroes:

I was just reading a review of a movie called Watchmen *that uses it, and the reviewer said "Can we please have a moratorium on 'Hallelujah' in movies and television shows?" And I kind of feel the same way. I think it's a good song, but I think too many people sing it.*[45]

Ever a gentleman, Cohen acknowledges the compliment, but it's not surprising that this outpouring of tributes from the unlikeliest places comes as something of a culture shock to him. After a half-century of meticulously crafted words, it seems that Cohen has, albeit accidentally, become what his fictional alter ego had perceived in a Montreal restaurant: "the kind of pet people wanted." As he powers through his eighth decade – and he's still singing 'Hallelujah' on tour, he wouldn't be permitted to leave it out – new generations are waking up to the peculiar charm of that deep, growly miaow; an acclamation of a special kind.

APPENDIX II
Leonard and Robert

"Dylan was what I'd always meant by the poet – someone about whom the word was never used."
– Leonard Cohen, 1967

Popular music, in common with any art form, is usually seen as something akin to a complex relay race, with each new artist picking up a baton of influences, and subsequently passing it on to the next lot. So someone like Ray Charles was influenced by the jazz, blues, gospel and R&B artists of his childhood; he melded them into what would now be known as soul music; and in turn gave a lead to Stevie Wonder, Aretha Franklin and others. Every so often something appears – the Beatles, Pablo Picasso, Samuel Beckett, Igor Stravinsky – that seems to have emerged fully formed, without apparent antecedents. But closer examination reveals that the influences are present; just radically reworked and remodelled to such an extent that it's harder to spot them.

And sometimes of course, it can go the other way; critics and public alike make a snap judgement that New Artist A is influenced by Established Artist B, and that's all there is to say about the matter. Which is rather what happened when Leonard Cohen appeared on the scene in the mid-late 1960s; he was a new Dylan. Of course, he wasn't alone in this, as dozens of musicians – including the compulsive self-reinventor Dylan himself – had the label applied to them.[46] Sometimes all it took was a harmonica solo or a corduroy jacket to prompt a connection. But in the case of Cohen, who had been pretty much divorced from the American musical mainstream for the best part of the decade, it made even less sense.

Obviously there were similarities. Dylan (*née* Zimmerman) and Cohen were both Jewish, and both looked it; both had Lithuanian grandparents; neither came from a region particularly renowned for its role in popular music (Dylan was from Minnesota). Both wrote songs with lyrics that veered wildly from the conventional memes of moonlight and romance; neither was blessed with a conventionally attractive voice. Both received a major career boost from the patronage of John Hammond, and they were signed to his record label, Columbia. Both hung out at Andy Warhol's factory; both love country music; both recorded albums with Bob Johnston in Nashville; both made memorable appearances at the Isle of Wight Festival, albeit one year apart. Both wrote songs rich with Biblical references, sometimes the same ones (for example, Dylan's 'Highway 61 Revisited' and Cohen's 'Story Of Isaac'); both would become heavily involved in religious traditions outside the faith of their parents, but neither would ever fully renounce their Jewish identities. And both are enthusiastic artists, but frankly not very good ones, who have been allowed on occasion to design their own album sleeves (Dylan's *Self Portrait*; Cohen's *Dear Heather*).

But there was so much that was different. The age gap was crucial, for a start. Although Cohen was only seven years older than Dylan, the cultural chasm between them is best characterised by the musical environment of their respective teenage years. Topping the Billboard Charts on Cohen's 15th birthday was Vic Damone and the quasi-operatic 'You're Breaking My Heart'; the equivalent for Dylan's was Elvis Presley's 'Heartbreak Hotel'. Cohen's adolescent alter-ego Breavman (and presumably Cohen himself, despite his frequent denials of the autobiographical elements in *The Favourite Game*) had to indulge in the excruciating conga-style dance known as 'Bunny Hop'; Dylan saw Buddy Holly at one of his last concerts. Cohen's first band was called the Buckskin Boys, cheery, outdoorsy, wholesome, the sort of outfit you wouldn't mind playing at your church social; Dylan's was the Shadow Blasters, dark and violent, almost apocalyptic, just the sort of thing to scare your parents.

Cohen would have been aware of the post-war changes in the role and expectation of teenagers, and felt some of their effects; but their manifestation in the primal energy of rock 'n' roll came just a little too late for him. When Cohen was a rebellious teen, poetry seemed to be as good an outlet as any for his creative urges; for Dylan, the *only* feasible course was to be a musician.

As a result of this, while Cohen was sitting on his terrace at Hydra, chatting to the daisies and squeezing three pages a day from his Olivetti, Dylan made straight for New York. His first, eponymous album was released in March, 1962, nearly six years before Cohen's debut; at the point when Cohen was only just discovering the Twist, as he approached his thirtieth birthday. *Bob Dylan* was a modest beginning, containing only two of Dylan's own compositions, but within a couple of years, he was being touted as the conscience of a generation, his lyrics scoured for meaning by those who wondered why the Baby Boom generation had suddenly adopted long hair, short skirts and a profoundly sceptical attitude to authority. He helped redefine the notion of what a pop star could be. Even Elvis Presley, quivering hips and lips notwithstanding, was still a polite, Godfearing Southern boy who loved his mother and called journalists "sir". Dylan was surly, uncooperative, rendering press conferences farcical with his bizarre non sequiturs – even his habit of wearing dark glasses was perceived as an affront to standards of civilised behaviour. This was displayed in 1966, a time when journalists from the *New Musical Express* still wore suits and ties and expected musicians at least to play along with the publicity game:

For posterity's sake, I framed a question which might be construed as "being aware". Why is it that the titles of his recent singles like 'Rainy Day Women #12 And #35' apparently bear no connection with the lyric?

"It has every significance," returned Dylan.
"Have you been down to North Mexico?"

"Not recently."

"Well, I can't explain it to you then."[47]

Although music journalists were often the victims of Dylan's prima donna antics, it was clear to them that he encapsulated the mood of the times in the same way that the Beatles did. The two acts were profoundly influential on each other. Dylan introduced the Beatles to cannabis, and encouraged them to be subtle, allusive, consciously difficult in their lyrics; the Beatles and the other British invasion groups reintroduced Dylan to the primal power of rock 'n' roll, encouraging him to "go electric", to the chagrin of the folkie purists.

By the time Cohen signed with Columbia in 1967, Dylan had redefined the notion of what a popular singer could be. It was inevitable that Cohen, Paul Simon, James Taylor and others who came to the public consciousness around that time would be considered in the context of Dylan, and it was equally inevitable that they would resent the fact that their own voices were not being heard as unique and valid.

It has long been reported that Cohen was more eager than most to adopt the mantle, and that in early 1966, he had startled a group of his friends from the Montreal poetry scene with the announcement that he wanted to become "Canadian Dylan".[48] More recently, however, he has denied ever having made such a claim, identifying it as a question posed to him (and one, we infer, that he never answered) rather than a statement of his own:

> *I'd never say that any more than I'd say I wanted to be the next* *Keats. You know how that arose? There was a party at Frank* *Scott's house. I had a record of Bob Dylan, and I brought it to this* *party...* It was probably Bringing It All Back Home. *It was one of* *his early records. I said, listen fellas, listen to this. This guy's a* *real poet. I put the record on, and it was greeted with yawns. They* *said, 'That's not a poet.' I said, 'No. I insist, let me play it again.'* *They said, 'Do you want to be that?' That's how it arose. But it's* *not my syntax. Anyway, they didn't like it. But I put it on a few* *more times, and by the end of the evening they were dancing.*[49]

There's no doubt that Cohen was an admirer, although his exile on Hydra had left him pretty much unaware of Dylan's central role in the contemporary pop pantheon. Performers such as the Byrds and Peter, Paul and Mary, who had first taken his songs into the higher reaches of the pop charts were just names to Cohen. Until he went to New York, he knew little of the politically oriented folk movement that had sprung up around the black-clad Minnesotan, and he had little idea of Dylan's image as a brooding, media-unfriendly contrarian, the voice of a generation who seemed not to want to be understood.

This is significant because, although Cohen was a lover of literature, his responses to it were often romantic as much as scholarly. His love for García Lorca and Yeats and Byron was to an extent informed by their life stories and the social and historical contexts in which their work arose; they were poets, but also poster boys for poetry. By contrast, he came to an appreciation of Dylan pretty much cold; his response was chiefly to the words and the music and the records, rather than the image. In Cohen's eyes and ears he was "a real poet", rather than the leader of a cultural revolution.

His fascination with Dylan came at a time when academics and music writers began to pay far more critical attention to (some) performers and writers from the world of pop, rock and folk music. The first to be so honoured were, inevitably the Beatles, with the notorious *Times* review that identified hints of Mahler and "Aeolian cadences" in 'Not A Second Time', a rather obscure song on their second album, *With The Beatles*.[50] But Dylan was next on the list for analysis, and very soon after, Leonard Cohen joined him there. Here's a piece comparing the work of the two men, first published in 1969:

Bob Dylan and Leonard Cohen represent two highly contrasting directions from which the attempt to restore significance and integrity of vision to the popular song can be made. Bob Dylan is the child runaway who became a professional songwriter by deliberate hard work, and whose emergence as a poet of some talent seems to have been accidental, almost as if he had unconsciously realized that good songs have to contain reasonably good lyric poetry. Leonard Cohen is a university-educated formalistic poet who has moved in an opposite direction with his recent discovery that a good lyric poem could equally be a good song. Dylan brings to poetry a spontaneity of rhythm and a resourcefulness in imagery that had long been qualities of American folk music, as in that of Huddie Ledbetter or of Dylan's own idol, Woody Guthrie. Cohen takes

219

to the poem as popular song a scholarly precision of language and an obsession for external form.[51]

Even if Cohen was wary of the 'New Dylan' tag, he can only have been pleased to have achieved sufficient credibility that the two men's work might be compared; especially because, at this point, he had released a mere two albums, compared with Dylan's ten. By this stage Cohen and Dylan had finally met face to face at the Kettle of Fish in Greenwich Village, and expressed their admiration for each other's work; although it is perhaps significant that it was Dylan who requested Cohen's attendance, rather than vice versa.[52] One wonders how Cohen's songwriting might have developed if he'd encountered Dylan in 1966, before he was established as a musician; whether he might have fallen more completely under the younger man's spell.

The mutual respect has endured, although some of this can be seen as a mutual protection pact. The sort of brickbats Cohen receives (the gloominess, the bad voice, the cleverness of his lyrics) can just as easily be thrown at Dylan. Here's Cohen in 1988 – the year in which Dylan began performing 'Hallelujah' on stage – dealing with the issue of his own vocal limitations, and spreading the net a little wider:

Most music criticism is in the nineteenth century. It's so far behind, say, the criticism of painting. It's still based on nineteenth-century art – cows beside a stream and trees and "I know what I like." There's no concession to the fact that Dylan might be a more sophisticated singer than Whitney Houston, that he's probably the most sophisticated singer we've had in a generation. Or that Tom Waits' whole personage is incredibly classy and chic, much more so than anybody around, mostly.
[Is that something you take to heart?]
Well, I'm actually talking about myself.[53]

Davey's 1969 article might have confirmed Cohen's status among the ranks of popular songwriters, but it also suggested the reason that, even if he was worthy of comparison with Dylan, his critical reputation would always lag. Both men achieved fame at a time when the old literary canon was coming under assault, that the universities and other centres of thought and learning had to shake off their centuries-old assumption that the key to understanding culture was contained in the writings of a select few; the notorious 'Dead White Males' whose position had been assured by opinion-formers who, for the most part, looked and sounded rather like them.

When university academics, most notoriously Christopher Ricks, began to suggest that Bob Dylan was not just a poet, but possibly equal or superior to those poets who had stood unchallenged on school and university syllabuses for generations, it was as much a social and political statement as a critical judgement: the fact that Dylan expressed his poetry through the medium of rock 'n' roll, rather than on the printed page was definitely something to be counted in his favour. The old order was rapidly fading, and youth and newness were suddenly the most desirable characteristics to possess in nearly every walk of life.

On the other hand, Cohen was, as Davey noted, a "university-educated formalistic poet" who brought precision and form to his songwriting. The brilliance of the University of Minnesota dropout Dylan was, one might infer, instinctive; Cohen learned it from books, the old way; he was probably trying too hard. Unsurprisingly, Dylan's chief academic cheerleader, Christopher Ricks, didn't and doesn't think that much of Cohen's work: or, to be as pedantically precise as textual criticism demands, he believes that the 'correct' answer to the conundrum "I love Leonard Cohen, so how come I don't love Bob Dylan?" should be "But I don't love Leonard Cohen, I find him somewhat tedious."[54]

In the febrile cultural atmosphere of the 60s and 70s, the distinction between Cohen and Dylan was as much a moral judgement as a literary one. Spontaneity was the order of the day; thoughtful, meticulous, learned craftsmanship was out. It would, for example, be many years before any self-respecting critic would be able to argue that Paul McCartney was more talented than John Lennon without attracting hoots of derision. This might be as good a moment as any to recount the oft-told story about Cohen and Dylan discussing songwriting methods, this time in Cohen's own words:

*A few years ago I helped out at a Dylan concert in Paris, after-
ward we went out to get coffee together. He mentioned one of my
songs that he played on stage, 'Hallelujah'. He asked me, "How
long did it take you to write it?" "Oh, I don't know. Two years
maybe, at least." Then I mentioned one of the songs from Slow
Train Coming, 'I And I'. "And for that, how long?" He answered,
"15 minutes."*[55]

The details of the story are open to question: for a start, 'I And I' is
on Dylan's album *Infidels* (1983), rather than on *Slow Train Coming*.
Cohen has offered various different estimates as to how long 'Hallelujah' took to compose; and Dylan himself is certainly not above a certain economy with the truth, especially if it helps maintain his own
mythology – if indeed he boasted of having written the song so quickly in the first place, as Cohen claims he did. But at the same time, the
exchange does encapsulate the differing approaches of the two men,
not to mention the contrast between Dylan's sometimes abrasive self-
assurance, and Cohen's lack of confidence in his own abilities.

It could of course be argued that Dylan's approach is popular with
academics because it gives them something to play with. Fast, sponta-
neous writing necessarily leads to ambiguity; the author doesn't take
time to ponder how the work might be received, which means that
multiple conflicting interpretations are possible. Patient rewriting and
revision brings clarity, a characteristic that academics claim to admire, but secretly loathe because it gives them relatively little to work
on. From about 1965, when he moved from political protest towards
a more surreal, stream-of-consciousness style, critics have indulged
themselves playing in the amusement parks of his language. In comparison, although Cohen's writing can be erudite and serious, it is rarely consciously obscure. There are exceptions in both cases, of course:
a piece such as 'The Butcher' (from *Songs From A Room*) does offer
the opportunity for a number of differing interpretations; while Dylan's 'Simple Twist Of Fate', from *Blood On The Tracks* (1975) is an el-
egantly transparent song of lost love. Interestingly, 'Sisters Of Mercy',
one of the few songs that Cohen finished at a single sitting, is also one
of his most ambiguous, provided the listener isn't aware of the story

that inspired it – a story which, in any case, is prone to occasional revisions: see Chapter Nine.

Plenty of academics, such as Ira Nadel and Stephen Scobie, have written about Cohen, of course. But the intensity of the interest in Dylan, the sheer volume of words devoted to him by literary critics has to make him the most discussed popular musician in modern academia. As I write, the Cambridge University Press has launched a new series of texts, The Cambridge Companion to American Studies. The first five subjects deemed worthy of analysis are two of the Founding Fathers of the United States, Thomas Jefferson and Benjamin Franklin; two major black leaders of the 20th century, WEB DuBois and Malcolm X; and Dylan. As the editor of the latter volume states, "Dylan has long since passed into the Academy."[56] The canon he was supposed to help destroy in the late 60s and early 70s has not in fact crumbled – it's just flexed and expanded a little to accommodate him. In some circles, Dylan's reputation has exceeded that of Keats or Byron, but by being placed alongside the likes of Jefferson, he has become a politician, a statesman, a philosopher – the sort of figure he used to excoriate in his early works. Dylan is analysed, dissected, admired, worshipped, placed in the iconography of the age not just with Elvis Presley and the Beatles, but alongside Che Guevara and Martin Luther King and the running Vietnamese girl, as a definitive image of his own lifetime, transcending the boundaries of the music business.

At the same time, Dylan is hugely successful in commercial terms, certainly in comparison with his label mate Cohen. In the 1960s and 1970s, 14 of his albums achieved Top Ten placings in the US charts; a feat not managed by a single one of Cohen's. The inverted snobbery that declares 'wide appeal must equal artistic compromise' does not seem to apply in this case. Moreover, Dylan has managed to balance academic and commercial success with the adulation of the music press, again something that has been a struggle for Cohen.

For example, when *Rolling Stone* magazine published its controversial (for being so uncontroversial) list of the 500 'greatest' albums, Dylan earned a total of 10 mentions, with two in the Top 10; Cohen was entirely ignored, although that can at least partly be explained by the extent to which the poll so utterly marginalised music that came from anywhere outside the United States or the British Isles.[57] A slightly less reverential list, published in Britain at around the same time, was a little more balanced, although Cohen still only warranted two albums (*Songs Of Leonard Cohen* and *I'm Your Man*) to Dylan's five.[58] Even with Dylan out of the picture on a list of Canadian albums, Cohen was eclipsed by Neil Young (seven places, including first and third) and Joni Mitchell (five places). Cohen's tally of three (*Songs Of Leonard Cohen* in 11th place; *I'm Your Man* at 29; *Songs Of Love And Hate* at 35) put him on a par with a previously little known Francophone progressive rock outfit called Harmonium.[59] It's possible, and probably quite sensible, to dismiss such lists as essentially meaningless self-indulgences; but collectively they are capable of reinforcing cultural structures, setting up a hierarchy of received opinions, according to which someone like Bob Dylan is somehow 'better' or 'more important' than someone like Leonard Cohen.

The number of books devoted to Dylan dwarfs those written about most other rock artists, let alone Cohen. (Consider this volume a modest attempt to redress the balance.) There are few other artists who could inspire a major critic such as Greil Marcus to write a full-length book about a single recording of a single song, as he did about 'Like A Rolling Stone', from *Highway 61 Revisited* (1965).[60]

Of course, we can go back to the Davey article from 1969; one obvious explanation is that Dylan is a musician whose work has often veered into poetry, whereas Cohen is a poet who picked up a guitar. In an age in which recorded sound is more important to most people than printed books (and you can multiply the difference a hundredfold when it comes to poetry books), it's inevitable that Dylan (and Young and the Beatles and Springsteen and many others) wins out. While both Dylan and Cohen specialise in singing their own words, the former also invests plenty of time in interpreting the works of others; to date, he has recorded five albums solely or mainly consisting of songs written by other people, with as yet unconfirmed rumours of a Christmas album for 2009. Cohen, on the other hand, very rarely performs cover versions, and *Dear Heather* was highly unusual in containing more than one track with lyrics by someone other than Cohen himself. People would, it is believed, rather hear Dylan (or Cave, or Joel, or Buckley, or Burke) sing Cohen than to hear Cohen sing Dylan.

But of course it's not that simple. Judy Collins, John Lissauer, Robert Christgau and many others have paid tribute to Cohen's musical gifts, his facility with a tune. Although he has adapted some of his poems to become songs, most are conceived as musical works. He's a real musician, not some sort of dilettante.

Dylan meanwhile, even if he'd not followed Cohen's path of public readings and bound volumes, was already being defined as something other than a songwriter. Although he's published several collections of his lyrics, Dylan has never gone out on a limb and produced a book that defines itself as poetry. Indeed, until his well-received memoir *Chronicles* was published in 2004, his most important piece of writing separate from his music was the bizarre novel *Tarantula*, written in the mid-1960s – around the same time that Cohen was bringing out *Beautiful Losers* – but not officially published until 1971, by which stage its quasi-Beatnik stream-of-consciousness styling seemed more than a little outmoded.

However, journalists befuddled by his lapses into uncooperative weirdness would reach for the catch-all justification that he was a "poet" or an "idyllic dreamer", something set apart from the common herd.[61] And even if he didn't necessarily choose the description of "poet" for himself (Cohen was often uneasy about it as well), he was clearly well aware of the contemporary canon of American poetry; in his autobiography, he describes long conversations with Archibald MacLeish, whom he describes as a "Poet Laureate of America", alongside Carl Sandburg and Robert Frost.[62] Although he's never explicitly conceded the point, it's quite likely that he took his pseudonym from the Welsh writer Dylan Thomas.

So they're both poets, and they're both musicians, and they're considered to be respectable subjects for academic study because they are clearly distinct from the most egregious manifestations of commercial pop. In Frank Davey's words:

> ...both are thoroughly disinterested in purveying the old and simplistic romantic lies which so many of today's pop artists – Dono-

van, the Bee Gees, the Fifth Dimension, the Association – consistently peddle. Both instead try to do the poet's job present the world as the world appears in the words and images which their separate visions demand.[63]

And yet, despite their professions of mutual respect, they're also both probably aware that in 100 years' time, it will be Dylan's music, rather than Cohen's, that is seen as defining the second half of the 20th century.

And yet Cohen has an advantage, in his relationship with his fans, although this has only become obvious in recent months. Maybe it's as a result of being the underdog for so long. Maybe it's a response to his financial troubles. Maybe it's because he's a Canadian. Maybe it's simply been there, hovering under the surface, sincerely felt but never consciously acknowledged.

Paradoxically – hell, let's all try for a piece of Zen once in a while – it can perhaps best be expressed by a description of what it's not. Here's Cohen describing a Dylan show he attended – part of the so-called Never-Ending Tour that has been in progress since 1988 – in May, 2008:

Bob Dylan has a secret code with his audience. If someone came from the moon and watched it they might wonder what was going on. In this particular case he had his back to half the audience and was playing the organ, beautifully I might say, and just running through the songs. Some were hard to recognise. But nobody cared. That's not what they were there for and not what I was there for. Something else was going on, which was a celebration of some kind of genius that's so apparent and has touched people so deeply that all they need is some kind of symbolic unfolding of the event. It doesn't have to be the songs. All it has to be is: remember that song and what it did to you.[64]

Which is probably a very worthwhile and memorable experience, but at the same time it doesn't sound like a whole lot of fun. In fact, it sounds more akin to a religious service than a rock 'n' roll show. Cohen saw Dylan play when both men found themselves in St John's, Newfoundland at the same time; this was on the opening leg of Cohen's comeback tour. And the contrast between the two events is significant; although he is fascinated by religion, and constantly returns to the subject in his songs, Cohen's own performances are not religious events. His own wariness of false, controlling teachers and gurus (see Conclusion) discourages him from that path. Reading reports of his gigs, listening to recordings, watching footage, it's plain to see the immense warmth generated between performer and audience. They laugh at his corny, well-honed one-liners; he acknowledges their reactions with a smile and a doff of the hat. Unhappy circumstances may have pushed this tour into existence, but he and they seem happy to be there. Yes, that word, Cohen haters: 'happy'. We can all put away the razorblades now, and their attendant clichés.

That happiness does not seem to prevail in Dylan's public world. Perhaps he's spent too long having his creative entrails picked over by academics, being given top-ten positions by list-compilers and taste-makers. His concerts seem designed to improve, to elucidate, like a lecture in a Victorian temperance hall. It may be unfair to judge someone's creative work in the light of his own personality and behaviour, but when it comes to live performance, and to the interaction between performer and audience, it surely matters. There was a time when a difficult reputation might even have been seen as a badge of honour. As Lester Bangs wrote in the early 1970s:

> *And even when word began to get out somewhere between* High-way 61 *and* Blonde On Blonde *that Dylan might actually have mutated into (or been all along) a nasty little punk who also happened to be the most gifted songwriter of his time, people just shrugged because, after all, it was Dylan.*[65]

Dylan is undoubtedly a great artist – Cohen says so himself. But there's something in the interface between Dylan's prickly demeanour and the nerdish, reverential obsessiveness of his fans, sometimes weirdly close to loathing – like the Dylanologist/garbologist AJ Weberman, who rooted through his trash in his quest to uncover the secrets of his life and work – that can seem a little cold, a little too male,[66] ever so slightly devoid of love.

And Cohen? Well, Cohen is loved. And Cohen – and surely Dylan as well – knows which is more important.

APPENDIX III
My favourite songs of Leonard Cohen

...my over serious Top Ten goose-stepping through my head like the generals of a junta who do not know the coup d'état has been staged the very night of the formal ball...
– Beautiful Losers (1966)

As I mentioned in the comparison with Bob Dylan, Leonard Cohen often seems to lose out when it comes to the modern-day obsession with moulding opinions about popular music into list formation, for which I hold Dave Marsh and Nick Hornby jointly to blame. Fans of other acts are always desperately keen to demonstrate either their in-depth knowledge of their idols' life and work, or their own exquisite taste, leading to interminable arguments about the five best Beatles songs on which Paul McCartney plays the drums; or the ten best B-sides that Radiohead never play live these days. Cohen fans avoid this – perhaps because they tend to be gentle, sensitive souls, who don't like hurting anyone's feelings, or even the feelings of the songs that might get missed out. Perhaps they're simply above such petty geekiness.

There is no particular justification for the existence of this list, nor of course is there any coherent explanation for why I prefer these songs to any others. It just felt like a good place to stop. A bit like 'Tacoma Trailer' (which isn't on the list). Note that these are my favourite Cohen *songs*; to haggle over the favourite version would be even more point-less, and probably induce apoplexy in a few fundamentalists.

I did wonder whether to include a bottom 10, but then I recalled the great man's own words:

My feeling about music that I don't like is to keep my mouth shut about it. I understand it's completely a matter of taste; a lot of peo-ple who don't like my music have insisted on writing and speaking widely about how bad it is.[67]

So here are 10 songs, some of them not so new:

1. 'Tower Of Song'
2. 'Famous Blue Raincoat'
3. 'Paper-Thin Hotel'
4. 'Hallelujah'
5. 'Bird On The Wire'
6. 'Who By Fire'
7. 'Anthem'
8. 'A Thousand Kisses Deep'
9. 'Suzanne'
10. 'The Great Event'

NOTES

[1] Billy Walker, 'The Sounds Interview', *Sounds*, October 23, 1971.

[2] *Arthur Smith Sings Leonard Cohen* (BBC Radio 4, February 5, 2004).

[3] Sheppard, pp. 105-106.

[4] Brian D Johnson, 'Hallelujah!', *Uncut*, December, 2008.

[5] *Ladies And Gentlemen... Mr Leonard Cohen* (1965)

[6] Tim de Lisle, 'Who held a gun to Leonard Cohen's head?', *The Guardian*, September 17, 2004.

[7] *Leonard Cohen Under Review, 1978-2006* (Sexy Intellectual, 2007).

[8] Biba Kopf, 'Lenny and *Jenny Sings Lenny*', *NME*, March 14, 1987.

[9] *Songs From The Life Of Leonard Cohen* (1988).

[10] Leon Wieseltier, 'The Prince Of Bummers', *The New Yorker*, July 26, 1993.

[11] *Leonard Cohen: Spring 96* (1997)

[12] Gavin Martin, 'Hello! I Must Be Cohen', *NME*, January 9, 1993.

[13] Nadel, p. 16.

[14] *Leonard Cohen: I'm Your Man* (2006).

[15] *Leonard Cohen: Spring 96* (1997). Cohen later said that "if Roshi had been a professor of physics in Heidelberg, I would have learned German and gone to Heidelberg." *Leonard Cohen: I'm Your Man* (2006).

[16] Robin Pike, 'September 15th 1974', *ZigZag*, October, 1974.

[17] Interview with the author, June, 2009.

[18] *Songs From The Life Of Leonard Cohen* (1988). Persistent optimists and Americans might with some justification observe that Ms Warnes was born in Seattle, which is close enough to Canada to raise their suspicions.

[19] Paul Saltzmann, 'Famous Last Words from Leonard Cohen (The poet's final interview, he hopes)', *Maclean's*, June, 1972.

[20] Paul Monk, 'Under The Spell Of Stranger Music: Leonard Cohen's Lyrical Judaism', *Australian Financial Review*, June 8, 2001.

21 Stephen Dalton describes him as "the Samuel Beckett of pop"; 'Leonard Cohen: Opera House, Manchester', *The Times*, June 18, 2008. Beckett is another artist whose mordant sense of humour has often been obscured by his reputation for bleakness.

22 Steven R Rosen, 'Nick Cave: *The Proposition*, Pop Music and Leonard Cohen', *Cincinnati CityBeat*, June 7, 2006.

23 *What Leonard Cohen Did For Me* (BBC4, September 2, 2005).

24 *Stephen Scobie, Intricate Preparations: Writing Leonard Cohen* (Toronto: ECW, 2000), p. 4.

25 Simon Houpt, Coffee And Candour With Cohen', *Globe and Mail* (Toronto), February 27, 2009.

26 Neil Strauss, 'Leonard Cohen, Down From The Mountain', *Rolling Stone*, March 19, 2009.

27 Robert Christgau, 'Sonic Refuges', *Village Voice*, November 2, 2004.

28 *The Fourth, The Fifth, The Minor Fall* (BBC Radio 2, November 1, 2008).

29 *Leonard Cohen Under Review 1978-2006* (2007). Hamlet is a good pick; Buckley's version could easily have adorned any of several recent productions of the play, featuring beautiful, damaged, troubled stars such as Ethan Hawke or Jude Law.

30 Starsailor would emulate Cohen in 2003, by engaging Phil Spector as a producer. Spector's interpersonal skills had not improved, and the resulting sessions were soon aborted, although no guns were pulled.

31 James Parker, 'Interview: Zack Snyder of Watchmen', *Boston Phoenix*, March 4, 2009. In fact, Snyder's first choice had been Allison Crowe, rather than Alison Krauss.

32 www.clapclap.org/2007/04/hallelujah.html

33 It may not have been coincidental that copyright for the song is owned by Sony, parent of Syco, the entertainment company run by *X Factor* presenter Simon Cowell.

34 *The Fourth, The Fifth, The Minor Fall* (2008). Williams recorded 'Hallelujah', alongside pieces by Nirvana, Lou Reed, Neil Young and others, on her album *Relations* in 2004.

35 Interview with the author, 2009.

36 *How The Heart Approaches What It Yearns*, interview with John McKenna (RTE, May 9, 1988).

37 *The Fourth, The Fifth, The Minor Fall* (2008).

38 And yet of course, people often don't listen to the words. How else can we explain the popularity of Dolly Parton's song 'I Will Always Love You' – which is clearly about the end of a relationship – as a wedding favourite?

39 Bryan Appleyard, 'Hallelujah!', *Sunday Times* (London), January 9, 2005.

40 Thomas Ryan, 'Nothing on my tongue but Hallelujah': Leonard Cohen and Catholicism', *National Catholic Reporter*, May 29, 2009. For another doomed attempt to squeeze the square peg of popular music into the round hole of religious dogma, see Steve Turner, *The Gospel According To The Beatles* (Louisville, Ky: Westminster John Knox Press, 2006).

41 Who recorded a version of 'Suzanne', and whose music, according to Cohen's 1977 poem 'The Other Village', Leonard Cohen prefers to Leonard Cohen's.

42 Greg Kot, 'Why Leonard Cohen's 'Hallelujah' Endures', *Chicago Tribune*, April 30, 2009.

43 Others include 'It's The Same Old Song' by the Four Tops (1965); 'Only A Northern Song' by the Beatles (1968); 'Your Song' by Elton John (1970); 'You're So Vain' by Carly Simon (1972); 'This Is Not A Love Song' by Public Image Limited (1983), 'My Iron Lung' by Radiohead (1994); 'This Song' by Ron Sexsmith (2001). Thanks to Barney Hoskyns and Bob Collum for ideas here; see also Tim Footman, *Welcome to the Machine: OK Computer and the Death of the Classic Album* (London: Chrome Dreams, 2007) pp.66-69.

44 Kate Kiefer and Jason Killingsworth, 'Stop Covering These Ten Songs', *Paste*, April 23, 2009.

45 Jian Ghomeishi, 'I'm blessed with a certain amnesia', *The Guardian*, July 10, 2009.

46 For Greil Marcus's list of 100 New Dylans, see Dave Marsh and James Bernard, *The New Book of Rock Lists* (New York: Fireside, 1994) p. 334.

47 Keith Altham, 'Dylan's Press Deception', *NME*, May 13, 1966.

[48] Sandra Djwa, *The Politics Of The Imagination: A Life Of FR Scott* (Toronto: McClelland & Stewart, 1987); quoted in Nadel, p. 141. Other contenders for the title of 'Canadian Dylan' would include Gordon Lightfoot, Joni Mitchell, Buffy Sainte-Marie and Neil Young.

[49] Brian D Johnson, 'Hallelujah!', *Uncut*. December, 2008. An extract from the journal of poet Ralph Gustafson, who was also present, suggests that "Cohen advocates Bob Dylan as present great poet-singer", although Gustafson himself describes Dylan as "mental chewing-gum"; Stephen Scobie, *Intricate Preparations: Writing Leonard Cohen* (Toronto: ECW, 2000), 89.

[50] William Mann, 'What Songs The Beatles Sang…', *The Times* (London), December 23, 1963. John Lennon said that he thought Aeolian cadences were exotic birds. See MacDonald, pp. 74-75.

[51] Frank Davey, 'Leonard Cohen and Bob Dylan: Poetry and the Popular Song', *Alphabet*, December 1969.

[52] See Nadel, p. 156. Dylan later claimed, presumably facetiously, that he wouldn't mind being country musician Roy Acuff, actor Walter Matthau, or Cohen.

[53] Mark Rowland, 'Leonard Cohen's Nervous Breakdown', *Musician*, July, 1988. This was also the interview in which Cohen first compared Dylan to Picasso.

[54] Ieva Lesinska and Christopher Ricks, 'A lesson in Dylan appreciation', *Eurozine*, November 4, 2008.

[55] Christian Fevret, 'Comme un guerrier', *Les Inrockuptibles*, August 21, 1991.

[56] Kevin JH Dettmar, *The Cambridge Companion To Bob Dylan* (Cambridge University Press, 2009).

[57] 'The 500 Greatest Albums Of All Time', *Rolling Stone*, November 18, 2003.

[58] Jim Irvin and Colin McLear, *The Mojo Collection* (Edinburgh: Canongate, 2003).

[59] Bob Mersereau, *The Top 100 Canadian Albums* (Fredericton, NB: Goose Lane Editions, 2007).

[60] Greil Marcus, *Like A Rolling Stone: Bob Dylan At The Crossroads* (New York: Public Affairs, 2005).

61 'When a poet fills in a form, you can expect anything!', *NME*, May 21, 1965.

62 Bob Dylan, *Chronicles: Volume One* (New York: Simon & Schuster, 2004), pp. 107-113. Dylan labels the three "the Yeats, Browning and Shelley of the New World". In 'A Thousand Kisses Deep', on *Ten New Songs*, Cohen practically quotes Frost; see Chapter Twenty-One.

63 Frank Davey, 'Leonard Cohen and Bob Dylan: Poetry and the Popular Song', *Alphabet*, December 1969. The Fifth Dimension *et al* could, of course, be replaced by any number of modern equivalents.

64 Brian D Johnson, 'Hallelujah!', *Uncut*. December, 2008.

65 Lester Bangs, 'James Taylor Marked For Death', *Who Put The Bomp*, Winter-Spring, 1971; included in *Psychotic Reactions And Carburetor Dung* (London: Serpent's Tail, 1996), p. 69.

66 I've never seen an authoritative analysis of the gender breakdown at concerts by Dylan or Cohen, or a similar study of the people who buy their records, but casual observation would suggest that Cohen has a far higher proportion of women among his admirers.

67 *Songs From The Life Of Leonard Cohen* (1988).

DISCOGRAPHY:
I can't remember one line or where to look

STUDIO ALBUMS

Songs Of Leonard Cohen
Suzanne / Master Song / Winter Lady / The Stranger Song / Sisters Of Mercy / So Long, Marianne / Hey, That's No Way To Say Goodbye / Stories Of The Street / Teachers / One Of Us Cannot Be Wrong Additional tracks on 2007 reissue: *Store Room / Blessed Is The Memory*
Columbia, February, 1968

Songs From A Room
Bird On The Wire / Story Of Isaac / A Bunch Of Lonesome Heroes / The Partisan / Seems So Long Ago, Nancy / The Old Revolution / The Butcher / You Know Who I Am / Lady Midnight / Tonight Will Be Fine Additional tracks on 2007 reissue: *Like A Bird / Nothing To One*
Columbia, April, 1969 (cassette – 1984; CD – 1990)

Songs Of Love And Hate
Avalanche / Last Year's Man / Dress Rehearsal Rag / Diamonds In The Mine / Love Calls You By Your Name / Famous Blue Raincoat / Sing Another Song, Boys / Joan Of Arc Additional track on 2007 reissue: *Dress Rehearsal Rag* (early version)
Columbia, March, 1971 (cassette – 1984)

New Skin For The Old Ceremony
Is This What You Wanted / Chelsea Hotel # 2 / Lover Lover Lover

/ Field Commander Cohen / Why Don't You Try / There Is A War /
A Singer Must Die / I Tried To Leave You / Who By Fire / Take This
Longing / Leaving Green Sleeves
Columbia, August, 1974 (cassette – 1986)

Death Of A Ladies' Man

True Love Leaves No Traces / Iodine / Paper-Thin Hotel / Memories
/ I Left A Woman Waiting / Don't Go Home With Your Hard-On /
Fingerprints / Death Of A Ladies' Man
Columbia, November 1977

Recent Songs

The Guests / Humbled In Love / The Window / Came So Far For
Beauty / The Lost Canadian (Un Canadian Errant) / The Traitor /
Our Lady Of Solitude / The Gypsy's Wife / The Smokey Life / Ballad
Of The Absent Mare
Columbia, September 1979

Various Positions

Dance Me To The End Of Love / Coming Back To You / The Law
/ Night Comes On / Hallelujah / The Captain / Hunter's Lullaby /
Heart With No Companion / If It Be Your Will
Columbia, February 1985

I'm Your Man

First We Take Manhattan / Ain't No Cure For Love / Everybody
Knows / I'm Your Man / Take This Waltz / Jazz Police / I Can't Forget
/ Tower Of Song
Columbia, February 1988

The Future

The Future / Waiting For The Miracle / Be For Real / Closing Time /

Anthem / Democracy / Light As The Breeze / Always / Tacoma Trailer
Columbia, November 1992

Ten New Songs
*In My Secret Life / A Thousand Kisses Deep / That Don't Make
It Junk / Here It Is / Love Itself / By The Rivers Dark / Alexandra
Leaving / You Have Loved Enough / Boogie Street / The Land Of
Plenty*
Columbia, October 2001

Dear Heather
*Go No More A-Roving / Because Of / The Letters / Undertow /
Morning Glory / On That Day / Villanelle For Our Time / There
For You / Dear Heather / Nightingale / To A Teacher / The Faith /
Tennessee Waltz*
Columbia, October 2004

LIVE ALBUMS

Live Songs
*Minute Prologue / Passing Through / You Know Who I Am / Bird On
The Wire / Nancy / Improvisation / Story Of Isaac / Please Don't Pass
Me By (A Disgrace) / Tonight Will Be Fine / Queen Victoria*
Columbia, April 1973

Columbia Radio Hour
*First We Take Manhattan / Ain't No Cure For Love / Coming Back To
You / Dance Me To The End Of Love / Democracy / Waiting For The
Miracle / The Future / I'm Your Man*
Columbia promo, 1993; only 100 copies released.

Cohen Live

Dance Me To The End Of Love / Bird On The Wire / Everybody Knows / Joan Of Arc / There Is A War / Sisters Of Mercy / Hallelujah / I'm Your Man / Who By Fire / One Of Us Cannot Be Wrong / If It Be Your Will / Heart With No Companion / Suzanne
Columbia, July 1994

Field Commander Cohen: Tour Of 1979

Field Commander Cohen / The Window / The Smokey Life / The Gypsy's Wife / Lover Lover Lover / Hey, That's No Way To Say Goodbye / The Stranger Song / The Guests / Memories / Why Don't You Try / Bird On The Wire / So Long, Marianne
Columbia, February 2001

Live In London

Dance Me To The End Of Love / The Future / Ain't No Cure For Love / Bird On The Wire / Everybody Knows / In My Secret Life / Who By Fire / Hey, That's No Way To Say Goodbye / Anthem / Introduction / Tower Of Song / Suzanne / The Gypsy's Wife / Boogie Street / Hallelujah / Democracy / I'm Your Man / Recitation w / N.L. / Take This Waltz / So Long, Marianne / First We Take Manhattan / Sisters Of Mercy / If It Be Your Will / Closing Time / I Tried To Leave You / Wither Thou Goest
Sony, March 2009

SELECTED BOOTLEGS

(Although most of these recordings were originally available on vinyl, cassette or CD, many have subsequently appeared as MP3s on the Web. Be aware that bootleg recordings are unauthorised and illegal.)

Live At The BBC 1968

You Know Who I Am / Bird On The Wire / The Stranger Song / So Long, Marianne / Master Song / There's No Reason Why You Should Remember Me (improvisation*) / Sisters Of Mercy / Dress Rehearsal Rag / Suzanne / Hey, That's No Way To Say Goodbye / Story Of Isaac / One Of Us Cannot Be Wrong / Bird On The Wire / So Long, Marianne / You Know Who I Am / Hey, That's No Way To Say Goodbye* (duet with Julie Felix)

Live In Israel 1972

Famous Blue Raincoat / Hey, That's No Way To Say Goodbye / Machines Song (improvisation*) / Sisters of Mercy / Chelsea Hotel #1 / Avalanche / Suzanne / We Shall Not Be Moved*

Paris 1976

Avalanche / Chelsea Hotel #2 / The Partisan / Story Of Isaac / Famous Blue Raincoat / Lover Lover Lover / Is This What You Wanted / Suzanne / Bird On The Wire / Who By Fire / Storeroom / I Tried To Leave You / Lady Midnight / There Is A War / Do I Have To Dance All Night / The Butcher / Do I have To Dance All Night (reprise)

Germany 1979 (aka Live In New York 1979)

So Long, Marianne / The Window / Famous Blue Raincoat / Passing Through / Memories / The Guests / Suzanne

Warsaw 1985

Who By Fire / The Law / Dance Me To the End Of Love / There Is A War / The Gipsy's Wife / The Partisan / Sisters Of Mercy / The Night Comes On / Diamonds In The Mine / Avalanche / Chelsea Hotel # 2 / Lover Lover Lover / Famous Blue Raincoat / Suzanne / Hallelujah / Passin' Thru / If It Be Your Will / Hey, That's No Way To Say Goodbye

/ So Long, Marianne / Tennessee Waltz / I Tried To Leave You

I'm Your Man (Bergen 1988)

Dance Me To The End Of Love / First We Take Manhattan / Ain't No Cure For Love / Everybody Knows / I'm Your Man / Take This Waltz / Heart With No Companion / Bird On The Wire / Joan Of Arc / The Partisan / So Long, Marianne / Suzanne / Whither Thou Goest / There Is A War / Coming Back To You / Sisters Of Mercy / Dance Me To The End Of Love

First We Take LA Then We Take Berlin (Los Angeles 1993)

First We Take Manhattan / Ain't No Cure For Love / Coming Back To You / Dance Me To The End Of Love / Democracy / Waiting For The Miracle / The Future / I'm Your Man / Bird On A Wire / Everybody Knows / Avalanche / Tower Of Song / I Can't Forget

New York 2009

Dance Me To The End Of Love / The Future / Chelsea Hotel # 2 / Tower Of Song / Suzanne / The Partisan / Hallelujah / A Thousand Kisses Deep / Take This Waltz / So Long, Marianne / First We Take Manhattan / Democracy

COMPILATION ALBUMS

Greatest Hits (aka The Best Of Leonard Cohen)

Suzanne / Sisters Of Mercy / So Long, Marianne / Bird On The Wire / Lady Midnight / The Partisan / Hey, That's No Way To Say Goodbye / Famous Blue Raincoat / Last Year's Man / Chelsea Hotel # 2 / Who By Fire / Take This Longing
Columbia, November 1975

More Best Of Leonard Cohen

Everybody Knows / I'm Your Man / Take This Waltz / Tower Of Song / Anthem / Democracy / The Future / Closing Time / Dance Me To The End Of Love (live) / Suzanne (live) / Hallelujah (live) / Never Any Good / The Great Event
Columbia, October 1997

The Essential Leonard Cohen

Suzanne / The Stranger Song / Sisters Of Mercy / Hey, That's No Way To Say Goodbye / So Long, Marianne / Bird On A Wire (sic) / The Partisan / Famous Blue Raincoat / Chelsea Hotel #2 / Take This Longing / Who By Fire / The Guests / Hallelujah / If It Be Your Will / Night Comes On / I'm Your Man / Everybody Knows / Tower Of Song / Ain't No Cure For Love / Take This Waltz / First We Take Manhattan / Dance Me To The End of Love (live) / The Future / Democracy / Waiting for the Miracle / Closing Time / Anthem / In My Secret Life / Alexandra Leaving / A Thousand Kisses Deep / Love Itself Additional tracks on 2008 reissue: *Seems So Long Ago, Nancy / Love Calls You By Your Name / A Singer Must Die / Death Of A Ladies' Man / The Traitor / By The Rivers Dark / The Letters*
Columbia, October 2002 / August 2008

MOJO Presents: An Introduction To Leonard Cohen

Suzanne / Sisters Of Mercy / One Of Us Cannot Be Wrong / The Old Revolution / Seems So Long Ago, Nancy / Bird On The Wire / Joan Of Arc / Famous Blue Raincoat / Diamonds In The Mine / Chelsea Hotel # 2 / I Tried To Leave You / Who By Fire / Iodine / The Smokey Life / Dance Me To The End Of Love / Hallelujah / If It Be Your Will / I'm Your Man / Take This Waltz / Tower Of Song / Light As The Breeze / The Gypsy's Wife / That Don't Make It Junk
Sony/Columbia, September, 2003

242

EP

Track Hits

Bird On The Wire / Lady Midnight / Joan Of Arc / Suzanne / Hey, That's No Way To Say Goodbye / So Long, Marianne / Paper Thin Hotel
Pickwick (UK), July 1983

SINGLES

Suzanne / So Long, Marianne
Columbia, March 1968

Bird On The Wire / Seems So Long Ago, Nancy
Columbia, May 1969

Joan Of Arc / Diamonds In The Mine
Columbia, July 1971

Sisters of Mercy / Winter Lady / The Stranger Song
Columbia, July 1972

Suzanne / Bird On The Wire
Columbia, March 1973

Bird On The Wire (live) / Tonight Will Be Fine (live)
Columbia, July 1974

Lover Lover Lover / Who By Fire
Columbia, November 1974

Suzanne / Take This Longing
Columbia, May 1976

Do I Have To Dance All Night? (live) / The Butcher (live)
CBS France, July 1976

Memories / Don't Go Home With Your Hard-On
Columbia, November 1977

True Love Leaves No Traces / I Left A Woman Waiting
Columbia, March 1978

Dance Me To The End Of Love / The Law
Columbia, February 1985

Take This Waltz
CBS Holland, June 1986

First We Take Manhattan / Sisters Of Mercy
Columbia, January 1988
12-inch adds *Bird On The Wire / Suzanne*

Ain't No Cure For Love / Jazz Police
Columbia, May 1988
12-inch adds *Hey, That's No Way To Say Goodbye / So Long, Marianne*

Closing Time / Anthem
Columbia, January 1993

The Future / Suzanne
Sony, April 2009; from the *Live In London* album. Promotional 7-inch single for Record Store Day (April 18, 2009)

APPEARANCES ON COMPILATIONS, SOUNDTRACKS, ETC

Six Montreal Poets
For Wilf And His House / Beside The Shepherd / Poem / Lovers / The Sparrows / Warning / Les Vieus / Elegy
Folkways, 1957 (Other poems written and performed by AJM Smith,

Irving Layton, FR Scott, Louis Dudek, AM Klein)
Natural Born Killers OST
Waiting For The Miracle (Edit) / The Future
Interscope, 1994

Born To The Breed: A Tribute To Judy Collins
Since You've Asked (Dialogue)
Wildflower, October 2008

GUEST APPEARANCES

Was Not Was: Are You Okay?
Elvis's Rolls Royce
Fontana, 1990

Various: Weird Nightmare: Meditations On Mingus
Eclipse (with Diamanda Galás)
Sony, 1992

Elton John: Duets
Born To Lose
MCA/Rocket, 1993

Herbie Hancock: River: the Joni Letters
The Jungle Line
Verve, 2007

COVERS OF COHEN SONGS

Oddly for someone whose technical proficiency is, by his own
admission, so modest, Leonard Cohen is a real musician's musician,
which means that the number of people attempting to cover his work

is very high in proportion to his overall sales; this has especially been the case since the hugely successful *Famous Blue Raincoat* and *I'm Your Fan* albums. Moreover, his popularity is international; France, Spain, Poland and the Scandinavian countries are particular hotbeds of fandom, and musicians in all these countries have been keen to pay homage to the great man.

Add to this the hundreds of acoustic-wielding wannabes on YouTube and MySpace keen to have a go at 'Hallelujah' or (less commonly) 'Don't Go Home With Your Hard-On' and it becomes clear that a truly definitive list of Cohen covers would fill this book and more. What's here then is a track listing of the major albums, by multiple or individual artists, containing solely cover versions of Cohen compositions; and then a mopping-up operation of individual tracks, with a focus on the more prominent recording artists. The website leonardcohenfiles.com offers a far more extensive, international and esoteric list of those who have paid tribute to Mr Cohen in song.

ALBUMS

Graeme Allwright Chante Leonard Cohen
Demain sera bien (Tonight Will Be Fine) / L'homme de l'an passe (Last Year's Man) / Suzanne / L'Etranger (Stranger Song) / Diamants dans la mine (Diamonds In The Mine) / Vagabonde (Winter Lady) / Les soeurs de la misericorde (Sisters Of Mercy) / Jeanne d'Arc (Joan Of Arc) / Avalanche
Mercury, France, 1973

Night Magic OST
I Have Counted What I Have / Wishing Window / The Throne Of Desire / Throne Variations / Angel's Eyes / The Law / The Promise / The Marriage March / The Third Invention / Clap! Clap! / Hunter's Lullaby / We Told You So / Fire / Song Of Destruction / The Walls /

Coming Back / Song To My Assassin / The Bells
RCA France, 1985 (Lyrics by Cohen)

Jennifer Warnes: Famous Blue Raincoat
First We Take Manhattan / Bird On A Wire / Famous Blue Raincoat / Joan Of Arc / Ain't No Cure For Love / Coming Back To You / Song Of Bernadette / A Singer Must Die / Came So Far For Beauty
Additional tracks on 2007 reissue: *Night Comes On / Ballad Of The Runaway Horse / If It Be Your Will / Joan Of Arc* (Live in Belgium)
Private Music, 1987

GG Gunn: Hot Romances
Suzanne / Lady Midnight / Hey, That's No Way To Say Goodbye / Tonight Will Be Fine / Joan Of Arc / I Left A Woman Waiting / Dance Me To The End Of Love / Bird On A Wire / Teachers / Famous Blue Raincoat / Death Of A Ladies' Man / Minute Prologue
Cassette only – Gramm Records, Iceland, 1988

I'm Your Fan
Who By Fire (House Of Love) / *Hey, That's No Way To Say Goodbye* (Ian McCulloch) / *I Can't Forget* (Pixies) / *Stories Of The Street* (That Petrol Emotion) / *Bird On The Wire* (Lilac Time) / *Suzanne* (Geoffrey Oryema) / *So Long, Marianne* (James) / *Avalanche IV* (Jean-Louis Murat) / *Don't Go Home With Your Hard-On* (David McComb & Adam Peters) / *First We Take Manhattan* (REM) / *Chelsea Hotel* (Lloyd Cole) / *Tower Of Song* (Robert Forster) / *Take This Longing* (Pete Astor) / *True Love Leaves No Traces* (Dead Famous People) / *I'm Your Man* (Bill Pritchard) / *A Singer Must Die* (Fatima Mansions) / *Tower Of Song* (Nick Cave & The Bad Seeds) / *Hallelujah* (John Cale)
Atlantic/EastWest, 1991 (There was also a promotional EP, *Voulez-*

Vous Chanter Cohen?, with the Pritchard, Astor and Oryema tracks, plus the Fatima Mansions' version of *Paper-Thin Hotel*)

Tower Of Song
Everybody Knows (Don Henley) / *Coming Back To You* (Trisha Yearwood) / *Sisters Of Mercy* (Sting with The Chieftains) / *Hallelujah* (Bono) / *Famous Blue Raincoat* (Tori Amos) / *Ain't No Cure For Love* (Aaron Neville) / *I'm Your Man* (Elton John) / *Bird On A Wire* (Willie Nelson) / *Suzanne* (Peter Gabriel) / *Light As The Breeze* (Billy Joel) / *If It Be Your Will* (Jann Arden) / *Story Of Isaac* (Suzanne Vega) / *Coming Back To You* (Martin Gore)
A&M, 1995

Red: Songs From A Room
Bird On The Wire / Story Of Isaac / A Bunch Of Lonesome Heroes / The Partisan / Seems So Long Ago, Nancy / The Old Revolution / The Butcher / You Know Who I Am / Lady Midnight / Tonight Will Be Fine
Rectangle, France, 2001 (Track-by-track re-recording of Cohen's second album)

John Bergeron: In The House Of Mystery
Bird On A Wire / Famous Blue Raincoat / Sisters Of Mercy / Joan Of Arc / Master Song / Suzanne / Take This Longing / Seems So Long Ago, Nancy / Story of Isaac / Winter Lady / If It Be Your Will
Musical Dreams, 2002

Maciej Zembaty: 35 x Leonard Cohen
Ptak na drucie (Bird On The Wire) / Kim jestem Ty wiesz (You Know Who I Am) / Dzis w nocy bedzie fajnie (Tonight Will Be Fine) / Nauczyciele (Teachers) / Wydaje sie tak dawno, Nancy (Seems So Long Ago, Nancy) / Kto w plomieniach? (Who By Fire?) / Lover

*Lover (Lover Lover Lover) / Wspomnienia (Memories) / Diamenty w
kopalni (Diamonds In The Mine) / Malenka, nie wolno sie zegnac w
ten spos / (Hey, That's No Way To Say Goodbye) / Slynny niebieski
prochowiec (Famous Blue Raincoat) / Zuzanna (Suzanne) / Czy to jest
to czego chcialas? (Is This What You Wanted) / Jedno z nas nie moze
sie mylic (One Of Us Cannot Be Wrong) / Partyzant (The Partisan) /
Tancz mnie po milosci kres (Dance Me To The End Of Love) / Wciaz
wojna trwa (There Is A War) / Prawo (The Law) / Zona Cygana
(The Gypsy's Wife) / Dzisiaj tu, jutro tam (Passin' Thru) / Lawina
(Avalanche) / Goscie (The Guests) / Kolysanka mysliwego (Hunter's
Lullaby) / Jesli wola twa (If It Be Your Will) / Alleluja (Hallelujah) /
Opowiadanie Izaaka (Story Of Isaac) / Siostry milosierdzia (Sisters
Of Mercy) / Zdrajca (The Traitor) / Joanna D'arc (Joan Of Arc) /
Upokorzona miloscia (Humbled In Love) / Madonna samotnosci (Our
Lady Of Solitude) / Manhattan (First We Take Manhattan) / Okno (The
Window) / Zamglone zycie (The Smokey Life) / Rzeznik (The Butcher)*
MTJ, Poland, 2002

Judy Collins Sings Leonard Cohen: Democracy
*Democracy / Suzanne / Thousand Kisses Deep / Hey, That's No Way
To Say Goodbye / Dress Rehearsal Rag / Priests / Night Comes On /
Sisters Of Mercy / Story Of Isaac / Bird On The Wire / Famous Blue
Raincoat / Joan Of Arc / Take This Longing / Song Of Bernadette*
CD – Rhino, 2004

Perla Batalla: Bird On The Wire: The Songs Of Leonard Cohen
*If It Be Your Will / Seems So Long Ago, Nancy / Coming Back To You
/ Dance Me To The End Of Love / So Long, Marianne / Came So Far
For Beauty / Ballad Of The Absent Mare / Famous Blue Raincoat /
Bird On The Wire / Suzanne*
CD – Mechuda Music, 2005

Anjani: Blue Alert

Blue Alert / Innermost Door / The Golden Gate / Half The Perfect World / Nightingale / No One After You / Never Got To Love You / The Mist / Crazy To Love You / Thanks For The Dance
Columbia, 2006 (Lyrics and production by Cohen)

Leonard Cohen: I'm Your Man, Original Motion Picture Soundtrack

Tower Of Song (Martha Wainwright) / *Tonight Will Be Fine* (Teddy Thompson) / *I'm Your Man* (Nick Cave) / *Winter Lady* (Kate McGarrigle) / *Sisters Of Mercy / Chelsea Hotel No. 2* (Rufus Wainwright) / *If It Be Your Will* (Antony) / *I Can't Forget* (Jarvis Cocker) / *Famous Blue Raincoat* (The Handsome Family) / *Bird On A Wire* (Perla Batalia) / *Everybody Knows* (Rufus Wainwright) / *The Traitor* (Martha Wainwright) / *Suzanne* (Nick Cave) / *The Future* (Teddy Thompson) / *Anthem* (Perla Batalia) / *Tower Of Song* (Leonard Cohen & U2)
Universal, 2006

Monsieur Camembert: Famous Blue Cheese

I'm Your Man / Gypsy Wife / Field Commander Cohen / Chelsea Hotel / First We Take Manhattan / The Guests / A Singer Must Die / Famous Blue Raincoat / Light As The Breeze / The Future / Take This Waltz / 1958 Manifesto / Seems So Long Ago, Nancy / Intro To Jazz Police / Jazz Police / Suzanne / Who By Fire / Bird On A Wire / Memories / Hallelujah / Everybody Knows / Closing Time / The Dove / Dance Me To The End Of Love
MGM Australia, 2007

Various Artists: Acordes Con Leonard Cohen

Mi Gitana (The Gypsy's Wife) (Duquende) / *A Thousand Kisses Deep*

(Jackson Browne) / *Chelsea Hotel* (Javier Muguruza) / *Diamonds In The Mine* (Elliott Murphy) / *Tú Sabes Quien Soy (You Know Who I Am)* (Santiago Auseron) / *Balada de la Yegua Ausente (Ballad Of The Absent Mare)* (Javier Solis) / *Thanks For The Dance* (Anjani Thomas) / *Susanna (Suzanne)* (Toti Soler) / *Titulos* / *Bird On The Wire* (Adam Cohen) / *Pequeño Vals Vienés (Take This Waltz)* (Adam Cohen) / *Suzanne* (Perla Batalla) / *Impermeable Azul (Famous Blue Raincoat)* (Christina Rosenvige) / *So Long, Marianne* (Javier Muguruza) / *Al Leluia (Hallelujah)* (Gerard Quintana) / *Half The Perfect World* (Anjani Thomas) / *El Futuro (The Future)* (Luis Eduardo Aute) / *Cualquier Sistema (Any System)* (Constantino Romero) / *El Carnicero (The Butcher)* (Javier Solis & Javier Mas) / *Oración Por el Mesías (Prayer For Messiah)* (Constantino Romero) / *Baila Conmigo (Hasta el Fin del Amor) (Dance Me To The End Of Love)* (Perla Batalla) Discmedi, 2007

Philip Glass: Book Of Longing
I Can't Make the Hills (Prologue) / I Came Down From The Mountain / A Sip Of Wine / Want To Fly / The Light Came Through The Window / Puppet Time / G–d Opened My Eyes / You Go Your Way / I Was Doing Something / Not A Jew / How Much I Love You / Babylon / I Enjoyed The Laughter / This Morning I Woke Up Again / I Want To Love You Now / Don't Have The Proof / The Night Of Santiago / Mother Mother / You Came To Me This Morning / I Am Now Able / Roshi's Very Tired / Merely A Prayer (Epilogue)
Orange Mountain, 2007 (Lyrics and recitation by Cohen)

Conspiracy Of Beards
Chelsea Hotel # 2 / Lady Midnight / Hallelujah / Famous Blue Raincoat / Tower Of Song
Conspiracy of Beards, 2008

251

Cohen Covered

Suzanne (Ian McCulloch) / *In My Secret Life* (Katie Melua) / *Hey, That's No Way To Say Goodbye* (Claudine Longet) / *Sisters Of Mercy* (Dion) / *Story Of Isaac* (Linda Thompson) / *Priests* (Eyeless In Gaza) / *Joan Of Arc* (Allison Crowe) / *Hallelujah* (Susanna And The Magical Orchestra) / *Avalanche* (Nick Cave & The Bad Seeds) / *Chelsea Hotel # 2* (Josh Ritter) / *Take This Longing* (Phil Campbell) / *Tower Of Song* (Martha Wainwright) / *Song For Bernadette* (Judy Collins) / *Famous Blue Raincoat* (The Handsome Family) / *Tonight Will Be Fine* (Mr David Viner)
With December, 2008 edition of MOJO

Stranger Music

Who By Fire (Schonwald) / *Diamonds In The Mine* (Le Luci della Centrale Ellettrica) / *A Singer Must Die* (Albanopower) / *Bird On The Wire* (His Clancyness) / *Lover Lover Lover* (Mickey Eats Plastic) / *Is This What You Wanted* (El Muniria) / *So Long, Marianne* (Finn) / *Famous Blue Raincoat* (Gismondi & Nuccini) / *I'm Your Man* (Wolther Goes Stranger) / *There Is A War* (Father Murphy) / *How To Speak Poetry* (Emido Clementi) / *Teachers* (Death In Donut Plains) / *Chelsea Hotel # 2* (Luca Giovanardi) / *The Partisan* (Giancarlo Frigeri) / *Stories Of The Street* (Arbdesatr) / *Suzanne* (Musica da Cucina)
Punk Not Died, Italy, 2009
(Proceeds to victims of the Abruzzo earthquake)

Leonard Cohen Revisited

Hallelujah (John Cale) / *Lover Lover Lover* (Ian McCulloch) / *The Partisan* (16 Horsepower) / *Bird On A Wire* (Johnny Cash) / *Hey, That's No Way To Say Goodbye* (Lemonheads & Liv Tyler) / *Paper-Thin Hotel* (Close Lobsters) / *Here It Is* (Jonathan Richman) / *There*

Is A War (Don Niño) / *Chelsea Hotel # 2 (live)* (Lambchop) / *Famous Blue Raincoat* (Marissa Nadler)
With May, 2009 edition of Les Inrockuptibles

SINGLES, ALBUM TRACKS

Adam and Mia: Adam and Mia *Hallelujah* (D and T, 2008).
Artery: Second Coming *Diamonds In The Mine*
(Golden Dawn, 1984)
Autorickshaw: So The Journey Goes *Bird On A Wire*
(La Tribu Can/Zoom, 2007)
Joan Baez: No Woman No Cry *Famous Blue Raincoat*
(Delta, 1992)
Joan Baez: Ring Them Bells *Suzanne* (Angel, 1995)
The Bobs: The Bobs Cover The Songs Of... *Bird On A Wire*
(Rounder, 1994)
Chris Botti: A Thousand Kisses Deep *A Thousand Kisses Deep*
(Sony, 2003)
Chris Botti: December *Hallelujah* (Columbia, 2006)
Broken Family Band: Balls *Diamonds In The Mine*
(Track and Field, 2006)
Till Brönner: Oceana *In My Secret Life* (feat. Carla Bruni)
(Emarcy, 2007)
Delmar Brown: Inner Spirit *The Land Of Plenty* (Ponderosa, 2008)
Michael Bublé: Call Me Irresponsible *I'm Your Man*
(!43/Reprise, 2007)
Roy Buchanan: The Prophet *Story Of Isaac*
(Hip-O Select/Polydor, 2004)
Jeff Buckley: Grace *Hallelujah* (Columbia, 1994)
Eric Burdon: My Secret Life *In My Secret Life* (SPV, 2004)

John Cale: Various Artists: Bleecker Street: Greenwich Village In The 60s *So Long, Marianne* (Astor Place, 1999)

Hamilton Camp: Welcome To Hamilton Camp *Hey, That's No Way To Say Goodbye* (Warner Bros, 1969).

Johnny Cash: American Recording *Bird On A Wire* (American, 1994)

Cobra Verde: Copycat Killers *So Long, Marianne* (Scat Records, 2005)

Joe Cocker: Joe Cocker! *Bird On A Wire* (A&M, 1969)

Joe Cocker: One Night Of Sin *I'm Your Man* (Capitol, 1989)

Joe Cocker: No Ordinary World *First We Take Manhattan* (Red Ink, 2000)

Adam Cohen: Various Artists: War Child Presents Heroes *Take This Waltz* (Astralwerks, 2009)

Coil: Horse Rotorvator *Who By Fire* (Some Bizzare, 1986)

Lloyd Cole: Various Artists: Rare On Air, Vol 2 *Famous Blue Raincoat* (Mammoth, 1995)

Christine Collister: Love *Hallelujah* (Stereoscout, 2005)

Concrete Blonde: Still In Hollywood *Everybody Knows* (Capitol, 1994)

Rita Coolidge: The Lady's Not For Sale *Bird On The Wire* (A&M, 1972)

Craig of Farrington: Easy Being *Joan Of Arc* (2005)

Allison Crowe: Secrets *Joan Of Arc* (Rubensesque, 2004)

Allison Crowe: Tidings *Hallelujah* (Rubensesque, 2004)

Jackie DeShannon: To Be Free *Bird On The Wire* (Imperial, 1970)

Neil Diamond: Stones *Suzanne* (MCA, 1971).

Barbara Dickson: For The Record *Song Of Bernadette* (Eagle, 2001)

Dion: Dion *Sisters Of Mercy* (Laurie, 1968).

Il Divo: The Promise *Hallelujah* (Syco/Sony, 2008).

Elizabeth & the Catapult: Taller Children *Everybody Knows* (Verve, 2009)

Marianne Faithfull: Vagabond Ways *Tower Of Song* (Instinct/EMI, 1998)

Fairport Convention: Jewel In The Crown *Closing Time* (Woodworm, 1995)

Julie Felix: The Rainbow Collection *Hallelujah* (Track, 2004).

Roberta Flack: First Take *Hey, That's No Way To Say Goodbye* (Atlantic, 1969)

Roberta Flack: Killing Me Softly *Suzanne* (Atlantic, 1973)

Flying Lizards: Top Ten *Suzanne* (Statik, 1984)

Aretha Franklin: Rare & Unreleased Recordings From The Golden Reign Of The Queen Of Soul *Suzanne* (Rhino, 2007)

Howe Gelb: Upside Down Home 2004: Year Of The Monkey *Tower Of Song* (OW OM Finished, 2004)

Anthony Michael Hall: Dead Zone OST *Hallelujah* (Image, 2004)

Tim Hardin: Bird On A Wire *Bird On A Wire* (Columbia, 1971)

Françoise Hardy: Comment Te Dire Adieu *Suzanne* (Vogue France, 1968)

Noel Harrison: Collage *Suzanne* (Reprise, 1967)

Noel Harrison: Santa Monica Pier *So Long, Marianne / Dress Rehearsal Rag* (Reprise, 1968)

Harvey Milk: Courtesy And Good Will Toward Men *One Of Us Cannot Be Wrong* (Relapse, 1996)

Richie Havens: Richard P Havens, 1983 *Priests* (Verve, 1969)

Lee Hazlewood: Poet, Fool Or Bum *Come Spend The Morning* (Capitol, 1973)

Engelbert Humperdinck: Don't You Love Me Anymore? *Come Spend The Morning* (Columbia, 1981)

Katherine Jenkins: Sacred Arias *Hallelujah* (Universal 2008)

Jesus & Mary Chain: The Sound Of Speed *Tower Of Song* (Blanco y Negro, 1993)

Aled Jones: Reason To Believe *Hallelujah* (UCJ, 2007)

Klezmer Conservatory Band: Dance Me To The End Of Love *Dance Me To the End Of Love* (Rounder, 2000).

kd lang: Songs Of The 49ᵗʰ Parallel *Bird On A Wire / Hallelujah* (Nonesuch, 2004)

Michael McDonald: Soul Speak *Hallelujah* (Motown, 2008).

Farhad Mehrad: Farhad *Hey, That's No Way To Say Goodbye / Master Song / Suzanne* (2003)

Bette Midler: Bathhouse Betty *Song Of Bernadette* (Warner, 1998)

Barbara Montgomery: Trinity *Alexandra Leaving / A Thousand Kisses Deep* (Mr Bean & Bumpy, 2005)

Enrique Morente & Lagartija Nick Cantando A Federico García Lorca Y Leonard Cohen *Pequeño Vals Vienés (Take This Waltz) / Manhattan (First We Take Manhattan) / Sacerdotes (Priests) / Aleluya (Hallelujah)* (El Europeo, Spain, 1996)

Sarah Jane Morris: August *Chelsea Hotel # 2* (Fallen Angels, 2001)

Nana Mouskouri: A Canadian Tribute *Ballad Of The Absent Mare / The Guests / Suzanne / You Know Who I Am* (Phantom, 2004)

Anne Murray: What A Wonderful World *Song Of Bernadette* (EMI, 1999)

Willie Nelson: Songbird *Hallelujah* (Lost Highway, 2006).

Neville Brothers: Brother's Keeper *Bird On A Wire* (A&M, 1990)

Stina Nordenstam: People Are Strange *Bird On A Wire / Came So Far For Beauty* (EastWest, 1998)

Patricia O'Callaghan: Real Emotional Girl *A Singer Must Die / Hallelujah / I'm Your Man / Joan Of Arc / Take This Waltz* (Atlantic, 2001)

Patricia O'Callaghan: Naked Beauty *True Love Leaves No Traces /
The Smokey Life* (Marquis, 2004)

Esther Ofarim: Esther Ofarim *You Know Who I Am / Bird On The
Wire / Please Don't Pass Me By* (Phonodor, Israel, 1969)

Esther Ofarim: Portrait *Suzanne / Hey, That's No Way To Say
Goodbye* (CBS, Israel, 1969)

Pearls Before Swine: Balaklava *Suzanne* (ESP-Disk, 1968)

Pearls Before Swine: Beautiful Lies You Could Live In *Bird On
The Wire* (Reprise, 1971)

Marti Pellow: Between The Covers *Suzanne* (Universal, 2004)

Madeleine Peyroux: Careless Love *Dance Me To The End Of Love*
(Rounder/Universal, 2004)

Madeleine Peyroux: Half The Perfect World *Blue Alert / Half The
Perfect World* (Rounder/Universal, 2006) (*Crazy To Love You* on
Japanese edition)

Gretchen Phillips & David Driver: Togetherness *Joan Of Arc*
(Bar/None, 2003)

Dianne Reeves: In The Moment *Suzanne* (Blue Note, 2000)

The Rhonda Harris: The Trouble With Rhonda Harris *Avalanche*
(Flower Shop, 2001)

Jonathan Richman: Because Her Beauty Is Raw And Wild
Here It Is (Vapor, 2008)

Sharon Robinson: Everybody Knows *Alexandra Leaving /
Everybody Knows / Summertime* (Freeworld, 2009)

**Linda Ronstadt & Emmylou Harris: Western Wall: The Tucson
Sessions** *Sisters Of Mercy* (Elektra, 1999).

Diana Ross: Red Hot Rhythm & Blues *Summertime* (RCA, 1987)
(Co-written with Sharon Robinson)

Buffy Sainte-Marie: Illuminations *God Is Alive, Magic Is Afoot*
(Vanguard, 1969) (Based on passages from *Beautiful Losers*)

Darrell Scott: Modern Hymns *Joan Of Arc* (feat. Alison Krauss,

Mary Gauthier) (Appleseed, 2008)

Ron Sexsmith: Ron Sexsmith *Heart With No Companion*
(Interscope, 1995)

Nina Simone: To Love Somebody *Suzanne* (RCA Victor, 1969)

Slow Dazzle: View From the Floor *Anthem* (Misra, 2005)

David Soul: David Soul *Bird On A Wire* (Private Stock, 1976).

Spanky & Our Gang: Like To Get To Know You *Suzanne*
(Mercury, 1968)

Status Quo: Rockers Rollin' *Democracy* (Polygram, 2002)

James Taylor: Covers *Suzanne* (Hear Music, 2008)

Christine Tobin: Yell Of The Gazelle *You Know Who I Am*
(Babel, 1999)

Christine Tobin: You Draw The Line *Tower Of Song* (Babel, 2003)

Christine Tobin: Secret Life Of A Girl *Everybody Knows*
(Babel, 2008)

Dave Van Ronk: Van Ronk *Bird On The Wire* (Polydor, 1971)

Kate Voegele: Don't Look Away *Hallelujah*
(Interscope, 2008: iTunes version only)

The Vogues: The Vogues Sing The Good Old Songs And Other Hits
Hey, That's No Way To Say Goodbye (Reprise, 1970)

**Rufus Wainwright: Shrek: Music From The Original
Motion Picture** *Hallelujah* (DreamWorks, 2001)

Jennifer Warnes: The Hunter *Way Down Deep* (Private Music,
1992) (Co-written with Warnes, Steve Forman, Amy La Television.)

Colm Wilkinson: Some Of My Best Friends Are Songs *Suzanne*
(Sony, 2004)

Kathryn Williams: Relations *Hallelujah* (EastWest, 2004)

Norma Winstone: It's Later Than You Think *Sisters Of Mercy*
(Provocateur, 2006)

Ygdrassil: Ygdrassil *Winter Lady* (VIA, Netherlands, 1995)

Thalia Zedek: Been Here And Gone *Dance Me To The End Of Love*
(Matador, 2001)

BIBLIOGRAPHY

POETRY AND LYRICS

Let Us Compare Mythologies
(Montreal: McGill Poetry, 1956)
The Spice-Box Of Earth
(Toronto: McClelland & Stewart, 1961)
Flowers For Hitler
(Toronto: McClelland & Stewart, 1964)
Parasites Of Heaven
(Toronto: McClelland & Stewart, 1966)
Selected Poems: 1956-1968
(Toronto: McClelland & Stewart, 1968)
The Energy Of Slaves
(Toronto: McClelland & Stewart, 1972)
Death Of A Lady's Man
(Toronto: McClelland & Stewart, 1978)
Book Of Mercy
(Toronto: McClelland & Stewart, 1984)
Stranger Music: Selected Poems & Songs
(Toronto: McClelland & Stewart, 1993)
Dance Me To The End Of Love
(New York: Welcome Books, 1995)
Book Of Longing
(Toronto: McClelland & Stewart, 2006)
Words Of Love And Hate: The Lyrics Of Leonard Cohen
(London: Omnibus, 2009)

FICTION

The Favourite Game (London: Martin Secker & Warburg, 1963)
Beautiful Losers (Toronto: McClelland & Stewart, 1966)
Books about Cohen and his work:

Devlin, Jim, *Leonard Cohen: In Every Style Of Passion*
(London: Omnibus, 1996)
Devlin, Jim, *Leonard Cohen: In His Own Words*
(London: Omnibus, 1998)
Dorman, LS & Rawlins, CL, *Leonard Cohen: Prophet Of The Heart*
(London: Omnibus, 1991)
Fournier, Michael & Norris, Ken, *Take This Waltz: A Celebration Of
Leonard Cohen At 60* (Toronto: The Muses, 1997)
Gnarowski, Michael (ed), *Leonard Cohen And His Critics*
(New York: McGraw-Hill Ryerson, 1976)
Green, Roger, *Hydra And The Bananas Of Leonard Cohen*
(New York: Basic Books, 2002)
Hendrickx, Marc, *Yesterday's Tomorrow: Leonard Cohen*
(Blackheath, NSW: Brandl & Schlesinger, 2008)
Middlehurst, Shelagh, *Sex With Leonard Cohen*
(Cardiff: Leaf Books, 2006).
Nadel, Ira B, *Leonard Cohen: A Life In Art*
(London: Robson Books, 1995)
Nadel, Ira B, *Various Positions: A Life Of Leonard Cohen*
(Toronto: Random House, 1996; Austin, University of Texas Press, 2007)
Needham, Pete, *The Diamond's Mine*
(Chesterfield, UK: Bannister, 2008)
Ondaatje, Michael, *Leonard Cohen (Canadian Writers series)*
(Toronto: McClelland & Stewart, 1970)
Rasky, Harry, *The Song of Leonard Cohen: Portrait Of A Poet,
A Friendship And A Film* (Oakville, Ontario: Mosaic, 2001)
Ratcliff, Maurice, *The Complete Guide To The Music Of Leonard
Cohen* (London: Omnibus, 1999)
Scobie, Stephen, *Leonard Cohen*
(Toronto: Douglas & McIntyre, 1979)
Scobie, Stephen (ed.), *Intricate Preparations: Writing Leonard Cohen*
(Toronto: ECW, 2000)
Sheppard, David, *Leonard Cohen (Kill Your Idols series)*
(London: Unanimous, 2000)
Wilde, Alex, *I Can Sleep For The Rest Of My Life: The Letters Of
Michael & Marianne* (London: HHO, 2001)
(A novel inspired by the lyrics of 'So Long, Marianne'.)

VIDEO/DVD / FILM

Bird On A Wire (Dir: Tony Palmer, 1974)
Dynamite Chicken (Dir: Ernest Pintoff, 1974)
The Ernie Game (Dir: Don Owen, 1967)
The Favourite Game (Dir: Bernar Hébert, 2003)
(Based on Cohen's first novel)
Guitare Au Poing (Dir: Daniel Szuster, 1973)
I Am A Hotel (Dir: Allan F. Nicholls, CBC, 1984)
Ladies and Gentlemen... Mr Leonard Cohen
(Dir: Donald Brittain, Don Owen, NFB, 1965)
Leonard Cohen: Everybody Knows (Dir: Jocelyn Barnabé, Festival
International de Jazz de Montreal, 2008)
Leonard Cohen: I'm Your Man (Dir: Liam Lunson, 2006)
Leonard Cohen, Spring '96 (Dir: Armelle Brusq, 1997)
Leonard Cohen Under Review: 1934-1977 (Sexy Intellectual, 2007)
Leonard Cohen Under Review: 1978-2006 (Sexy Intellectual, 2008)
Leonard, Light My Cigarette (Dir: Tony Babinski, 1996)
Live In London (Sony, 2009)
Message To Love: The Isle Of White Festival
(Dir: Murray Lerner, 1997)
Night Magic (Dir: Lewis Furey, 1985)
(Cohen co-wrote the screenplay and wrote the lyrics.)
Poen (Dir: Josef Reeve, 1967)
The Song Of Leonard Cohen (Dir: Harry Rasky, CBC, 1980)
Songs From The Life Of Leonard Cohen
(Dir: Bob Portway, BBC, 1988)
This Beggar's Description (Dir: Pierre Tétrault, 2005).
What Leonard Cohen Did For Me (Dir: Martina Hall, BBC, 2005)

FURTHER READING

Bangs, Lester, *Psychotic Reactions And Carburetor Dung*
(London: Serpent's Tail, 1996)
Cave, Nick, *And The Ass Saw The Angel*
(London: Black Spring, 1989)
Chusid, Irwin, *Songs In The Key Of Z: The Curious Universe Of*

Outsider Music (London: Cherry Red, 2000)

Collins, Aileen (ed.), *CIV/n: A Literary Magazine Of The 1950s*
(Montreal: Vehicule Press, 1983)

Kevin JH Dettmar, *The Cambridge Companion To Bob Dylan*
(Cambridge University Press, 2009)

Sandra Djwa, *The Politics Of The Imagination: A Life Of FR Scott*
(Toronto: McClelland & Stewart, 1987)

Dylan, Bob, *Chronicles, Volume One*
(New York: Simon & Schuster, 2004)

Eliot, TS, *Complete Poems And Plays* (London: Faber & Faber, 2004)

Footman, Tim, *Welcome To The Machine: OK Computer And The
Death Of The Classic Album* (New Malden: Chrome Dreams, 2007)

Frost, Robert, *The Poetry Of Robert Frost* (New York: Holt, 2002)

Fukuyama, Francis, *The End Of History And The Last Man*
(New York: Free Press, 1992)

García Lorca, Federico, *Selected Poems*
(New York: New Directions, 2005)

Ginsberg, Allen, *Howl And Other Poems*
(San Francisco: City Lights, 1956)

Greene, Graham, *The Power And The Glory*
(London: William Heinemann, 1940)

Havers, Richard, *Sinatra* (London: Dorling-Kindersley, 2004)

Hutcheon, Linda, *The Canadian Postmodern: A Study of
Contemporary English-Canadian Fiction*
(Don Mills, Ontario: Oxford University Press, 1988)

Irvin, Jim, and Colin McLear, *The Mojo Collection*
(Edinburgh: Canongate, 2003)

Johnson, BS, *The Unfortunates* (London: Secker & Warburg, 1969)

Joyce, James, *A Portrait Of The Artist As A Young Man*
(New York: BW Huebsch, 1916)

Kerouac, Jack, *On The Road* (New York: Viking, 1957)

Klein, AM, *The Collected Poems Of AM Klein*
(Toronto: McGraw-Hill Ryerson, 1974)

Lawrence, DH, *Lady Chatterley's Lover* (London: Penguin, 1960)

Layton, Irving, *A Wild Peculiar Joy: The Selected Poems*
(Toronto: McClelland & Stewart, 2004)

Longfellow, Henry Wadsworth, *Poems And Other Writings*
(New York: Library of America, 2000)

MacDonald, Ian, *Revolution In The Head* (London: Pimlico, 1995)

Marcus, Greil, *Like A Rolling Stone: Bob Dylan At The Crossroads*
(New York: Public Affairs, 2005)
Marsh, Dave and James Bernard, *The New Book of Rock Lists*
(New York: Fireside, 1994)
Mersereau, Bob, *The Top 100 Canadian Albums* (Fredericton, NB:
Goose Lane Editions, 2007)
Nabokov, Vladimir, *Pale Fire* (New York: GP Putnam, 1962)
O'Grady, Jean, & Staines, David (eds), *Northrop Frye on Canada*
(Toronto: University of Toronto Press, 2003)
Parker, Dorothy, *The Collected Dorothy Parker*
(London: Penguin, 2001)
Perec, Georges, *Life: A User's Manual (La Vie mode d'emploi)*
(Paris: Hachette Littératures, 1978)
Pratt, EJ, *Complete Poems*
(Toronto: University of Toronto Press, 1989)
Ricks, Christopher, *Dylan's Visions Of Sin* (London: Viking, 2003)
Selby, Jr, Hubert, *Last Exit To Brooklyn*
(New York: Grove Press, 1964)
Turner, Steve, *The Gospel According To The Beatles*
(Louisville, Ky: Westminster John Knox Press, 2006)
Wilson, Colin, *The Outsider* (London: Victor Gollancz, 1956)
Woodcock, George, *Odysseus Ever Returning*
(Toronto: McClelland & Stewart, 1970)
Yeats, WB, *WB Yeats* (London: Faber & Faber, 2009)

Periodicals to which I have referred include: *Alphabet, Australian Financial Review, Blitz, Boston Phoenix, Buzz* (Los Angeles), *Canadian Literature, Chicago Tribune, Cincinnati CityBeat, Commentary, Crawdaddy, Eurozine, The Fiddlehead, The Globe and Mail* (Toronto), *Goldmine, The Guardian* (London), *Hollywood Reporter, The Independent* (London), *Les Inrockuptibles, LA Phonograph, Literary Review of Canada, Maclean's, Melody Maker, Mojo, Musician, National Catholic Reporter, New York Magazine, New York Review Of Books, New York Times, New Yorker, NME, The Observer* (London), *Paste, Prospect, Q, Rock CD, Rolling Stone, Sing Out!, Sounds, Sunday Times* (London), *Sydney Morning Herald, The Times* (London), *Toronto Star, Uncut, University of Toronto Quarterly, Weekend, Who Put The Bomp, The Word, Your Flesh, ZigZag.*

WEBSITES

www.leonardcohen.com
The official site.

www.leonardcohenfiles.com
The best, fullest repository of Cohenabilia, since 1995. Cohen himself has been known to communicate directly.

www.leonardcohenforum.com
Talk site, affiliated with the above.

www.leonardcohensite.com
En français.

1heckofaguy.com
With an emphasis on the often neglected lighter side of Cohen's life and work; includes a splendid discussion of the affinity of certain Cohen songs for movie scenes set in strip clubs.

www.cohencovers.com
Identifies versions of Cohen songs on iTunes.
speakingcohen.com Portal to sites hosted by Marie Mazur, including the Leonard Cohen webring.

leonardcohen.search.com

www.tea-and-oranges.de

www.mbzc.com
The official site of the Mount Baldy Zen Center.

More generally, *allmusic.com* and *rocksbackpages.com* are also excellent sources for factual nuggets and archive material.

INDEX